"Dissociative disorder in adults – 'the presence of two or more distinct identity or personality states' – is well known. Despite the fact that the majority of traumatic experiences associated with Dissociative Disorder derive from Adverse Childhood Experiences, there is less familiarity with the condition in childhood and young people. This detailed text aims to redress this failure, by describing the latest clinical and trauma research, integrating attachment, neurobiology, child development, mental health and family systems offering unique perspectives on the phenomena of dissociation, and presentations in children and young people.

Through clinical examples of detailed highly skilled therapeutic work with seriously traumatised children and young people, the concept of dissociation is brought to life – a key response to overwhelming toxic and damaging traumatic stress through the life-course. These result in the presence of self-states that influence the child either internally or directly by taking executive control over their bodies. An elemental dramatic relationship is enacted in the inner world of the child or young person, between figures who can guide, protect and cope, or are destructive to the self or other.

The detailed therapeutic task is described, understanding the nature and origins of dissociative responses, and the extensive work of creating a coherent narrative of experiences. Separate self-states need to be integrated to establish a coherent, mature individual, who can put their experiences in memory to be open to relationships, to be creative, and not to repeat and promulgate disastrous toxic ways of being."

Arnon Bentovim, Child and Adolescent Psychiatrist;
Formerly Great Ormond Street Children's Hospital and
the Tavistock Clinic, UK

"This is a long awaited and much needed book. Brave, theoretically deep, imbued with rich clinical experience, daring to state what we fear to hear, and written by some of the finest and most experienced clinicians in this field, this is a must-read for anyone trying to get to grips with this complex and challenging area of work."

Graham Music, PhD; Consultant Psychotherapist,
Tavistock Centre, London; Author, Nurturing Natures,
The Good Life *and* Nurturing Children

"Offering detailed case histories and guidelines for treatment of children with complex symptoms (including discrete dissociative states of consciousness), this rare book takes us deep into the under-explored realm of multiple types of extreme trauma suffered by young victims, ranging from family violence, emotional or sexual abuse, to cyber-crime exploitation on the darknet. Experienced practitioners sensitively elucidate the 'undoing' of seemingly inexplicable disturbances in memory, identity, affect, soma and behaviour as aftereffects of protective dissociation, regarded here as a 'psychological escape hatch – the only getaway at the time of the trauma'."

Professor Joan Raphael-Leff, PhD;
Retired Psychoanalyst/Transcultural Psychologist;
Fellow of the British Psychoanalytical Society;
Member, IPA; Leader, Academic Faculty for
Psychoanalytic Research, Anna Freud Centre

Treating Children with Dissociative Disorders

This book provides a comprehensive overview of research into dissociation in children and adolescents and challenges conventional ideas about complex behaviours.

Offering a new perspective to those who are unfamiliar with dissociation in children, and challenging prevalent assumptions for those who are experienced in the field, the editors encourage the professional to ask questions about the child's internal experiences beyond a diagnosis of the external symptoms. Chapters bring together a range of international experts working in the field, and interweave theories, practice, and challenging and complex case material, as well as identifying mistakes that therapists can avoid while working with children who dissociate.

Filled with practical tools and examples, this book is a vital resource for professionals to enrich their practice with children who dissociate.

Valerie Sinason, PhD, is a widely published writer and psychoanalyst. She has pioneered disability and trauma-informed therapy for over 30 years, is President of the Institute of Psychotherapy and Disability, is Founder and Patron of the Clinic for Dissociative Studies and is on the Board of the ISSTD.

Renée Potgieter Marks specialises in working with children with complex trauma and dissociation. She is a national and international trainer on attachment, complex trauma and dissociation, and founder of Integrate Families and BICTD.

Treating Children with Dissociative Disorders

Attachment, Trauma, Theory and Practice

Edited by
Valerie Sinason and
Renée Potgieter Marks

LONDON AND NEW YORK

Cover image: © Martin Barraud | Getty Images

First published 2022
by Routledge
2 Park Square, Milton Park, Abingdon, Oxon OX14 4RN

and by Routledge
605 Third Avenue, New York, NY 10158

Routledge is an imprint of the Taylor & Francis Group, an informa business

© 2022 selection and editorial matter, Valerie Sinason and Renée Potgieter Marks; individual chapters, the contributors

The right of Valerie Sinason and Renée Potgieter Marks to be identified as the authors of the editorial material, and of the authors for their individual chapters, has been asserted in accordance with sections 77 and 78 of the Copyright, Designs and Patents Act 1988.

All rights reserved. No part of this book may be reprinted or reproduced or utilised in any form or by any electronic, mechanical, or other means, now known or hereafter invented, including photocopying and recording, or in any information storage or retrieval system, without permission in writing from the publishers.

Trademark notice: Product or corporate names may be trademarks or registered trademarks, and are used only for identification and explanation without intent to infringe.

British Library Cataloguing-in-Publication Data
A catalogue record for this book is available from the British Library

Library of Congress Cataloging-in-Publication Data
A catalog record has been requested for this book

ISBN: 978-1-032-15975-1 (hbk)
ISBN: 978-1-032-15976-8 (pbk)
ISBN: 978-1-003-24654-1 (ebk)

DOI: 10.4324/9781003246541

Typeset in Times New Roman
by codeMantra

Contents

List of contributors ix
Acknowledgements xv

Introduction 1
VALERIE SINASON AND RENÉE POTGIETER MARKS

1 **Attachment and dissociation** 7
KARL HEINZ BRISCH

2 **Infant attachment and dissociative psychopathology: an approach based on the evolutionary theory of multiple motivational systems** 10
GIOVANNI LIOTTI

3 **Importance of attachment in the presence of a perceived threat** 27
MARY SUE MOORE

4 **"You will not believe me if I tell you!" – prenatal trauma and dissociation** 34
RENÉE POTGIETER MARKS

5 **A case series of 70 victims of exploitation from child sexual abuse imagery** 49
JOYANNA SILBERG

6 **The Star Theoretical Model: an integrative model for assessing and treating childhood dissociation** 73
FRAN WATERS

7 The power of care: the healing that comes from teaching non-offending parents how to regulate their child after physical and sexual abuse 98
CHRISTINE C. FORNER

8 Structuring treatment for dissociative children with the Sleeping Dogs method 116
ARIANNE STRUIK

9 Genesis of a dissociative child: Kayleigh's story – how 'I' became 'us' 139
JO RUSSELL

10 The Inside-Outside Technique: exploring dissociation and fostering self-reflection 155
SANDRA BAITA

11 Severe and unusual self-harm in DID: motive, means and opportunity 168
ADAH SACHS

12 I didn't know where you were: in the play space of treatment with a young dissociative boy 180
EVA TEIRSTEIN YOUNG

13 A journey of discovery 198
JOY HASLER

14 The price that society and the individual victim pay 213
ZOE HAWTON

15 Covid-19 – the challenge, the solution and the unknown: treating dissociative children online 237
RENÉE POTGIETER MARKS

Resources for treating complex trauma in children and adolescents 251
Index 259

Contributors

Sandra Baita is a clinical psychologist, child therapist and EMDR approved consultant in private practice in Buenos Aires, Argentina. A fellow member of ISSTD, and a member of the Child & Adolescent committee of the same organisation, she has worked in different public programmes for child abuse victims in the City of Buenos Aires. She has given training in the field of child developmental trauma and dissociation in many countries of Latin America, the USA, Spain, Italy and Holland. She is the author of the first book published in Spanish language on the topic *Rompecabezas. Una guía introductoria al trauma y la disociación en la infancia*, which was recently translated into Italian.

Karl Heinz Brisch, MD, is a specialist for child and adolescent psychiatry and psycho-therapy, adult psychiatry, psychotherapeutic medicine, psychoanalysis and group psychoanalysis. He is head of the Department of Paediatric Psychosomatic Medicine and Psychotherapy at the Dr Von Hauner Children's Hospital University of Munich, Germany. He is a lecturer at the university and also at the Psychoanalytic Institute in Stuttgart, Germany. His main research topic is early child development with special impact on attachment processes and disorders. His publications are about attachment development of high-risk infants and clinical attachment research. He is a past president of the German Speaking Association for Infant Mental Health (GAIMH).

Christine C. Forner, BA, BSW, MSW, RSW, has more than 30 years of clinical experience working with individuals with trauma, PTSD, traumatic dissociation and developmental trauma. Christine works in private practice at Associated Counselling in Calgary Alberta, Canada. She has presented locally and internationally on issues of traumatic dissociation and mindfulness and dissociation, the power of care in treating complex trauma and dissociation, and the intersection of patriarchy and misogyny in the role of child abuse and neglect. Christine was the treasurer of the International Society for the Study of Trauma and Dissociation (2012–2017) and was the President of the ISSTD in 2019. Being awarded several president awards for her service to the ISSTD, she is an ISSTD

Fellow and won an award for her article, "What Mindfulness can learn about Dissociation and what Dissociation can learn from Mindfulness" (*Journal of Trauma & Dissociation*, 2019). She is the author of *Dissociation, Mindfulness and Creative Meditations: Trauma Informed Practices to Facilitate Growth* (Routledge, 2017).

Joy Hasler, MA ALCM Cert Ed, has been a teacher in inner city schools and a SEN School. In 1993, she became a Music Therapist specialising in working with children affected by developmental trauma. She has been a short- and long-term foster carer and is an adoptive parent. In 2001, she founded Catchpoint Consultancy CIC in Bristol, which is a registered adoption support agency, offering creative arts therapies focusing on developing positive attachments within adoptive and foster families. Joy is a Music Therapy supervisor and trainer. She co-edited *Creative Therapies for Complex Trauma* (JKP 2017).

Zoe Hawton is a therapist and supervisor based in London and Manchester. She has 15 years' experience working in clinical, private and educational setting. Zoe specialises in using a Rogerian inspired base, in conjunction with trauma-focused techniques, to treat extreme dissociation and relational trauma in young people and adults. A significant aspect of her work is engaging clients who are traditionally disenfranchised from accessing therapy and trying to bridge the "digital divide."

Giovanni Liotti, who sadly died in April 2018, was founder and past president of the Italian Society of Cognitive Behavioural Therapy. He advanced the understanding of attachment disorganisation as a potential precursor of dissociation in 1992 and became a close colleague of John Bowlby. His use of two therapists to dilute the transference and his focus on the relational link between patient and therapist to be one of collaborating peers impacted on many clinicians worldwide. In 2005, he was honoured with the Pierre Janet Writing Award by the International Society for the Study of Trauma and Dissociation.

Renée Potgieter Marks, PhD, is a Consultant Therapist and Clinical Lead at Integrate Families, National Centre for Child Trauma and Dissociation in England. She specialises in children and adolescents who suffered complex trauma. Renée published articles and chapters in various books. She is an international trainer and involved in online training with BICTD (www.bictd.org), on assessing and treating dissociative children and adolescents. She is the chair of the Child and Adolescent Committee of the ESTD (European Society on Trauma and Dissociation) and also a member of the Child and Adolescent Committee of the ISSTD (International Society on Studies of Trauma and Dissociation).

Mary Sue Moore is a clinical psychologist, psychotherapist and educator in Colorado. She has taught and participated in a variety of clinical research projects in the USA, the UK and Australia over the past 25 years. Her research has focused on attachment theory and the impact of trauma on the developing brain. From 1986 to 1988, Mary Sue undertook a Fulbright Research Fellowship in London, where she worked with John Bowlby at the Tavistock Clinic. Moving to Boulder in 1989, she worked as a clinician and consultant for a local CAMH service, where she pursued long-standing educational, research and clinical training interests, while continuing to teach in London twice a year, at the Tavistock Clinic. She is also writing a book on the impact of trauma and disturbed attachment relationships in children's drawings.

Jo Russell is a Consultant Child and Adolescent Psychotherapist and the Professional Lead responsible for the development and delivery of child psychotherapy services within NHS CAMHS across West Sussex, Brighton and Hove. Jo completed doctoral research in 2014 entitled "Dissociative Identities in Childhood: An Exploration of How Children with Dissociative Identities May Present in Psychotherapy. Are There Implications for Psychoanalytic Technique?" Until recently she was the Senior Editor for *The Journal of Child Psychotherapy*, the professional journal of the Association of Child Psychotherapy, curating special issues on themes of working with refugee and asylum-seeking young people, working with issues of gender identity, and psychotherapy with fostered and adopted children. Before training as a child psychotherapist, Jo worked in therapeutic communities for children in care and retains a special interest in work with hard-to-reach young people who have experienced complex developmental trauma in their early years.

Adah Sachs is an attachment-based psychoanalytic psychotherapist and a member of the Bowlby Centre. She has worked for decades with adults and adolescents in psychiatric care, was a consultant psychotherapist at the Clinic for Dissociative Studies and had recently retired from heading the NHS Psychotherapy Service for the London borough of Redbridge. Adah lectures and supervises worldwide and publishes regularly on attachment and dissociation, including two co-edited books, *Forensic Aspects of DID* (2008) and *The Abused and the Abuser: Victim-Perpetrator Dynamics* (2018). She is a fellow of the International Society for Study of Trauma and Dissociation.

Joyanna Silberg, PhD, is the president of the Leadership Council on Child Abuse & Interpersonal Violence and scientific consultant to CHILDUSA. Her psychotherapy practice specialises in children and adolescents suffering from dissociative symptoms and disorders, and her forensic practice specialises in child sexual abuse. She is past-president of the International Society for the Study of Trauma and Dissociation (ISSTD). She has presented nationally and internationally on child abuse, psychotherapy and protecting abused children in family court. Her newest book *The Child*

Survivor: Healing Developmental Trauma and Dissociation (2013, new edition, release 2020) received the annual media award from ISSTD.

Valerie Sinason, PhD PGTC MACP M Inst Psychoanal, is a poet, writer, child psychotherapist and adult psychoanalyst. She worked at the Tavistock and Portman NHS Trust and St George's Hospital before becoming Founder Director of the Clinic for Dissociative Studies, until her retirement from long-term clinical work in December 2016. Dr Sinason specialises in work with abused, abusing and dissociative patients, including those with a learning disability, and has been used as an expert witness in court cases. She speaks nationally and internationally, and has published over 150 papers and 15 books. She won a lifetime achievement award from the ISSTD in 2016 and is on the Board of the ISSTD.

Arianne Struik is a clinical psychologist, family therapist and EMDR consultant, and director of the Institute for Chronically Traumatized Children (ICTC) in Australia. She provides specialised trauma treatment and teaches internationally on the treatment of trauma and dissociation in children. She is a member of the Child and Adolescent Committee of the European Society for Trauma and Dissociation.

Fran Waters, DCSW, LMSW, LMFT, is an internationally recognised trainer and consultant in the field of childhood trauma, abuse and dissociation. As an invited presenter, she has conducted extensive training programmes nationally and internationally ranging from a day to five days in Europe, Africa, Australia, South America and North America on a variety of related topics. She is the author of *Healing the Fractured Child: Diagnosing and Treating Youth with Dissociation* and the comprehensive Checklist on Indicators of Trauma & Dissociation in Youth, CIT-DY (2020). She is past president of the International Society for the Study of Dissociation (ISSTD) and is a Fellow of the ISSTD. She is the recipient of ISSTD's Presidential Award and Cornelia Wilbert Award, the Media Award from American Professional Society on Abuse of Children for her three part DVD on Trauma and Dissociation of Children, and the William Friedrich Memorial Child Sexual Abuse Research, Assessment and/or Treatment Award from Institute on Violence, Abuse and Trauma. She maintains a private practice in Marquette, MI.

Eva Teirstein Young, MFA, MPS, ATR-BC, LCAT, is a licenced Creative Arts Therapist with a private practice in New York City. She treats children, adolescents and adults, and specialises in the treatment of Dissociative Disorders and DID. She holds an Advanced Trauma Certificate from the Center for Advanced Studies in Trauma and Dissociation awarded by the International Society for the Study of Trauma and Dissociation (ISSTD). She is a graduate of the Child and Adolescent Psychoanalytic

Psychotherapy Program at the William Alanson White Institute, where she is currently on faculty. Eva Young is an Assistant Professor in the Graduate Art Therapy Department at Pratt Institute in Brooklyn, NY. She has presented clinical work at various institutes and conferences including the ISSTD annual conference, the William Alanson White Institute, Institute for Contemporary Psychotherapy, NY Center for Children and Pratt Institute.

Acknowledgements

To all the brave children and families who inspired this book. And to all the adults with DID whose child selves had to wait years to be heard.

With thanks to the ESTD, ISSTD, FPP, PODS, MIND, RAINS, CDS UK, CCMH, Bowlby centre and all those who have continued to shine a light on this subject.

With thanks to our husbands, children and families.

With thanks to Sandy Dilip for her invaluable aid, and with great gratitude to Jo Russell for her rapid editing of complex proofs at the eleventh hour. Finally with thanks to all at Routledge for providing a space for children with DID.

Introduction

Valerie Sinason and Renée Potgieter Marks

"I think I am very bad and that is why Mummy wants me to die," said the five-year-old. She was sitting on the floor in a therapy room in the largest National Health Service Treatment and Training Centre in the UK. She burst into tears and continued. "And they passed me round and people touched me and hurt me." The therapists felt the deep level of fear and hurt.

"The problem," one of us said to colleagues later (Sinason, 2002), "was that this 5-year-old, who tugged at our heart strings and made us feel like weeping, is the child part of a 22-year-old who has Dissociative Identity Disorder." It is one thing, however awful, to feel the pain of a self-injuring adult whose relationships have all been damaged by childhood abuse. It is a step nearer to the original pain to hear a child alter-personality or state express this in five-year-old language and affect which brings lived child experience powerfully into the room. And it is another level of impact altogether for an adult professional to see a child, a small person, who has felt the full weight of adult sadism and perversion literally and symbolically in their tiny body, mind and soul. We can rarely bear it.

It is therefore not surprising that whilst adult psychiatrists, psychologists and mental health units across the world struggle with the lack of training provided to properly diagnose and treat adults with dissociative disorders, the situation is even more grave for children. In most clinical or educational units for children with emotional problems, dissociation is misdiagnosed, unrecognised, unknown or, even more worryingly, the very existence of child dissociation is still debated. At one level this is not surprising. Dissociative Identity Disorder is a forensic condition (Sachs & Galton, 2008) in which the vast majority of such cases owe their origins to disorganised attachment and early abuse from attachment figures. This means that the child is living evidence of a current crime. Schools and child facilities find it painful and frightening to consider current as opposed to past abuse. It means involvement with the law and with reality. Sometimes it is parents who have the courage to back their child's disclosures and validate their symptoms; sometimes it is foster parents or adoptive parents who provide the first safety; sometimes it is teachers. But all too often the child gives up telling anyone or asking for help. Often it waits until adulthood for us to hear their awful disclosures and the appalling abuse which went on for years longer because of our societal failure to listen to what children are saying. Or there is an attempt to scapegoat those the child trusted rather than face the possibility of such trauma (Sinason, 2020).

As Midgley comments (2002, p. 39):

> we come across a paradox: almost all articles on dissociation speak of childhood abuse, both physical and sexual, as a prime causal factor, and yet the converse does not hold; the majority of articles on child abuse barely even mention dissociation.

The tragedy is that whilst the fearful jury is out on whether dissociation in children 'exists' and 'can be treated' increasing numbers of mental health professionals are successfully treating dissociative children daily. Within this book we meet some of the key international heroes and heroines who are changing the lives of children.

Children and adolescents presenting with serious suicide risks are successfully treated as they finally uncover that one dissociative self-state is trying to kill another part of the self. Extremely aggressive children, for whom multiple therapies have failed, are now successfully treated as they find that an 'angry', 'violent', 'aggressive dissociative state' or 'perpetrator introject' is responsible. Children who are exceptionally controlling are finally released from the grip of an 'internal mother' dissociative state or a 'bossy' dissociative state. They learn that such states are acting in defence of a younger part of the self and protecting against parents, adults and other children. The regressed and infantile behaviour of many children and adolescents is enabled to develop age-appropriate behaviours as the trauma and 'stuckness' of these younger and infantile dissociative states are finally released to develop in order to match the chronological age of the child.

We celebrate each professional who is brave enough to free these children and adolescents from a long-term journey in the mental health services by 'seeing', 'hearing' and working directly with these dissociative states. However we continue to be deeply saddened by the thousands of children who are working very hard to broadcast their internal distress and display their dissociative states but who are met with denial, ignorance or lack of knowledge by their mental health professionals. Almost all of us can look back and recognise, with shame, cases we have missed. Indeed, one of us (Sinason, 1990) even published a paper that showed her surprise at the different voices one child expressed herself in. She learned from this. However, in a fearful environment many professionals continue to turn a blind eye.

There are more concerns. In the PhD study of Madden (2004), she found that only 17.6% of professionals who indicated that they are knowledgeable about dissociation accurately diagnosed the DID vignette, which was used during the study. 'It is ironic that 47.1% of participants for this survey strongly disagreed that DID is under-diagnosed, while almost twice as many respondents (82.4%) for this survey provided various false negative diagnoses' (Madden, 2004, p. 72). This disconcerting information only emphasises the urgent need for more in-depth training for mental health professionals working with children and adolescents, specifically in the area of dissociation. And that will exclude the majority, who are still denying the existence of dissociation in children and adolescents.

Dissociation in children and adolescents is not new. The first child dissociation case was described in 1840 by Antoine Despine, a French physician. He diagnosed a child, Estelle, with multiple personality disorder and expressed his concerns that the future generations might "not attend to their predecessor's original mistakes" (Fine, 1988, p. 38). According to Putnam (1989), DID was seen as a rare disorder and rarely mentioned in psychology textbooks. Alvardo (1989) reported four cases of adolescents with some form of multiple personality disorders and one case of a child with a multiple personality disorder. Steinberg (1996) noted no cases of DID in children and adolescents between 1840 and 1997. Kluft (1990) expressed the view that journal reviewers are reluctant to print information about DID in children and adolescents.

Child dissociation is generally underdiagnosed and under-recognised. Some of the reasons include fear, denial and a high level of scepticism in professionals involved with children and adolescents (Putnam, 1991), the smaller number of clinicians in the field of child dissociation (Ross, 1996) and the child's fear of ridicule and disbelief by others about the internal experiences (McElroy, 1992). Clinicians' disbelief that the child would or could assume a defensive posture against trauma might also be a cause for misdiagnosis (Goodwin, 1995). It is also worth considering if some clinicians feel a need to rescue the child from a controversial diagnosis such as DID (McElroy & McElroy, 1991). Additionally, the lack of a secure attachment is a predisposing factor to the development of a dissociative disorder. Disorganised attachment activates a desperate attempt to take the blame for an attachment figure who cannot provide a secure home. This tragic loyalty, akin to trauma-bonding, adds to the problem.

Silberg and Dallam (2004) referred to Zoroglu et al. (1996) who stated that many children are misdiagnosed because of comorbid symptomatology – for instance, ADHD, conversion and somatoform disorders, conduct and oppositional defiant disorders, schizophrenia and various forms of epilepsy and affective disorders. Kluft (1984) also argues that dissociation in children is often not recognised due to a lack of familiarity with dissociative symptoms in children, differences in the presentation in dissociative adults and dissociative children, the availability of more familiar diagnoses and the normative nature of fluctuating behaviours in children. Further, the normative dissociative experiences of children can make it hard to differentiate between a pathological process and imagination involved in play (Haugaard, 2004).

Silberg et al. (2004) also conclude that children and adolescents might not report dissociative symptoms as they may consider it as normal. It is still very difficult for professionals to accept that in children and adolescents 'the self may no longer be whole,' and 'the dissociated memories and sensations may be perceived as not being under the control of the conscious and executive self' (Silberg & Wieland, 2013).

Over the past 30 years multiple books and articles have seen the light on dissociative disorders in adults. But, as stated earlier, child dissociation literature remains a rare gem. Finally, in 1996, Silberg and Shirar each released the first books on dissociative children. Silberg and Waters describe their theories and experiences with dissociative children from the 1980s onwards. The following year, in 1997, Putnam released his book on dissociative children and adolescents. For many years these two books became the main handbooks for many clinicians working with dissociative children. In 2004 the Child and Adolescent Guidelines of the ISSTD was published.

With the exception of selected articles on child dissociation, a severe literature drought followed for many years with no further books published on the topic of child and adolescent dissociation. Although this time produced no books, it was perhaps the most fruitful time in the lives of multiple clinicians working with dissociative children and adolescents who used trainings and conferences like the ISSTD annual conferences to share their thoughts, experiences and amazement that across the world there were similar cases of children sharing and recovering from their apparently bizarre internal experiences, all related to dissociative disorders.

At an ISSTD meeting in 2010, there was a decision made for the Child and Adolescent Committee to finally write about professional experiences. The book, edited by Sandra Wieland, was published in 2011 and very quickly more books followed on child dissociation, written by Struik (2014 & 2019), Silberg (2013), Baita – Spanish (2015), Baita – Italian (2018), Yehuda (2016) and Waters (2016). Weiland's book was reprinted in 2015 and also translated into German in 2018. In 2016 the ESTD's Child and Adolescent Guidelines were published and updated in 2017.

This book is the brainchild of Valerie Sinason, a child psychotherapist and adult psychoanalyst in the UK who is a member of the ESTD and a Board Member of the ISSTD. She wanted there to be a major UK-based book on the subject and brought in Renée Potgieter Marks as co-editor, who has probably assessed the largest number of children with DID in the UK. A huge variety of theory, experience, history, information and cases shape the turbulent landscape of this book. Most of the key thinkers and practitioners in Europe and the USA are included in the book or in the resource list. The book is depressing, uplifting, exhilarating and challenging. In essence it is reflecting the true nature and reality of child dissociative disorders in the world. It will provide a new perspective to those who are unfamiliar with dissociation in children, confirmation to those who have already encountered dissociation in children, answers to those who are treating dissociative children and challenges to those who are experienced in the field of working with dissociative children.

Detecting self-states when children are younger and providing appropriate treatment will facilitate early recovery with a more favourable prognosis for the future (Waters, 2016).

Sometimes it is easier to focus only on the internal narratives to defend against trauma in the external world. Putnam et al. (1986) in looking at 100 DID adult patients found that 97 had experienced major early trauma with almost half having witnessed the violent death of someone close to them.

By facing the possibility of trauma in the aetiology of childhood dissociative states, this book will give hope. Hope that the suffering of adult DID and dissociative clients can be prevented if more therapists are aware, willing and able to hear the voices of thousands of children and adolescents. These children and adolescents are trying to convey their complex internal experiences of fragmentation, internal voices, loss of control when dissociative states take over and intense confusion by multiple symptoms, bizarre drawings, inexplicable 'fantasy' and complex behaviours, which there appears to be no resolution for. This book will encourage the professional to ask different questions about the child's internal experiences. All too often there is only a diagnosis of the external symptoms, medication or short-term therapy. Hopefully forensic services will be educated through this in parallel to relieve the burden from the therapist when the child is not in a safe environment. The therapeutic task is to enable meaning to be established within a safe environment. Sometimes this can take us to terrible places. We need good sound supervision and protection.

As de Zulueta states (1993):

> A refusal on the part of psychiatrists and therapists to validate the horrors of their patients' tortured past implies a refusal to take seriously the unconscious psychological mechanisms that individuals need to use to protect themselves from the unspeakable. Such a denial is, however, no longer ethical, for it is this human capacity to dissociate that is part of the secret of both childhood abuse and the horrors of Nazi genocide, both forms of human violence so often carried out by respectable men and women.
>
> (ibid., p. 190)

References and bibliography

Baita, S. (2015). *Rompecabezas: Unaguíaintroductoria al trauma y la disociación en la infancia*. Amazon: CreateSpace.

Fine, C.G. (1988). The work of Antoine Despine: The first scientific reports on the diagnoses and treatment of a child with multiple personality disorder. *American Journal of Clinical Hypnosis*, 31(1), pp. 33–39.

Goodwin, J. (1995). Credibility problems in multiple personality disorder patients and abused children. In R.P. Kluft (Ed.), *Childhood Antecedents of Multiple Personality Disorder*, pp. 1–20. Washington, DC: American Psychiatric Press Inc.

Haugaard, J.J. (2004). Recognizing and treating uncommon behavioral and emotional disorders in children and adolescents who have been severely maltreated: Introduction. *Child Maltreatment*, 9(2), pp. 123–130. doi: 10.1177/1077559504264304.
Kluft, R.P. (1984). Multiple personality in childhood. *Psychiatric Clinics of North American*, 7, pp. 121–134.
Kluft, R.P. (1990). Thoughts on childhood MPD. *Dissociation*, 3, pp. 1–2.
Madden, Nancy E. (2004). "Psychologists' skepticism and knowledge about dissociative identity disorders in adolescents". PCOM Psychology Dissertations. Paper 90.
McElroy, L.P., & McElroy, R.A. (1991). Countertransference issues in the treatment of incest families. *Psychotherapy*, 28(3), pp. 48–54.
McElroy, L.P. (1992). Early indicators of pathological dissociation in sexually abused children. *Child Abuse and Neglect*, 16, pp. 833–846.
Midgley, N. (2002). Child dissociation and its "roots" in adulthood. In V. Sinason (Ed.), *Attachment, Trauma and Multiplicity*, pp. 37–51. London: Routledge.
Putnam, F.W. (1989). *Diagnosis and Treatment of Multiple Personality Disorder*. New York: Guildford Press.
Putnam, F.W. (1991). Dissociative disorders in children and adolescents: A developmental perspective. *Psychiatric Clinics of North America*, 14, pp. 519–531.
Ross, C.A. (1996). Epidemiology of dissociation in children and adolescents. *Psychiatric Clinics of North America*, 5, pp. 273–274.
Sachs, A., & Galton, G. (2008). *Forensic Aspects of Dissociative Identity Disorder*. London: Karnac Books.
Silberg, J. (2013). *The Child Survivor: Healing Developmental Trauma and Dissociation*. New York: Routledge.
Silberg, J., & Wieland, S. (2013). Dissociation focussed therapy. In J. Ford & C. Courtois (Eds.), *Treating Complex Traumatic Stress Disorder in Children and Adolescents*. Guildford: Guildford Press.
Sinason, V. (1990). Passionate lethal attachments. *British Journal of Psychotherapy*, 7(1) pp. 66–76. United Kingdom.
Sinason, V. (2002). The shoemaker and the elves. In V. Sinason (Ed.), *Attachment, Trauma and Multiplicity*, pp. 125–139. London: Routledge.
Sinason, V. (2020). *The Truth about Trauma and Dissociation: Everything You Didn't Want to Know and Were Afraid to Ask*. London: Confer Books.
Steinberg, M. (1996). Diagnostic tools for assessing dissociation in children and adolescents. *Psychiatric Clinics o/North America*, 5, pp. 333–349.
Struik, A. (2014). *Treating Chronically Traumatized Children. Don't Let Sleeping Dogs Lie!* London: Routledge.
Struik, A. (2019). *Treating Chronically Traumatized Children. The Sleeping Dogs Method*. 2nd Edition. London: Routledge.
Waters, F.S. (2016). *Healing the Fractured Child: Diagnoses and Treatment of Youth with Dissociation*. New York: Springer Publishing Company.
Yehuda, N. (2016). *Communicating Trauma: Clinical Presentations and Interventions with Traumatized Children*. New York: Routledge.

Chapter 1

Attachment and dissociation

Karl Heinz Brisch

The development of attachment is fundamental to the healthy physical, intellectual, and social development of the child. It is critically important that a child has sensitive parents who are able to perceive her signals, enable her to regulate stress and affect appropriately, and in this way anchor a secure emotional representation of the attachment in the child's neuronal networks. Normally, children with a secure attachment have an integrated and coherent internal working model of attachment. Children with an insecure attachment also have an organised inner working model of attachment – for example avoidant or ambivalent attachment – but it is insecure; however, children with the disorganised attachment have a model in which a variety of working models of attachment coexist simultaneously. In other words, such a type of attachment tends to be dissociated.

A disorganised attachment model develops when children perceive that their parents are afraid of them, sometimes frighten and threaten them, but then collapse into a helpless state in which they are incapable of responding sensitively to their child's signals. In essence, they do not perceive their parents as consistent, coherent entities when dealing with stressful, emotional situations in daily life. This becomes especially important when a child is under stress and frightened and is searching for a secure attachment figure for protection. If an attachment figure signals that she, too, is fearful in these situations, perhaps because she has not yet worked through her own childhood traumas, she may be triggered by the child's normal behaviour such as crying or throwing a tantrum. Because of the parent's own agitation or anxiety, she may not be available to provide the protection and security that her child is seeking or respond when he signals that he needs calming, security, and help with affect regulation. Under these circumstances, the child may be prone to developing a disorganised working model. Longitudinal studies involving psychological testing at the end of the second year have shown that children who exhibit a disorganised attachment pattern during the first year of infancy tend to develop symptoms of a borderline personality disorder during adolescence. As has been shown in numerous studies, dissociated self and ego-states are more frequent in such persons.

The situation becomes all the more complex when the children have been subjected to deprivation, neglect, violence in various forms, or emotional rejection during the early months of infancy. When this happens, the children may develop not only disorganised attachment but, as early as the second or third year, signs of an attachment disorder, which may manifest in promiscuous or indifferent attachment behaviour or in an attachment disorder with inhibited attachment behaviour. I have discussed other types of attachment disorders elsewhere, such as those involving addiction, role reversal, aggressive behaviour, and psychosomatic symptoms. These persons live with an internal working model of attachment that is characterised by pathological attachment behaviours.

For example, a child with an indiscriminate attachment disorder may run towards a completely unknown person when frightened and try to find protection and comfort there. We frequently encounter this sort of behaviour in children who were cared for in institutions under circumstances of great deprivation. Children with an attachment disorder do not typically vacillate between various working models of attachment with different behaviours such as seeking closeness and then running away; rather behaviours have become anchored in a pathological attachment pattern, and these behaviours have become their predominant pattern. In other words, these children live in a sort of pathological ego state that remains unchanged despite changing external circumstances, such as switches between foster parents or homes. And even if such children have received loving emotional support from adoptive parents over many years, the parents frequently report that their children continue in this indiscriminate, promiscuous pattern, for example, seeking out a stranger on the street when they are frightened or in danger. These children live in a sort of dissociated attachment state that seems to be highly resistant to external influence.

In our experience, it may require intensive inpatient psychotherapy with the aim of modelling new ways of relating in attachment relevant situations or get these children to attach to specific persons. This process is generally associated with powerful emotions and fear. As a result, these children require careful one-on-one attention to open them up to experiencing new emotions and modes of attachment in frightening situations. If the entire therapeutic team responds promptly and sensitively to these affective states, a new and more coherent attachment pattern may emerge or form. This may lead to attachment behaviours that focus on individual attachment figures and, in the best-case scenario, on adoptive or foster parents. But for this to happen, the entire family must be involved in the therapeutic process, with the parents making full use of counselling. The aim is to support and promote similar co-regulatory behaviours in the parents so that the child experiences similar responses from all attachment figures, team members, parents, and other family members.

If therapy is successful, the child becomes better able to regulate these emotions in stressful situations and less dependent on the presence of an actual attachment figure. To the extent that the child is able to self-regulate, he will be better able to integrate into groups of children in school or at the playground.

Reference

ESTD Newsletter, 4 (4), December 2015.

Chapter 2

Infant attachment and dissociative psychopathology

An approach based on the evolutionary theory of multiple motivational systems

Giovanni Liotti

The possibility of tracing back to infant attachment patterns the origins of mental disorders and of both healthy and untoward interpersonal styles has been of great appeal, in the past four decades, both to developmental psychopathologists (e.g. Sroufe & Rutter, 1984) and to psychotherapists (e.g. Obegi & Berant, 2008; Slade, 2008; Wallin, 2007). The interest of clinicians and researchers for the roots in early attachment patterns of clinically very relevant aspects of personality development is reflected in abundant clinical reflections and in a mushrooming of controlled studies. However, the careful examination of the rich and manifold literature on the applications to psychotherapy of attachment theory and research may be somehow disappointing to clinicians, for at least two main reasons. First, research on attachment across the life span has yielded a proliferation of different assessment procedures and different classification schemes. Second, while the phrase "attachment-based psychotherapy" is often used (Obegi & Berant, 2008), it has been authoritatively argued that although attachment theory and research may be key in informing psychotherapy, they are insufficient for devising a specific type of psychotherapy entirely based on it (Slade, 2008). One reason for this contention is that the relational dynamics on which attachment theory is focused are only one aspect of the manifold components of human relatedness that should be considered by psychotherapists in their daily practice.

This chapter will try to clarify the problems posed to the clinician by the different assessment procedures and related classification schemes used by researchers in classifying infant and adult attachment styles, and then expand on the main psychobiological (motivational) systems that, together with attachment, control, since the first years of life, human behaviour in general and human relatedness in particular. It will be argued that the nature of infant attachment patterns and of their developmental sequels are captured in a clinically more useful way when one focuses on the dynamic tensions between attachment and other motivational systems rather than on attachment alone. The implications of the important finding of two longitudinal studies – that attachment disorganization is a much more powerful predictor of dissociation than exposure to psychological trauma (Dutra, Bureau, Holmes et al., 2009; Ogawa, Sroufe, Weinfield et al., 1997) – justify the attention paid in this chapter more to disorganization of infant attachment than to the organized attachment patterns (secure, insecure-avoidant and insecure-ambivalent).

Classification schemes in the research on attachment

Much of the appeal exerted on clinicians by research on attachment follows the empirically evidenced correlation between states of mind related to attachment in the caregivers and patterns of attachment in the infants they are caring for. Infant attachment patterns are universally classified on the basis of observations in the Strange Situation Procedure (SSP: Ainsworth, Blehar, Waters & Wall, 1978) into three main organized patterns, called secure, insecure-avoidant and insecure-ambivalent (or resistant). These three organized patterns are classified according to the dimension security-insecurity in approaching the attachment figure. To them it must be added the classification of disorganized attachment, obtained by considering a dimension of coherence (organization-disorganization) of behaviour and attention (Main & Solomon, 1990; Solomon & George, 2011).

There is a strong statistical link between each pattern of infant attachment and a corresponding mental state of the caregiver assessed through a semi-structured interview called the Adult Attachment Interview (AAI: George, Kaplan & Main, 1985;). Table 2.1 summarizes in a very schematic way the results of an impressive amount of empirical research on infant attachment patterns and mental states related to attachment in the caregiver (for a meta-analysis and a review, see Bakermans-Kranenburg & Van IJzendoorn, 2009 and Van IJzendoorn, 1995).

In contrast with the universal use of the SSP to assess attachment styles in infants in their second year of life, and with the wide acceptance of the consequent classification of infant attachment into three organized patterns and a dimension of disorganization, there are different methods and different classification schemes used by researchers to categorize adult mental states related to attachment.

Besides the AAI, self-report questionnaires (Bartholomew & Horowitz, 1991; Hazan & Shaver, 1987) and the Adult Attachment Projective system (AAP: George & West, 2001) are widely used by researchers. The problem for clinicians who wish to consider the relevance for their clinical practice of the wide body of research on adult attachment is that the categories obtained through self-report measures do not have strong statistical correlation with

Table 2.1 Correlations between mental states of the caregiver and infant attachment patterns

AAI coding	Adult mental state	SSP coding	Infant behaviour
Free Autonomous	Values attachment and related experiences as influential on healthy personality development. Objective (free from defences) in reporting childhood attachment experiences. Coherence of thought and discourse	Secure	Cries at separation from the caregiver and is promptly comforted at reunion
Dismissing	Devalues the influence of attachment needs in personality development. Idealizes parents but has difficulties in remembering specific childhood experiences supporting the idealization	Avoidant	Does not cry at separation and avoids actively, without behavioural signs of fear, the caregiver at reunion
Preoccupied Enmeshed	Ambivalent attitudes towards attachment relationships. Has access to specific childhood memories but shows confusion and enmeshment about their meaning and value	Ambivalent Resistant	Cries at separation, but resists to comfort offered by the caregiver at reunion (accepts it but continues to cry or displays mild aggression)
Unresolved or Hostile Helpless	Unresolved memories of attachment trauma and losses. Defective mentalization, dissociation. Either frightened and/or frightening (FF) or hostile/helpless (HH) style of caregiving	Disorganized	Simultaneous contradictory behaviour towards the caregiver (e.g. fearful every cry at separation followed by fearful avoidance at reunion three minutes later; approaches the caregiver with the head averted; freezes or collapses to the ground in the middle of an approach to the caregiver

the AAI categories (De Haas, Bakerman-Kranenburg, Van IJzendoorn, 1994; Roisman, Holland, Fortuna et al., 2007). The lack of correspondence between AAI and self-report measures of adult attachment is particularly confusing even when these diverse measure and coding systems use the same name for a category. Therefore, clinicians must be wary of using as an assessment tool a self-report questionnaire, and infer from such a way of assessing their patient's attachment style any characteristic that has been linked to mental states related to attachment by research based on the AAI.

Let us consider an example relevant to the theme of this book. Suppose that a clinician is dealing with dissociative symptoms of a pre-adolescent child that do not seem to have their origin in straightforward violence or emotional and sexual abuse. The clinician might know that infant disorganized attachment in the children of non-maltreating parent may explain dissociation (Dutra et al., 2009), and may wish to gather information supporting this hypothesis in the specific case of her patient. The clinician may ask the child's parents to fill up a questionnaire – a much easier way of assessing adult attachment than the AAI. Let us suppose that the clinician resorts to Bartholomew and Horowitz's (1991) self-report measure, the Relationship Questionnaire, and the two parents both turn out fearful in their attachment style. Given the apparent correspondence between the fearful coding of the Relationship Questionnaire and those adult attachment styles that seem to be the likely outcome of early disorganized attachment, the clinician may conclude that she has found evidence, in the light of what is known about the intergenerational transmission of attachment patterns (e.g. Obegi, Morrison & Shaver, 2004), that her patient has indeed been disorganized in her infant attachments. This is a reasonable clinical hypothesis, however, not an evidenced assertion. The only way for reliably inferring infant attachment disorganization in adults and children on the basis of their parents' adult attachment is, on the basis of existing controlled research, only the assessment of the parents' mental states related to attachment through the AAI or the Caregiving Interview (George & Solomon, 2011; Solomon & George, 2011). There is no controlled study that links the fearful coding of the Relational Questionnaire to the unresolved coding of the AAI.

Attachment and other motivational systems: Bowlby's view and beyond

Although the many gaps to be filled in attachment research and the confusing terminology consequent to different ways of studying adult attachment may somehow hinder the clinical applications of attachment theory, the main obstacle for devising a psychotherapy entirely based on attachment theory and research is the one hinted at by Slade (2008): human behaviour and inner experience are too complex to be explained only by the dynamics of the attachment system. This was also John Bowlby's opinion: attachment must be distinguished from, and always considered together with, other systems that control different aspects of social behaviour (Bowlby, 1969, pp. 230–234), and that are constructed, as the attachment system, on the basis of inborn disposition to be viewed as Darwinian adaptations.

In Bowlby's view, the control system governing attachment is mainly concerned with seeking care, help and soothing in moments of fear or distress: it is therefore linked to protection from threats and to soothing the physical or mental pain following injury and trauma (Bowlby, 1969, pp. 224–228 and 257–260). This means that activation of the inborn motivational system concerning direct defence from environmental danger (the fight-flight or defence system) is a quite frequent antecedent of the activation of the attachment system. The adaptive value for the immature offspring of birds and mammals in general and primates in particular to be protected by their parents in the face of actual or potential attacks by predators was hypothesized by Bowlby (1964, 1969, pp. 224–228) as a major environmental pressure in the evolution of the attachment system. Thus, the attachment system is attuned in its operations with the defence (fight-flight) system on the infant's side, and with the caregiving system on the caregivers' side.

The caregiving system is an evolved control (motivational) system – i.e. it has an inborn basis – just like the defence and the attachment systems. It is not simply the outcome in adults of childhood memories of how their requests for soothing and help were met by attachment figures. Babies as old as 18 months can be observed displaying caregiving behaviour: a hint at its evolved nature. The caregiving system, called by Panksepp and Biven the NURTURANCE system, is represented in brain areas different from those related to the attachment system, and is influenced by different brain chemicals (e.g. oxytocin): a further and stronger hint at the inborn separate basis of the caregiving system with respect to the attachment system. George and Solomon (2008, 2011) inquiries provide detailed information concerning the characteristics of the caregiving system and the methods for exploring them.

Besides defence and caregiving, other systems selected by evolutionary processes are involved in complex interactions and sometimes tensions or conflicts with the attachment system. Bowlby (1969, pp. 230–232) devoted some attention to the different nature of the attachment system and the sexual system, that we now know to be represented in different brain areas and to operate through different brain biochemistry with respect to the attachment system (Panksepp and Biven, who relate attachment to what they call the PANIC system and sexuality to what they call the LUSTFUL system, provide a review of neuroscience and evolutionary evidence on this topic). The complex dynamics linking, often harmoniously, attachment to sexuality in the interaction between sentimental partners are quite different from the conflicting ones involved in the interactions between a child and a sexually abusive although not violent adult caregiver. The serious conflict between attachment and sexuality may help in clarifying the psychopathological consequences of childhood sexual abuse within the family.

Other motivational systems to which Bowlby (1969) paid heed, hinting at their interplay and dynamic tensions with the attachment system, are the exploratory system and the cooperative system. The exploratory system is so strongly interacting with the attachment system that it lies at the very ground of the concept of secure base (Ainsworth, Blehar, Waters & Wall, 1978; Bowlby, 1969, 1988). When the goal of the attachment system is achieved through the protective proximity and availability of an attachment figure, the child's exploratory system becomes often active: the child becomes curious of the surroundings and begins to explore them having the attachment figure as a secure heaven to which it is easy to come back in case of trouble. Quite similar are the interactions between the attachment system and the cooperative system. If children have experiences of former secure attachment, and if they are not distressed, they usually do not ask for help and comfort but rather they tend to play or to cooperate with their caregivers. We now know that the cooperative system is an evolved system (just as attachment, exploration, defence from threats, sexuality and caregiving are), mainly thanks to the work by Tomasello and his collaborators (Hare & Tomasello, 2004; Tomasello, 1999, 2009; Warneken, Chen & Tomasello, 2006).

Finally, we must consider at least another evolved behavioural control system (or motivational system): the competitive, ranking one whose goal is to define the hierarchies of dominance-submission in social interactions. The specific type of behaviour controlled by the ranking system is called by ethologists ritualized aggressive behaviour, whose goal is not damaging, but rather forcing the opponent to submit (Gilbert, 1989). To carefully distinguish ritualized aggression (e.g. spanking children to achieve obedience) from malignant aggression (a predator-like form of aggression aimed at damaging or killing the victim and able to activate in the victim the defence fight-flight system, as tragically observed in child abuse) is of obvious importance for clinicians dealing with children raised in maltreating families.

Disorganized infant attachment and its developmental sequels provide illustrations of the utility of considering the complex interplay between the attachment system and other behavioural systems in understanding psychopathology – particularly the dissociative psychopathology that characterize traumatic development – and in planning psychotherapy interventions.

Disorganized attachment: an analysis based on the interaction between the attachment and the defence systems

According to the multi-motivational theory summarized above, infant attachment disorganization is characterized by a conflict between the attachment system and the defence system during the interactions between the infant and the caregiver. Securely attached infants – and to a lesser degree also babies with insecure but organized attachments – ask for help and comfort from the attachment figure when their defence system is activated by threatening environmental or inner conditions, and the soothing they find in the proximity of the caregiver deactivates their defence system.

In striking contrast with the absence of abnormal tensions between the attachment and the defence systems in babies whose attachment to the caregiver is organized, the defence system is activated in babies whose attachment is disorganized by the very proximity to a maltreating, neglecting or helpless attachment figure, so that a conflict between the two systems is established in the infant's experience.

While the attachment system motivates disorganized infants to approach the caregiver in times of distress, the defence system motivates these babies to try to flight from the attachment figures or to fight against them. This is very different from the condition of organized avoidant attachment, where avoidance is a strategy for keeping at least a degree of proximity to the attachment figure, and the infant's defence system is not simultaneously activated by a dismissing – but not abdicating, frightened or straightforwardly frightening – caregiver. Insofar as avoidant infants restrain from bothering the caregivers (who are dismissing the value of attachment needs, but not neglecting or frightened/frightening) with requests for physical closeness (that the attachment figures regard as unnecessary), they prevent being reproached (without physical or emotional maltreatment) or left momentarily alone (as a way, in the caregivers' view, of disciplining their babies and avoid what they believe amounts to spoiling them).

Such an organized avoidant strategy for dealing with a dismissing but not maltreating or neglecting caregiver does not involve the activation of the defence system, and is quite different from the attachment behaviour that is disorganized by the intrusion of defence responses (freezing, fight or flight) primed in the infant by the mere presence and proximity of a maltreating or severely neglecting caregiver.

While the intrusion of defence behaviour in the child's activities governed by the attachment (careseeking) system is easily explained by overt hostility or violent responses of the caregivers, it may seem less obvious that infant attachment disorganization and therefore the activation of the defence system are brought over by caregivers' attitudes that are "abdicating" (Solomon & George, 2011) – i.e. characterized by fear or helplessness but not by overt maltreatment and aggression. The cause of the conflict between the attachment and the defence system in the children of helpless and abdicating but not maltreating parents is explained by the strong evolutionary link between the two systems, already hinted at by Bowlby (1969, pp. 224–228). When the caregiver does not respond to the infant communications of fear and distress, the attachment system tends to be partially deactivated in the infant and the defence system becomes active by default even in the absence of environmental threats.

In a Darwinian perspective, when the attachment system is active but there is no response to the baby's basic need for protection the defence system must become active in preparation to cope alone with the always possible (and quite frequent in the evolutionary niche where humans evolved) environmental threats. Schore (2009) provides detailed illustration of this mechanism by analysing how the still face experimental procedure (the caregiver keeps a totally inexpressive face for up to three minutes during the interaction with the infant) involves the activation in the infant first of the attachment and immediately thereafter of the defence system.

The simultaneous and conflicting activation of the attachment and the defence system is encoded in the Internal Working Model (IWM: Bowlby, 1969) of disorganized attachment. It has been argued that the encoding of representations linked to the two conflicting systems is reflected in a compartmentalization (Holmes, Brown, Mansell et al., 2005) or structural dissociation (Van der Hart, Nijenhuis & Steele, 2006) between the representations of self-with-other linked to careseeking/caregiving exchanges and those, conveying the experience of being threatened within the very same exchanges, linked to the defence system. Representations of the self as vulnerable and of the caregiver as a rescuer, linked to careseeking-caregiving exchanges, coexist with dissociated representations of the self as the victim of a threatening adult, linked to interactions controlled by the defence system (Liotti, 1999, 2004).

The idea that the IWM of disorganized attachment is dissociated is supported by clinical observations, theoretical reflections and data from research studies (e.g. Hesse, Main, Abrams & Rifkin, 2003; Liotti, 1992, 2004, 2009, 2013, 2014; Lyons-Ruth, 2003; Pasquini, Liotti, Mazzotti et al., 2001).

Two longitudinal controlled studies (Dutra et al., 2009; Ogawa et al., 1997) provide robust evidence that children and adolescents who had been infants disorganized in their attachments are more prone to dissociative mental processes than their peers who have histories of organized (secure, insecure-avoidant and insecure-ambivalent) early attachments. Moreover, these longitudinal research studies, and particularly Dutra et al. (2009) study, provide evidence that early disorganized attachment is a much more powerful predictor of dissociation during later developmental years than memories of traumatic events during childhood and adolescence.

The possibility that disorganized early attachment interacts, through the dissociated IWM, with later traumatic events and plays a major role in causing dissociative symptoms throughout personality development and in adult life justifies further reflections on the abnormal tensions between the attachment and the defence systems. It has been convincingly argued that the symptoms of post-traumatic stress (numbing, avoidance, irritability, fright, autonomic unbalance) can be seen as the normal, evolved responses of the defence system activated by a traumatic event that become abnormal because of their duration, not of their nature that is expression of evolutionary adaptations (Cantor, 2004). It is likely that the activation of defence system after a traumatic event is usually terminated by soothing responses provided during careseeking-caregiving interactions involving the attachment system. However, if the attachment system is governed by a disorganized IWM, it will tend to stimulate from the inside the operations of the defence system and therefore fail to deactivate it. Hence the powerful and protracted activation of the defence system expressed in post-traumatic symptoms, and hence also the prolonged activation of the attachment system together with the dissociative influences of the compartmentalized IWM. In other words, traumatic events in people with histories of infant disorganized attachment will cause a re-enactment of the situation of fright without solution that characterizes attachment disorganization, and that in infancy is caused by the fact that the source of potential comfort is also, at the same time, the source of fear. There is no solution to the fright because infants cannot find relief from fear in responses mediated by the defence system (e.g. flying from the threatening caregiver), nor in responses controlled by the attachment system (e.g. approaching her or him in search for comfort). Throughout the developmental years and in adult life fright without solution gives origin and maintains what have been called the simultaneous and opposite phobias of inner states (Van der Hart et al., 2006): phobia of wishes for attachment (linked to the activation of the defence system primed by the expectation of threats from attachment figures) and phobias of feelings of impending separations and losses (linked to the simultaneous hyper-activation of the attachment system). These two phobias of inner states are held to play a key role in the structural dissociation of the personality (Van der Hart et al., 2006).

The mental mechanisms responsible for the dissociative influences exerted by the disorganized IWM whenever the attachment system becomes active are likely to involve the dynamics of implicit (non-verbal, or sub-symbolic: Bucci, 1997). Being constructed during the first two years of life, the representations of any IWM, organized or otherwise, necessarily pertain to the non-verbal domain of self-knowledge, that is, they operate at the implicit level of memory and expectations (Amini Lewis, Lannon et al., 1996). In other words, they are aspects of the ongoing implicit relational knowing that, besides characterizing the early phases of personality development, persists operating throughout the life span (Lyons-Ruth, 1998). Implicit relational knowing manifests itself in communication as intersubjective enactments (Lyons-Ruth, 1999) rather than as verbalized (explicit) meaning structures.

In the case of the IWM of disorganized attachment, such an enactment takes the form of a non-integrated coexistence of emotions and behaviours linked to the attachment system (e.g. wish to approach a potential attachment figure) with emotions and behaviours linked to the defence system (e.g. fear and tendency to flight). While this condition can be understood as a conflict between two basic motivational systems, at the level of representations it must be understood as a structural dissociation (rather than a conflict) between the incompatible sub-symbolic representations of self-with-other linked to the two different inborn systems. Since integration in consciousness of incompatible sub-symbolic representations involves first the elaborations of these representations into the explicit (verbalizable) realm – what Bucci (1997) calls referential activity or referential process of the mind – with the construction of an explicit super-ordinate meaning structure, the incompatible representations of the IWM remain dissociated in the intersubjective exchanges of implicit relational knowing.

The structurally dissociated (compartmentalized) representations of disorganized attachment, together with the dramatic re-experiencing of fear without solution during later attachment interaction, tend to hamper the higher (conscious and regulatory) mental functions during personality development, so that mentalization deficits, emotional dysregulation and impulsivity tend to follow infant attachment disorganization (Bateman & Fonagy, 2004). It should be emphasized that both dissociation among representations of self-with-other and mentalization deficits tend to occur, in people with disorganized attachment, during the experience of attachment needs and wishes rather than in moments where interpersonal behaviour is motivated by systems different from attachment, such as the competitive, the sexual, the caregiving or the cooperative systems (Liotti & Gilbert, 2011).

Developmental sequels of infant disorganized attachment: tensions between the attachment system and other motivational systems

The above analysis of disorganized attachment in terms of an unsolvable tension between the attachment and the defence system, expressed in a dissociative process, implies an important question: why this dissociative process does not manifest itself in pervasive and clinically evident dissociative symptoms during the personality development of most children and adolescents coming from an infant history of attachment disorganization? The answer is that, remarkably, disorganized attachment in infancy develops into rigid, controlling behaviour in middle childhood (Lyons-Ruth & Jacobvitz, 2008; Solomon, George & DeJong, 1995), which seems aimed at restraining the activation of the disorganized IWM (Hesse et al., 2003; Liotti, 2011a, 2011b).

There is robust evidence (for a review, see Lyons-Ruth & Jacobvitz, 2008) that most infants disorganized in their attachments either become bossy children who strive to obtain dominance by exerting aggressive competitiveness towards the caregiver (controlling-punitive strategy), or become children who invert the attachment relationship and display precocious caregiving towards their parents (controlling-caregiving strategy). These controlling strategies seem to compensate for disorganization in the child-parent interactions: they allow for organized interpersonal exchanges with the caregivers, thus reducing the likelihood of dissociative processes during these exchanges. The unconscious mental processes that generate the controlling strategies, it has been argued (Liotti, 2011a, 2011b), involve the activation of interpersonal motivational systems different from the attachment system but based as the attachment system on Darwinian adaptations, and therefore universally available to human beings. Whenever the attachment system tends to become dominant in governing the interpersonal behaviour and experience, children who have been disorganized in their infant attachments become prone to activate another motivational system instead of attachment. If this other system is the caregiving one, a controlling-caregiving strategy takes shape. If the other system is the competitive one (ranking ritualized aggression aimed at achieving dominance won the antagonist in interpersonal exchanges), the controlling-punitive strategy is generated.

If this analysis of the controlling strategies, based on the hypothesis of abnormal tensions between the attachment system and the caregiving or the competitive system, is correct, then we may expect that the attitudes of the caregivers play a major role in determining the type of controlling strategy a child will generate. A major cause of the controlling caregiving strategy is the relationship with a vulnerable, helpless parent who encourages the child to invert the normal direction of the attachment-caregiving strategy. A parent who perceives the child as powerful and evil may be one condition for the development of a controlling-punitive strategy. It is noteworthy that children with a controlling-punitive strategy are more prone than other children to develop externalizing disorders characterized by impulse dyscontrol, while children with a controlling-caregiving strategy tend to develop internalizing disorders, characterized by anxiety and depression (Moss, Smolla, Cyr et al., 2006). It can be hypothesized that a controlling-punitive strategy mediates between infant attachment disorganization and adult cluster B personality disorders (including BPD: Liotti, 2014), while a controlling-caregiving strategy is a risk factor for anxiety disorders, mood disorders or cluster A personality disorders.

The controlling strategies can put a brake on the activation of a child's attachment system in the usual daily situations where children's attachment needs are stimulated, such as brief separations from the caregiver. However, these strategies collapse in the face of events (e.g. traumas, threats of prolonged or separation), which stimulate intensely and durably the child's attachment system (Hesse et al., 2003). During the phases of collapse of the controlling strategies, the child's thought and behaviour suggest that dissociative processes are at work, presumably because of the reactivation of the disorganized IWM (Hesse et al., 2003; Liotti, 2004, 2011a, 2011b, 2012, 2013, 2014) causing disorganization of behaviour and narratives, panic (fright without solution), or even clear-cut dissociative symptoms (e.g. depersonalization). An important implication of this view of the developmental psychopathology of syndromes rooted in infant attachment disorganization is that dissociative tendencies underpin the clinical manifestations of the disorder even in moments when clear-cut dissociative symptoms are not to the fore because the controlling strategies temporarily restrain the activation of the disorganized IWM. This psychopathological theory invites the psychotherapists, both those working with children and those dealing with adult patients, to pay heed at signs of activation of the attachment system in the patient and at features of ongoing attachment exchanges whenever they try to understand the reasons for outbursts of dissociative symptoms.

Concluding remarks

The model of dissociative psychopathology outlined above, which explores the roots of manifest or latent dissociative processes in the manifold possible tensions between the disorganized attachment system and other motivational systems (defence, caregiving, competitive aggressiveness), illustrates both the key role of attachment dynamics and the need to consider these dynamics within the complex interplay with other system governing different basic aspects of human relatedness. It can be seen as an example of possible answers to the problem hinted at by Slade (2008), that a type of psychotherapy entirely based on attachment theory is impossible because human relations are governed by multiple motivational systems and by their complex reciprocal interactions, during personality development, in individualized and changing relational contexts. By taking into account the role of different types of tensions between attachment and other systems in shaping psychopathological syndromes – as exemplified by the diverse disorganized/controlling strategies – models of the kind outlined in this chapter can indeed guide the psychotherapist in making sense of abnormal interpersonal schemes and related psychopathological symptoms that do not seem to involve, prima facie, attachment-caregiving interactions. Quite often, however, the developmental roots of these interpersonal schemes can be traced back to abnormal tensions between attachment and other motivational systems. The identification of these developmental roots within the psychotherapy process could be a rewarding endeavour in clinical practice (see Liotti, 2013).

Although psychotherapy cannot be based only on the consideration of present and past attachment interactions, the dynamics of the attachment system may thus be acknowledged in the key role they often play in the genesis of psychopathology – a key role that is recognized by many experts of the treatment of chronic traumatization.

The phobias of attachment and attachment loss are pervasive in survivors of chronic traumatization and manifest in the therapy relationship through all phases of treatment. Overcoming these phobias is essential for further therapeutic gains, as attachment is the matrix in which all therapy takes place (Van der Hart et al., 2006, p. 278).

Much more basic research than is nowadays available, and the collection of clinical experiences based on the multi-motivational model outlined in this chapter are needed before psychotherapists can reliably apply it to their clinical practice. Just to give an example of the type of new questions posed by this model that should be addressed by basic research studies let us consider those related to the nature and genesis of the dissociated parts of the personality, or dissociated self-states, that constitute the essence of the Dissociative Identity Disorder (DID).

The nature and the genesis of the dissociated parts of the personality in DID is held, by the model presented in this chapter, to be traceable back to the abnormal tensions, throughout development, between the disorganized attachment system and other inborn motivational systems. The model predicts that DID is (1) linked to a relative failure in the construction of controlling strategies in childhood – so that shifts between self-representations related to attachment needs and dissociated self-representations related to the defence system are evident since childhood and are pervasive during personality development– or else is (2) the consequence of cumulative traumas during childhood, adding to the sequels of infant disorganized attachment in creating an increasingly rigid compartmentalization of self-representations related to controlling strategies. Each dissociated part of the personality, in this perspective, could be based on one motivational system, or else on a characteristic type of tensions between different motivational systems.

An example of dissociated self-states related to the attachment system could be the needy, suffering part of the personality that strives in vain for help and comfort, showing what has been described as the phobia of attachment loss (Van der Hart et al., 2006). Usually such a part of the personality alternates with a dissociated self-state related to the defence system, which displays the opposite phobia of attachment needs and frightfully avoids asking for help in the expectation of being re-traumatized (for a clinical illustration, see Liotti, 2013). Another example of self-states related to defence system is the dissociated part of the personality that aims at endless revenge, though destructive aggressiveness. Still another aspect that dissociated self-states constructed on the basis of the defence system turned against the self is the one prone to self-harming or repeatedly considering suicide.

One example of self-states related to the controlling strategies, and therefore displaying an abnormal tension between attachment/defence and a third motivational system, is the dissociated part of the personality that is compulsively caregiving. Another is the hypercritical, punitive self-state deriving from the controlling-punitive strategy, which sometimes appears as grandiose and narcissistically dominant over other people and sometimes is turned against the self in a sort of masochistic repetitive, severe self-shaming. To this list of dissociated self-states generated by the dissociative dynamics of disorganized attachment and by the tensions between the attachment system and other motivational systems one should add those related to the sexual system (e.g. self-states characterized by sexual promiscuity or by sexual perversions), that not infrequently enters into tension with a disorganized attachment in sexually abusing family environments. Mark Erickson (2000), reconsidering the theme of the Oedipus complex in the light of what we know about disorganized attachment, has argued that abnormal metal states related to sexuality may indeed be one outcome of being raised in sexually abusing families.

Such a taxonomy of the basic features of the dissociated self-states observed that the syndromes caused by chronic traumatization during the developmental years, based on the abnormal tensions with other motivational systems created by disorganized attachment and later cumulative trauma, seem to make sense in the light of the literature on DID that reports clinical observations of dissociated parts of the personality. Whether it is exhaustive or not, or whether it may be instrumental in the psychotherapeutic understanding of the genesis of dissociated self-states are questions to be answered by clinical research focused on this topic, and by process and outcome studies of psychotherapy.

References

Ainsworth, M.D.S., Blehar, M.C., Waters, E. & Wall, S. (1978). *Patterns of Attachment: A Psychological Study of the Strange Situation.* Hillsdale, NJ: Erlbaum.
Amini, F., Lewis, T., Lannon, R., Louie, A., Baumbacher, G., McGuinnes, T. & Zirker, E. (1996). Affect, attachment, memory: Contributions toward psychobiologic integration. *Psychiatry,* 59, pp. 213–239.
Bakermans-Kranenburg, M.J., & Van IJzendoorn, M. (2009). The first 10.000 adult attachment interviews: Distribution of adult attachment in clinical and nonclinical groups. *Attachment & Human Development,* 11, pp. 223–226.
Bartholomew, K. & Horowitz, L.M. (1991). Attachment styles among young adults: A test of a four-category model. *Journal of Personality and Social Psychology,* 61, pp. 226–244.
Bateman, A. W. & Fonagy, P. (2004). *Psychotherapy for Borderline Personality Disorder: Mentalization Based Treatment.* Oxford: Oxford University Press.
Bowlby, J. (1964). Note on Dr Lois Murphy's paper "Some aspects of the first relationship". *International Journal of Psychoanalysis,* 45, pp. 44–46.
Bowlby, J. (1969). *Attachment and Loss,* Vol. 1. (2nd edition 1982). London: The Hogarth Press.
Bowlby, J. (1988). *A Secure Base.* London: Routledge.
Bucci, W. (1997). *Psychoanalysis and Cognitive Science: A Multiple Code Theory.* New York: Guilford Press.
Cantor, C. (2004). *Evolution and Post-Traumatic Stress.* London: Routledge.
De Haas, M.A, Bakerman-Kranenburg, M.J. & VanIJzendoorn, M.H. (1994). The adult attachment interview and questionnaires for attachment style, temperament, and memories of parental behavior. *Journal of Genetic Psychology,* 155, pp. 471–487.

Dutra, L., Bureau, J., Holmes, B., Lyubchik, A. & Lyons-Ruth, K. (2009). Quality of early care and childhood trauma: A prospective study of developmental pathways to dissociation. *Journal of Nervous and Mental Disease*, 197, pp. 383–390.

Erickson, M.T. (2000). The evolution of incest avoidance: Oedipus and the psychopathologies of kinship. In P. Gilbert & K.G. Bailey (Eds), *Genes on the Couch: Explorations in Evolutionary Psychotherapy*, pp. 211–231. Hove: Brunner-Routledge.

George, C., Kaplan, N. & Main, M. (1985). *Adult Attachment Interview*. Unpublished manuscript, University of California, Berkeley.

George, C. & Solomon, J. (2008). The caregiving system: A behavioural systems approach to parenting. In J. Cassidy & P.R. Shaver (Eds), *Handbook of Attachment*, 2nd edition, pp. 833–856. New York: Guilford Press.

George, C. & Solomon, J. (2011). Caregiving helplessness: The development of a screening measure for disorganized maternal caregiving. In J. Solomon & C. George (Eds), *Disorganization of Attachment and Caregiving*, pp. 133–166. New York: Guilford Press.

George, C. & West, M. (2001). The development and preliminary validation of a new measure of adult attachment: The Adult Attachment Projective. *Attachment & Human Development*, 3, pp. 30–61.

Gilbert, P. (1989). *Human Nature and Suffering*. London: Erlbaum.

Hare, B. & Tomasello, M. (2004). Chimpanzees are more skilful in competitive than in cooperative cognitive tasks. *Animal Behavior*, 68, pp. 571–581.

Hazan, C. & Shaver, P. (1987). Romantic love conceptualized as an attachment process. *Journal of Personality and Social Psychology*, 52, pp. 511–524.

Hesse, E., Main, M., Abrams, K.J. & Rifkin, A. (2003). Unresolved states regarding loss or abuse can have "second-generation" effects: Disorganized, role-inversion and frightening ideation in the offspring of traumatized non-maltreating parents. In D.J. Siegel & M.F. Solomon (Eds), *Healing Trauma: Attachment, Mind, Body and Brain*, pp. 57–106. New York: Norton.

Holmes, E., Brown, R.J., Mansell, W., Fearon, R.P., Hunter, E., Frasquilho, F. & Oakley, D.A. (2005). Are there two qualitatively distinct forms of dissociation? A review and some clinical implications. *Clinical Psychology Review*, 25, pp. 1–23.

Liotti, G. (1992). Disorganized/ disoriented attachment in the etiology of the dissociative disorders. *Dissociation*, 5, pp. 196–204.

Liotti, G. (1999). Understanding the dissociative processes: The contribution of attachment theory. *Psychoanalytic Inquiry*, 19, pp. 757–783.

Liotti, G. (2004). Trauma, dissociation and disorganized attachment: Three strands of a single braid. *Psychotherapy: Theory, Research, Practice, Training*, 41, pp. 472–486.

Liotti, G. (2009). Attachment and dissociation. In P.F. Dell & J.A. O'Neill (Eds), *Dissociation and the Dissociative Disorders: DSM-V and Beyond*, pp. 53–66. New York: Routledge.

Liotti, G. (2011a). Attachment disorganization and the clinical dialogue: Theme and variations. In J. Solomon & C. George (Eds), *Disorganized Attachment and Caregiving*, pp. 383–413. New York: The Guilford Press.

Liotti, G. (2011b). Attachment disorganization and the controlling strategies: An illustration of the contributions of attachment theory to developmental psychopathology and to psychotherapy integration. *Journal of Psychotherapy Integration*, 21, pp. 232–252.

Liotti, G. (2012). Disorganised attachment and the therapeutic relationship with people in shattered states. In K. White & J. Yellin (Eds), *Shattered States: Disorganised Attachment and Its Repair*, pp. 127–156. London: Karnac.

Liotti, G. (2013). Phobias of attachment-related inner states in the psychotherapy of adult survivors of childhood complex trauma. *Journal of Clinical Psychology*, 69, pp. 1136–1147.

Liotti, G. (2014). Disorganized attachment in the pathogenesis and the psychotherapy of borderline personality disorder. In A.N. Danquah & K. Berry (Eds), *Attachment Theory in Adult Mental Health: A Guide to Clinical Practice*, pp. 113–128. London: Routledge.

Liotti, G. & Gilbert, P. (2011). Mentalizing, motivation and social mentalities: Theoretical considerations and implications for psychotherapy. *Psychology and Psychotherapy: Theory, Research and Practice*, 84, pp. 9–25.

Lyons-Ruth, K. (1998). Implicit relational knowing: Its role in development and psychoanalytic treatment. *Infant Mental Health Journal*, 19, pp. 282–289.

Lyons-Ruth, K. (1999). The two-person unconscious: Intersubjective dialogue, enactive relational representation, and the emergence of new forms of relational organization. *Psychoanalytic Inquiry*, 19, pp. 576–617.

Lyons-Ruth, K. (2003). Dissociation and the parent-infant dialogue: A longitudinal perspective from attachment research. *Journal of the American Psychoanalytic Association*, 51, pp. 883–911.

Lyons-Ruth, K. & Jacobvitz, D. (2008). Attachment disorganization: Genetic factors, parenting contexts and developmental transformations from infancy to adulthood. In J. Cassidy & P.R. Shaver (Eds), *Handbook of Attachment*, 2nd edition, pp. 666–697. New York: Guilford Press.

Main, M. & Solomon, J. (1990). Procedures for identifying infants as disorganized/disoriented during the Strange Situation. In M.T. Greenberg, D. Cicchetti & E.M. Cummings (Eds), *Attachment in the Preschool Years*, pp. 121–160. Chicago, IL: Chicago University Press.

Moss, E., Smolla, N., Cyr, C., Dubois-Comtois, K., Mazzarello, T. & Berthiaume, C. (2006). Attachment and behavior problems in middle childhood as reported by adult and child informants. *Development and Psychopathology*, 18, pp. 425–444.

Obegi, J.H. & Berant, E. (2008). Introduction. In J.H. Obegi & E. Berant (Eds), *Attachment Theory and Research in Clinical Work with Adults*, pp. 1–15. New York: The Guilford Press.

Obegi, J.H., Morrison, T.L. & Shaver, P.R. (2004). Exploring intergenerational transmission of attachment style in young female adults and their mothers. *Journal of Social and Personal Relationship*, 21, pp. 625–638.

Ogawa, J.R., Sroufe, L.A., Weinfield, N.S., Carlson, E.A. & Egeland, B. (1997). Development and the fragmented self: Longitudinal study of dissociative symptomatology in a nonclinical sample. *Development and Psychopathology*, 9, pp. 855–879.

Pasquini, P., Liotti, G., Mazzotti, E., Fassone, G. & Picardi, A. (2001). Risk factors in the early family life of patients suffering from dissociative disorders. *Acta Psychiatrica Scandinavica*, 104, pp. 1–7.

Roisman, G.I., Holland, A., Fortuna, K., Fraley, R.C., Clausell, E. & Clarke, A. (2007). The adult attachment interview and self-reports of attachment style: An empirical rapprochement. *Journal of Personality and Social Psychology*, 92, pp. 678–697.

Schore, A.N. (2009). Attachment trauma and the developing right brain: Origins of pathological dissociation. In P.F. Dell & J.A. O'Neil (Eds), *Dissociation and the Dissociative Disorders: DSM-V and Beyond*, pp. 259–276. New York: Routledge.

Slade, A. (2008). The implications of attachment theory and research for adult psychotherapy: Research and clinical perspectives. In J. Cassidy & P. Shaver (Eds), *The Handbook of Attachment Theory and Research*, second edition, pp. 762–782. New York: The Guilford Press.

Solomon, J. & George, C. (2011). Disorganization of maternal caregiving across two generations: The origins of caregiving helplessness. In J. Solomon & C. George (Eds), *Disorganized Attachment and Caregiving*, pp. 25–51. New York: The Guilford Press.

Solomon, J., George, C. & De Jong, A. (1995). Children classified as controlling at age six: Evidence of disorganized representational strategies and aggression at home and school. *Development and Psychopathology*, 7, pp. 447–464.

Sroufe, L.A. & Rutter, M. (1984). The domain of developmental psychopathology. *Child Development*, 55, pp. 17–29.

Tomasello, M. (1999). *The Cultural Origins of Human Cognition.* Cambridge, MA: Harvard University Press.

Tomasello, M. (2009). *Why we cooperate.* Cambridge, MA: The MIT Press.

Van der Hart, O., Nijenhuis, E. & Steele, K. (2006). *The Haunted Self: Structural Dissociation and the Treatment of Chronic Traumatization.* New York: Norton.

Van IJzenddorn, M.H. (1995). Adult attachment representations, parental responsiveness and infant attachment: A meta-analysis on the predictive validity of the adult attachment interview. *Psychological Bullettin*, 117, pp. 387–403.

Wallin, D.J. (2007). *Attachment in Psychotherapy.* New York: The Guilford Press.

Warneken, F., Chen, F. & Tomasello, M. (2006). Cooperative activities in young children and chimpanzees. *Child Development*, 77, pp. 640–663.

Chapter 3

Importance of attachment in the presence of a perceived threat

Mary Sue Moore[1]

When Selma Fraiberg published her ground-breaking paper, "Pathological Defences in Infancy" in 1982, it was considered by many to be a radical departure from accepted psychoanalytic theory. However, she catalysed a major paradigm shift in the fields of psychoanalysis and child development. Since that time, many carefully conducted research studies and clinical observations have established that infants and children, as well as adults, have an innate capacity to "dissociate" conscious awareness of bodily sensations as one of several neurologically organized survival mechanisms (Chu & Dill, 1990; Fraiberg, 1982; Lyons-Ruth & Spielman, 2004).

These capacities are found in human infants since birth. Whether the innate capacity to dissociate is triggered in any particular situation depends on the infant's awareness and experience of danger. Innate capacities to try to escape the situation or to fight to reduce the pain—impulses to flee or fight—are based on adrenergic reactions to fear. Apart from distress cries, which may bring a responsive adult to alleviate the fear, infants have minimal ability to alter the experience of extreme cold or hunger, for example.

Similarly, despite recognizing angry or hostile emotion in the facial expression of the other, an infant cannot fend off an abusive adult. If experience teaches an infant that actively reacting to an interpersonal attack with cries or flailing results in greater pain, a third innate neurobiological survival mechanism, one that is non-adrenergic and produced parasympathetically by the infant's body, will be triggered. This mechanism causes the sensations of fear or pain to be "blocked" from the infant's consciousness. This survival mechanism evolved, apparently, to allow humans to endure unavoidable, unbearable pain without consciously experiencing it at the time. This tertiary mechanism is triggered innately when flight or fight adrenergic responses are perceived to increase rather than decrease danger (Baldwin, 2013; Bowlby, 1973; Briere, 2006; McEwen, 2013).

Detailed research studies have verified these innate infant neurobiological survival responses, two of which are adrenergic, or sympathetic, and will trigger an action on the part of the infant to survive: The "flee" response is key when the threatened individual perceives that the danger can be reduced

DOI: 10.4324/9781003246541-4

or eliminated by actively distancing her/himself from the environment, and the secondary "fight" response will be activated when fleeing is perceived as likely to increase the survival risk, but there is some expectation of being able to mount a physical defence against the danger (Schore, 2003).

Included in the attachment survival response are the ability to recognize and remember the vision, smell, and touch of a protective other in addition to activating behaviours in the "flee" or "fight" range that are likely to ensure the protective proximity of another. These include gaze avoidance, or arching of the back when held, when the protective figure is not responding ("flee" reactions), and cries of distress and/or flailing, to bring a protective figure into close proximity ("fight" responses) (Ellis, Boyce, Belsky, Bakermans-Kranenburg, & van IJzendoorn, 2011; Lyons-Ruth, 1998).

The third brain-activated mechanism differs in that it is a parasympathetic response, designed to be triggered when neither "fleeing" nor "fighting" is perceived to enhance chances of survival. This parasympathetic, dissociative reaction is not an overt action of defence but is an internal "shutting down" of awareness of incoming body sensations. This mechanism does not allow for active defence against the danger but may enable the infant to survive otherwise unbearable pain. This tertiary survival response is of particular importance for human infants, as they are born in a state of such physical helplessness that most perceived life threats cannot be reduced or avoided by attempting to flee or to fight (Fraiberg, 1982; Gaensbauer, Chatoor, Drell, Siegel, & Zeanah, 1995; Grossmann et al., 2011; Zou et al., 2019).

To these three neurobiological mechanisms is added a fourth innate, intersubjective, and ideally, reciprocally interactive, survival mechanism: Humans and other primates are social species. Infants born in a very vulnerable state, unable to protect themselves from threats, have the innate capacity to use interpersonal behaviours to "attach" to a specific protective figure, or a few such specific figures (Bowlby, 1969; Nagy et al., 2010; Sander, Chappell, & Snyder, 1982).

One important feature of the environment of human infants and children is whether a specific, known, attachment figure is perceived to be nearby. If so, this awareness can trigger an infant's "flee" or "fight" response in an attempt to alert the protector to the infant's danger and draw her/him closer. Alternatively, when the protective attachment figure and the infant are simultaneously in danger, the protective attachment figure can respond in a way that becomes a model for survival, by fleeing while carrying the infant.

However, when an infant is isolated or alone when danger is experienced, her/his instantaneous reaction is not to try to flee or show distress but to "freeze," or dissociate; that is, the infant tries to become insensate, to appear to the predator to be dead. This does not allow the infant or child to protect him/herself against abuse, but it can allow the pain to be experienced without it being consciously registered by the infant.

In other words, the triggering of a dissociative response in an infant or child will depend on two things in addition to the perception of a life-threatening danger: an awareness of whether a known protective figure is present or absent, and an awareness of the specific context within which danger has been perceived (Cassidy, Ehrlich, & Sherman, 2013; Murray & Trevarthen, 1985).

In her recent chapter (Cassidy et al., 2013), Cassidy, Erlich, and Sherman summarize the essential elements of an infant's or child's response to threat in relation to the attachment figure's anticipated level of responsiveness, also citing John Bowlby (Bowlby, 1973):

> Most infants balance these three behavioural systems, responding flexibly to a specific situation after assessing both the environment's characteristics and the caregiver's availability and likely behaviour. ...

According to Bowlby (1973), "the degree to which each of us is susceptible to fear turns in great part on whether our attachment figures are present or absent" (ibid., p. 201).

Cassidy et al. continue:

> Bowlby described as important not only the physical presence of an attachment figure, but also the infant's confidence that the attachment figure will be available as needed.
> (Cassidy et al., 2013, p. 128)

In addition, a great deal has been written about the categories of attachment relationships in infants, children, and adults since the publication of Bowlby's trilogy *Attachment, Separation and Loss* (1969–1980). In 1978, three identifiable, organized patterns of attachment dyads—Avoidant (A), Secure (B), and Ambivalent/Resistant (C)—were described and classified by Mary Ainsworth, using her experimental design of a "Strange Situation" test (Ainsworth, Blehar, Waters, & Wall, 1978). One of Ainsworth's students, Mary Main, and her colleagues completed an analysis of the remaining "unclassifiable" attachment dyad tapes from the original Ainsworth studies. These were tapes of dyads where the infant seemed to reflect idiosyncratic responses or a mixture of behaviours normally classified into one group or another, upon reunion with the mother (Fearon, Lapsley, Bakermans-Kranenburg, van IJzendoorn, & Roisman, 2010; Lyons-Ruth, Yellin, Melnick, & Atwood, 2005; Main & Solomon, 1990).

Main and her student, Judith Solomon, proposed a fourth classification for these dyads, using the label "Disorganized / Disoriented Attachment" to reflect what appeared to the observing researchers to be odd infant behaviours upon reunion with the attachment figure that seemed to show simultaneous or sequential infant approach and avoid responses towards the returning attachment figure, among other "suddenly reunion-avoidant" behaviours (Liotti, 1999, 2004; Main & Solomon, 1986; Rayson, Bonaiuto, Ferrari, & Murray, 2017; Reisz, Duschinsky, & Siegel, 2018).

In his seminal research Liotti eloquently made the connection that is at the heart of our understanding today, developmentally linking the apparently disoriented/disorganized infant-parent attachment dyad behaviours to our understanding of adult dissociative behaviours and personality configurations (Liotti, 1995, 1999, 2004). Liotti's work, and that of dozens of others have exponentially added to our deeper understanding of dissociative dynamics and their earliest expressions in infant attachment dyads. All are worth reading (Baldwin, 2013; Briere, 2006; Duchinsky, 2018; Liotti, 1999, 2004; Lyons-Ruth, 2003a; Lyons-Ruth et al., 2005; Peltola, van IJzendoorn, & Yrttiaho, 2018; Sinason, 2002; Tucker, Poulsen, & Luu, 2015; Zou et al., 2019).

In closing, I would like to consider the following quote from Marcel Proust: "The real voyage of discovery consists not in seeking new landscapes but in having new eyes."

I believe our understanding of human development risks becoming distorted and misleading when our theories rely too heavily on our being able to observe behaviour visually. Perhaps we need new eyes. It is hoped that the above chapter will offer a new point of view both on the meaning of infant dissociation—from within a neurobiological, attachment-based understanding of the human infant's evolutionary preparedness to survive trauma—and on the crucial role of a protective, responsive, psychologically present attachment figure.

Key concepts

- First, the importance of a protective attachment figure being present in an infant's earliest days and months, to ensure the infant's survival (Bowlby, 1988; Cassidy et al., 2013).
- Second, the capacity of infants and children continually to assess the mental state of a known attachment figure, allowing the infant to ascertain whether a physically present other is psychologically "present" and aware of the infant's environment, as well as the needs of the infant or child (Fraiberg, 1982; George & Solomon, 1989; Lyons-Ruth, 1998, 2003b).
- Third, when an infant's or child's innate dissociative behaviours are triggered during an interaction with an attachment figure who is recognized by the infant to be physically present, but mentally, psychologically absent, the resulting infant behaviours, despite seeming "disoriented" to an outside observer, are, in fact, not being volitionally or consciously organized, but "innately survival-oriented." Thus, we should be thinking of attachment dyads who might be classified as "D,"

as "survival-oriented"—each towards the other—but not Dis-oriented or Dis-organized.

Note

1 I would like to acknowledge my gratitude to G. Liotti for his brilliant cross-discipline studies and publications, bringing the growing attachment literature of studies of "D" attachment dyads into the awareness of those studying adult dissociation and responses to trauma. We are deeply indebted to him for sharing his understanding and creative thinking with so many.

References

Ainsworth, M. D. S., Blehar, M. C., Waters, E., & Wall, S. (1978). *Patterns of Attachment: A Psychological Study of the Strange Situation*. Hillsdale, NJ: Lawrence Erlbaum.

Baldwin, D. (2013). Primitive mechanisms of trauma response: An evolutionary perspective on trauma-related disorders. *Neuroscience and Biobehavioral Reviews*, 37, pp. 1549–1566.

Bowlby, J. (1969). *Attachment and Loss: Attachment* (Vol. 1: Attachment). London: The Hogarth Press and The Institute of Psycho-Analysis.

Bowlby, J. (1973). *Attachment and Loss: Separation* (Vol. 2. Separation: Anxiety and Anger). London: The Hogarth Press and The Institute of Psycho-Analysis.

Bowlby, J. (1988). On knowing what you are not supposed to know and feeling what you are not supposed to feel. *A Secure Base: The Clinical Application of Attachment Theory*. London: Routledge.

Briere, J. (2006). Dissociative symptoms and trauma exposure: Specificity, affect dysregulation, and posttraumatic stress. *The Journal of Nervous and Mental Disease*, 194(2), pp. 78–82.

Cassidy, J., Ehrlich, K. B., & Sherman, L. J. (2013). Child-parent attachment and response to threat: A move from the level of representation. In M. Mikulincer & P. R. Shaver (Eds), *Nature and Development of Social Connections: From Brain to Group*, pp. 125–144. Washington, DC: American Psychological Association.

Chu, J. A., & Dill, D. L. (1990). Dissociative symptoms in relation to childhood physical and sexual abuse. *The American Journal of Psychiatry*, 147, pp. 887–892.

Duchinsky, R. (2018). Disorganization, fear, and attachment: Working toward clarification. *Infant Behavior and Development*, 39(1), pp. 17–29.

Ellis, B. J., Boyce, W. T., Belsky, J., Bakermans-Kranenburg, M. J., & van IJzendoorn, M. H. (2011). Differential susceptibility to the environment: An evolutionary–Neurodevelopmental theory. *Development and Psychopathology*, 23(1), pp. 7–28.

Fearon, R. P., Lapsley, A. M., Bakermans-Kranenburg, M. J., van IJzendoorn, M. H., & Roisman, G. I. (2010). The significance of insecure attachment and disorganization in the development of children's externalizing behavior: A meta-analytic study. *Child Development*, 81(2), pp. 435–456.

Fraiberg, S. H. (1982). Pathological defenses in infancy. *Psychoanalytic Quarterly*, 51, pp. 612–635.

Gaensbauer, T., Chatoor, I., Drell, M., Siegel, D., & Zeanah, C. H. (1995). Traumatic loss in a one-year-old girl. *Journal of the American Academy of Child & Adolescent Psychiatry*, 34(4), pp. 520–528.

George, C., & Solomon, J. (1989). Internal working models of caregiving and security of attachment at age six. *Infant Mental Health Journal*, 10(3), pp. 222–237.

Grossmann, T., Johnson, M. H., Vaish, A., Hughes, D., Quinque, D., Stoneking, M., & Friederici, A. D. (2011). Genetic and neural dissociation of individual responses to emotional expressions in human infants. *Developmental Cognitive Neuroscience*, 1(1), pp. 57–66.

Liotti, G. (1995). Disorganized/disoriented attachment in the psychotherapy of the dissociative disorders. In S. Goldberg, R. Muir, & J. Kerr (Eds), *Attachment Theory: Social, Developmental and Clinical Perspectives*, pp. 343–363. Hillsdale, NJ: The Analytic Press.

Liotti, G. (1999). Disorganization of attachment as a model for understanding dissociative psychopathology. In J. Solomon & C. George (Eds), *Attachment Disorganization*, pp. 291–217. New York and London: The Guilford Press.

Liotti, G. (2004). Trauma, dissociation, and disorganized attachment: Three strands of a single braid psychotherapy. *Theory, Research, Practice, Training*, 41(4), pp. 472–486. doi: 10.1037/0033-3204.41.4.472.

Lyons-Ruth, K. (1998). Implicit relational knowing: Its role in development and psychoanalytic treatment. *Infant Mental Health Journal*, 19, pp. 282–289.

Lyons-Ruth, K. (2003a). Dissociation and the parent-infant dialogue: A longitudinal perspective from attachment research. *Journal of the American Psychoanalytic Association*, 51, pp. 883–911.

Lyons-Ruth, K. (2003b). The two-person construction of defenses: Disorganized attachment strategies, unintegrated mental states, and hostile/helpless relational processes. *Journal of Infant, Child and Adolescent Psychotherapy*, 2(4), pp.105–114.

Lyons-Ruth, K., & Spielman, E. (2004). Disorganized infant attachment strategies and helpless-fearful profiles of parenting: Integrating attachment research with clinical intervention. *Infant Mental Health Journal*, 25, pp. 318–335.

Lyons-Ruth, K., Yellin, C., Melnick, S., & Atwood, G. (2005). Expanding the concept of unresolved mental states: Hostile/helpless states of mind on the adult attachment interview are associated with disrupted mother-infant communication and infant disorganization. *Development and Psychopathology*, 17(1), pp. 1–23.

Main, M., & Solomon, J. (1986). Discovery of a new, insecure-disorganized/disoriented attachment pattern. In M. Yogman & T. B. Brazelton (Eds), *Affective Development in Infancy*, pp. 95–124. Norwood, NJ: Ablex.

Main, M., & Solomon, J. (1990). Procedures for identifying infants as disorganized/disoriented during the Ainsworth Strange Situation. In M. Greenberg, D. Cichetti, & M. Greenberg (Eds), *Attachment in the Preschool Years*, pp.121–160. Chicago, IL: University of Chicago Press.

McEwen, B. (2013). The brain on stress: Toward an integrative approach to brain, body and behavior. *Perspectives on Psychological Science*, 8(6), pp. 673–675. doi: 10.1177/1745691613506907.

Murray, L., & Trevarthen, C. (1985). Emotional regulation of interactions between two-month olds and their mothers. In T. Field & N. Fox (Eds), *Social Perception in Infants*, pp. 177–197. Norwood, NJ: Ablex.

Nagy, E., Liotti, M., Brown, S., Waiter, G., Bromiley, A., Trevarthen, C., & Bardos, G. (2010). The neural mechanisms of reciprocal communication. *Brain Research*, 1353, pp. 159–167.

Peltola, M. J., van IJzendoorn, M. H., & Yrttiaho, S. (2018). Attachment security and cortical responses to fearful faces in infants. *Attachment & Human Development*, pp. 1–14. doi: 10.1080/14616734.2018.1530684.

Rayson, H., Bonaiuto, J. J., Ferrari, P. F., & Murray, L. (2017). Early maternal mirroring predicts infant motor system activation during facial expression observation. *Scientific Reports*, 7, p. 11738.

Reisz, S., Duschinsky, R., & Siegel, D. J. (2018). Disorganized attachment and defense: Exploring John Bowlby's unpublished reflections. *Attachment and Human Development*, 20(2), pp. 107–134.

Sander, L., Chappell, P., & Snyder, P. (1982). An investigation of change in the infant-caregiver system over the first week of life. In R. Emde & R. Harmon (Eds), *The Development of Attachment and Affiliative Systems*, pp. 119–136. New York: Plenum Press.

Schore, A. N. (2003). Early relational trauma, disorganized attachment, and the development of a predisposition to violence. In D. Siegel & M. Solomon (Eds), *Healing Trauma: Attachment, Mind Body, and Brain*, pp. 107–167. New York: W.W. Norton.

Sinason, V. (Ed.). (2002). *Attachment, Trauma and Multiplicity: Working with Dissociative Identity Disorder*. New York: Brunner-Routledge. Taylor Francis.

Tucker, D. M., Poulsen, C., & Luu, P. (2015). Critical periods for the neurodevelopmental processes of externalizing and internalizing. *Development and Psychopathology*, 27, pp. 321–346.

Zou, R., Tiemeier, H., van der Ende, J., Verhulst, F.C., Muetzel, R.L., White, T., Hillegers, M. & El Marroun, H. (2019). Exposure to maternal depressive symptoms in fetal life or childhood and offspring brain development: A population-based imaging study. *American Journal of Psychiatry*, 176 (9), pp. 702–710.

Chapter 4

"You will not believe me if I tell you!" – prenatal trauma and dissociation

Renée Potgieter Marks

Introduction

"You will not believe me if I tell you". The big brown eyes of Rachel studied me intently. "Well, I usually do, why don't you try?", I replied. "It was when I was in my mum's tummy", Rachel stated emphatically. Rachel was rummaging through the sand tray toys. "Aaaah!" Rachel exclaimed and took out an 'alien pod'. This is a plastic dome with a soft rubber alien in it (the alien with its big head looks very much like a foetus). "This is 'Baby Me'! This is how big I was when he tried to kill me!" she exclaimed. "Somebody tried to kill you when you were that small? Can you tell me about it?" I asked, but there was no answer. It was only the buzzers[1] of the EMDR[2]/BLS[3] that were making a sound. "How did I get here?" I wondered? The previous week Rachel identified "Baby Me is living in my head". Now, I only asked Rachel when "Baby Me" came to live with her, and this is the result!

Rachel studied the "foetus" and then buried it under the sand. She made sure that it was not visible at all. Rachel picked out a very big male figure and put it beside the tiny heap of sand under which "Baby Me" was buried. Rachel sat back, as if she tried to move away from the scene in front of her. "Rachel, I see that you are showing me something very important. Baby Me is under the sand and I cannot see her any longer. There is somebody very big close to her. What is happening?", I asked. Without lifting her head, she quietly said "Kill me". Silence. "Bad man". "They shouted". Silence. "He punched me". "He wanted me dead". Rachel moved forwards and started to pour more sand over the area where "Baby Me" was buried.

The possibility of children recalling pre-birth memories might raise questions and even objections. "But a foetus has no memory", most people might argue. "How can a child, like Rachel, recall what happened before she was born?" Some might argue that this is only 'fantasy'. Others might be convinced that Rachel knew her history of being exposed to severe domestic violence before she was born, while, in actual fact, she had no knowledge of these incidents, other than implicit memory which was busy surfacing.

DOI: 10.4324/9781003246541-5

Framing the discussion

The concept of prenatal trauma has been a divisive topic for a long time because there remains a lack of evidence for making detailed hypotheses and there is an urgent need to consider it for the purposes of treating people. The possibility of prenatal dissociation appears to be in its infant shoes.

I propose the conversation focuses on the question of how practitioners can treat trauma and dissociation, rather than trying to find evidence for the capacity of foetuses and infants to recall exact details from an event.

Framing the conversation in this way will allow practitioners to explore the possibility of pre-birth trauma and dissociation ahead of the scientific evidence.

Key hypotheses

The evidence available on this matter is sparse and vastly inadequate to meet the need for clinicians to treat their patients. I therefore made a few hypotheses to bear in mind when interpreting the data:

- Capacities such as memory are multidimensional. To remember that something is dangerous differs from remembering when and how that thing was first encountered.
- One can possess certain memory capacities and not others. One can remember that something is dangerous without remembering when and how that thing was first encountered.
- Human capacities for memory develop gradually over a long period of time. It might be thus possible for young infants to be adversely affected by traumatic experiences without yet having the capacity to recall details of the experience.
- Both children and adults confabulate when recalling past experiences, and some details of their recollection will be more accurate than others. It is thus possible to reflect critically on some of the recollected details while being confident about others.
- Due to the evolutionary advantage of responding to danger, the human capacity for remembering danger or being mentally influenced by dangerous events develops earlier than other capacities for memory.
- Practitioners do not need to know that all the details recalled of a traumatic event are accurate in order to deal with the dissociation and treat the trauma.
- Prenatal stress is not necessarily different from any other kind of early life stress.

Prenatal influences in birds

Dr Mylene Mariette and her team uncovered significant information with their research on the Zebra Finch in Australia. In hot weather, the Zebra Finch sings to their eggs in the days before hatching, which appears to have a physiological effect on their unborn offspring. Mariette and Buchanan (2016) found in their research that apparently the parents prepare the chicks for the temperature that they will experience after hatching. These sounds are made at a time that the chicks can potentially hear the parents. From this research it appears that the sounds that chicks hear from their parents can not only be heard, but the chicks can also respond on these sounds. If this is true of birds singing to the embryos in their eggs, the question needs to be asked how sound in the external environment might impact the human foetus.

Prenatal influences in animals

Prenatal stress increases the risk of shortened gestational length that is present across multiple generations of rats (Yao, Robinson, Zucchi, Robbins, Babenko, Kovalchuk et al., 2014). Various experiments with rodents resulted in evidence that stress in rodents can affect their behaviour on long term. DiPietro (2004, p. 71) states:

> Stress responses in rodents can be reliably induced by a variety of experimental methods. Deliberate exposure of pregnant laboratory animals to stressful events (e.g., restraint) produces effects on offspring. These include deficits in motor development, learning behaviour, and the ability to cope effectively in stressful situations.

DiPietro (2004) also refers to experiments with rhesus monkeys, where exposure to repeated loud noises in the prenatal phase resulted in delayed motor development and reduced attention in infancy.

Impact of early life stress (ELS)

"Early life stress (ELS) is defined as any such incident occurring within the defined development period from gestation through to either the onset of puberty or 18 years of age" (LaPrairie, Heim & Nemeroff, 2010). MacKinnon, Kingsbury, Mahedy, Evans and Colman (2018, p. 100) refer to the developmental programming hypothesis which "suggests that a foetus adapts to maternal cues about the external environment during critical periods of development". They also state that these "small adaptations" which occur in utero can have long-term consequences on the child's behaviour, health as well as mental and behavioural disorders. The prenatal stress may permanently "alter the hypothalamic-pituitary-adrenal axis" of the stress response in the foetus and cause long-term maladaptive stress responses.

In humans, the maternal prenatal depression and anxiety are associated with externalizing problems of their children (Korhonen, Luoma, Salmelin & Tamminen, 2014; Lahti, Savolainen, Tuovinen, Pesonen, Lahti, Heinonen, et al., 2017; Van Batenburg-Eddes, Brion, Henrichs, Jaddoe, Hofman, Verhulst, et al., 2013;). These disorders involve aggressive or antisocial behaviour, high levels of activity as well as difficulty with emotional regulation. In long term, these externalizing disorders are closely linked to school failure, substance abuse and criminal activity (Farmer, Compton, Burns & Robertson, 1998; Liu, 2004). MacKinnon et al. (2018, p. 101) refer to Barker and Maughan (2009) and state "for example results from one prospective study using the Avon Longitudinal Study of Parent and Children (ALSPAC) cohort suggested that high maternal anxiety during pregnancy was associated with a trajectory of persistent conduct problems throughout childhood". Exposure to specific prenatal stressful events correlates with symptoms of ADHD in two studies. Symptoms of ADHD are also associated with the death of a loved one during pregnancy (Class, Abel, Khashan, Rickert, Dalman, Larsson et al., 2014; Grizenko, Fortier, Zadorozny, Thakur, Schmitz, Duval & Joober, 2012; Grizenko, Shayan, Polotskaia, Ter-Stepanian & Joober, 2008; Li, Olsen, Vestergaard & Obel, 2010).

MacKinnon et al. (2018, p. 105) concluded:

> This 16-year prospective study of more than 10,000 mother – offspring pairs demonstrated an association between maternal stressful life events during pregnancy and subsequent risk of conduct disorder and hyperactivity symptoms in the offspring. Prenatal stress increased the risk for conduct disorder and hyperactivity symptoms throughout childhood in those with high maternal stress (i.e., top quartile), persisting until 16 years of age.

Babenko, Kovalchuk and Metz (2015) hypothesize that stress during pregnancy may affect the mental health in the offspring on long term. All these studies imply that exposure to significant prenatal stress might need at least some form of health/therapeutic intervention during their lifetime for these externalizing behaviours. Although medication is available to treat ADHD in most children, there is no specific medication which is able to treat all these externalizing behaviours effectively on long term. The question that might be of specific importance here is: whether any of these behaviours might be moderated or treated efficiently through an age-appropriate process of trauma processing? Trauma processing implies mostly at least some form of memory recall of the traumatic event that caused the stress. But will the child be able to retain or recall any prenatal memories relating to the initial traumatic event that happened in the external environment?

Prenatal memories

Controversial opinions still exist about the existence of prenatal memories. While many professionals still argue that prenatal memories do not exist, other writers and researchers are of a different opinion. Karr-Morse and Wiley (1999, p. 87) explain that although the memories of these first experiences of the foetus in utero will not be remembered in language and rational thoughts, the "limbic brain remembers, and our body remembers". They also state that the first environment that is actively shaping the human brain is the womb.

Chamberlain (1987) postulates that there is increasing evidence for a theory describing cellular memory which originated during the prenatal period. According to him these memories are usually behavioural rather that verbal memories. It is called cellular memory as specific parts if the body appears to hold and express these memories. In practice, this can often be seen in children who have no other way to explain the prenatal memory than through body movements and complex behaviours. If these 'behaviours' are treated with conventional behaviour modification, it merely increases the sense of helplessness and hopelessness in the child. It is often necessary to access the original prenatal experience and process this in order to enable these body or cellular memory to reduce its impact on the body and behaviour.

Dr Piontelli – medical practitioner, psychotherapist and psychoanalyst who observed foetuses from 16 weeks until birth and then followed them up until they were four years old – reports that there were some behaviours that the children displayed, which were very similar to behaviours they displayed prenatally. Piontelli (1992) observed that twins in utero were stroking each other in the womb through the dividing membrane and by the age of one year, their favourite game was to stroke each other being either side of a curtain. In another observation, Piontelli observed another set of twins hitting each other in utero and then continued to do so as soon as their motor development allowed it. "My central finding, as described above, is that there is a remarkable consistency in behaviour before and after birth and that many small children show signs after birth of being influenced by experiences they had before birth" (Piontelli, 1992, p. 22). She also treated children where their foetal past seemed to play a significant part in their current pathology. It appears possible that the foetus at least retains some form of 'memory' that allows intra-uterine behaviour to continue post-birth.

Is it possible that some of the neurons in the brain, somewhere, would also store prenatal sensory experiences? To be clear, the question is not whether the foetus has a fully developed sense of self before birth, whether it has the language capacity to identify trauma or whether it can think to itself in the womb. Prenatal trauma can have an impact without any of these factors being the case. Van der Kolk (2014) discussed traumatic memories and argues that the imprints of traumatic experiences are not organized in a logic way but are rather fragmented sensory and emotional traces of images, sounds and physical sensations.

How can trauma be remembered before the brain is fully functional? It can because not all memories are created equal. Decades of research have revealed that fear memories are processed through much simpler connections than other types of memory (LeDoux, 2015). This allows for faster reactions, conferring the evolutionary advantage of being able to respond quickly when in danger. Conserved among all mammals that have been tested, this feature is no less prominent in humans. If we have good reason to believe that a foetus of any species responds to outside stimulation, should we not prepare for the possibility that human infants might as well?

LaPrairie et al. (2010) found in the use of rodent models that early life adversity can have profound and permanent consequences on the behaviour and stress responses later in life. This also appears to be true in children who were exposed to prenatal stress as discussed above. Piontelli (1992) states that prolonged anxiety in pregnancy may be one of the emotions that affect the foetus and also hypothesize that the fears of the mother might impact the foetus and the child's behaviour at a later stage.

Impact of sound

If the song of the zebra finch pre-hatching of their chicks can impact the growth and development of the chicks to prepare them for better adaptation to the external environment, could the soothing voice of parents, songs of calming music also have a potential impact on the unborn child? The human cochlea and peripheral sensory end organs complete their normal development by 24 weeks of gestation. The thalamus that connects sensory organs to the amygdala develops at 31 weeks' gestation. There is also continued maturation of the neural acoustic networks until birth (Etzel, Balk, Bearer, Miller, Shea, Simon & Schell, 1997). This information is confirmed by Tasker, McClure and Aserni (2013).

Jones (2001) refers to the research of Psychologist Alexandra Lamont who found that babies can remember things from the womb for much longer than was originally thought. "Year-old babies still recognized and had a preference for musical pieces that were played to them before being born. Previous studies have only shown babies being familiar with prenatal experiences when they were a few days old".

Yehuda (2016, p. 6) states that the foetus "can hear during the last trimester of pregnancy". Yehuda (2016, p. 187) also states that "Foetuses hear their mother's heartbeat and body rhythms, and our nervous system remains attuned to rhythm through the interplay of our own heartbeat and autonomic system" (Nazzi et al.,1998; Ninio & Snow, 1996; Schore, 2012; Van der Kolk, 2014).

With these facts in mind, the question should also be asked what is the impact of harsh voices, fighting, violence, shouting, anger and aggression on the foetus before birth. This question might be a very sensitive one, especially in the light of the fact that domestic violence is commonplace in families around the world. Domestic violence is also often seen as acceptable, albeit by the silence of the professionals, leaving the children in continued domestic violent circumstances, as if we accept that they will 'survive' the domestic violence with minimum or no harm.

But what are the internal experiences of the child? Over the years, multiple children have recalled pre-birth experiences, which indicated that they suffered trauma during this period in their lives. In the early 90s, I treated a girl of four years who lived in foster care. She had significant attachment difficulties. One day she drew herself. The drawing was more unclear than normal and depicted a very small figure in a circle. According to Susie, this figure was her. With further exploration, she told me in no uncertain terms that this was when "I was in my mummy's tummy". I had to take a deep breath before knowing how to continue this exploration, as it was the first time I heard such information from a child and I was uncertain what to do next. "How does she feel?" I finally asked. "She is crying", Susie stated and added tears to the little figure. "I wonder what is happening that she is crying?" I explored further. With staccato answers, Susie finally explained that she heard very "loud music, shouting, fighting and screaming". Susie was covering her ears with her hands while she was providing this information. According to her, she was "very scared" and "crying".

Of course, I was very eager to discuss this information with the social worker, who referred the case to me. Fortunately, the social worker knew the case well and explained that before her birth, Susie's mother lived in a commune where there were multiple problems. The neighbours often complained about extremely loud music from the apartment where Susie's mother lived. Persistent violence, shouting and screaming was common, and the police often became involved. Due to the dire circumstances of her mother, Susie never lived with her but moved to foster care after birth. But Susie somehow was able to recall information to match these traumatic experiences. After my session with her, I discovered that this information had never been disclosed to Susie.

Impact of touch

The second sense the children reported, which affected them before birth, was specific types of touch, which originated from the external environment. Many of the children reported direct blows to them during what appeared like domestic violent incidents. In most cases, the files of social workers, and direct interviews with parents or family members substantiated this information. Some children are struggling to verbally express their experiences, and others are only able to show body movements, reminiscent to prenatal domestic violent incidents.

One four-year-old boy reported that the perpetrator "punched my mummy's belly button". A 15-year-old girl stated, "I was the target... he wanted me dead", referring to her prenatal experiences. Some children used a toy or doll to explain the sudden jerking movements and clearly indicated that they 'felt' these as a physical body sensation. Although all the children were not able to remember much detail, the sensory experiences that were recalled were sufficient to process the traumatic prenatal experiences with positive outcomes.

Case Vignette A

I vividly remember the eight-year-old boy who displayed extreme emotional outbursts at home. After one of these exceptional emotional outbursts, where he was screaming for 40 minutes and also tried to hurt himself by punching himself, his parents brought him for a therapy session. During the session, when asked what happened, Adam shrugged and said, "It was not me". "Well, Adam, if it was not you, can you please draw the one who was so upset?", I asked. Adam drew an infantile person. There were tears streaming down the face of the little figure. Adam then drew a circle around the figure and another bigger person attached to the circle. Suddenly the picture in front of me appeared to have a different meaning. "What did you draw Adam?", I asked. Adam ran to his adopted mother. He curled up on her lap. I moved closer and gave the mother the EMDR/BLS buzzers. She placed in on Adam's back. There was no response. Suddenly Adam made faint squeaking noises and his body was jerking. I reflected what I was seeing. More jerking movements followed. I was wondering what was happening with the little baby inside Sarah's tummy. Hesitantly, Adam said "Not want me". Silence. "Hit me". After some time where the adoptive mother reassured Adam of her love for him, Adam sat up again. "Adam, I wonder if you can help me? How old are you in this drawing?". Adam looked at me and said. That is not me, that is Zero. "Aaaah, and how old is Zero?", I asked. Without hesitation, Adam formed a 0 with his thumb and forefinger. "Mmmm, is that just after you were born?" I asked. "No, Renée", Adam sounded irritated. "You don't understand, Zero is unborn".

Over the next half an hour Adam was able to provide a more coherent narrative. Zero could not be born as he was "too afraid". Zero came to live with Adam to take all the "scary feelings away". It all happened because of the "punching" that the mother did to Adam as she "did not want to have a baby". It took many months before Adam finally felt safe enough to start to work with Zero and another couple of months before Zero felt safe enough to be born and adopted into this family. The screaming episodes and self-harm stopped permanently.

Development of the self

Is it possible to develop any form of dissociation, when there is no developed sense of self? Daniel Stern (1998, p. 38) states that during the period between birth and two months of age the infant is "actively forming a sense of an emerging self", which would be active for the rest of the child's life. A very important part of the life of the infant during the 'emerging self' phase is sensory experiences. If the sense of an emergent self can be developing while the infant is having multiple sensory experiences, is it also possible that an earlier self can develop prenatally where there are limited sensory experiences?

Is it possible that the "sensory self" starts to develop with the first flickering and awareness of intra-uterine sensory experiences? It appears from the subjective experiences of multiple children that the foetus might have at least some capacity to experience preferences, likes and dislikes, pleasure and unease, comfort and discomfort, pain and peace, all on a very elementary level, but vivid enough that the body, cells and senses will be able to recall some of these experiences later in life.

Prenatal dissociation

As if the memory and recall of pre-birth trauma does not pose enough difficulties, many traumatized children, during therapy, introduced a 'part' of the self that has not been born. Multiple children drew foetus-like figures: some inside a mother figure, others inside a round shape. The children mostly reported that these parts of the self were 'sad', 'scared' or 'unhappy'. Many of them reported that the 'baby' "did not want to be born".

When sensory experiences in utero are explored, it becomes evident that the sound in the external world played the most significant role in creating 'fear' and 'anxiety' in the foetus. These disclosures, of course, spark off another question. How is it possible for children to experience that 'part of the self' was left in utero while they were actually born? This question in itself might open another debate on 'prenatal dissociation', perceived dissociation, or the result of using 'parts' language during therapy with the children. Nevertheless, there is a clear indication that this group of children subjectively experience and report a separation from some part of the self before birth. In all cases, this separation from the self was induced by external traumatic experiences, often verified by external sources.

Piontelli (1992, p. 144) suggests that "foetuses may have some awareness of 'me/not me' sensations". She described how one child in utero was touching the wall of the uterus and then his face, back to the wall and then back to his face. The question was asked by one of the parents who observed these foetal activities during an ultrasound scan, whether the child could have been trying to feel "this is me, this is not me... me... not me...me...me?" (Piontelli, 1992, p. 128).

Piontelli also argues that the 'Me' and 'Not me' sensations might reach the foetus each time it moves. This might happen through the proprioceptive feedback, sensory stimulation as well as the enteroceptive and kinaesthetic stimuli. "From the moment the foetus begins to have sensory experiences, it seems to show highly individual preferences and reactions" (Piontelli, 1992, p. 234).

There might be two different ways that we can look at prenatal dissociation. The first is that perhaps the foetus has the capacity to dissociate but this is very difficult to prove. The other possible consideration is that the prenatal trauma can contribute to the development of dissociation later in the life of the child and somehow connect to traumatic prenatal experiences. Either way, we as practitioners need to be aware of the possibility of prenatal trauma in order to treat the children.

Anxiety and stress

A common denominator in these children is that they all present with very high levels of anxiety and also appear to be living with anticipatory anxiety. They all struggle with their attachment to their parents, foster carers or adoptive parents. Most children also at times display very high levels of externalizing behaviours – for instance anger and aggression, with significant change in voice, demeanour and physical stance during these episodes. Many children also report that the aggression is somehow related to the "baby that is not born" or prenatal experiences. There is a sense that part of the self might still rebel against the fact that the body of the child was finally expelled into the external world where the harsh sounds and touch originated from, with a lingering anticipation that this will repeat forever. Karr-Morse and Wiley (1997) state that the quality of the prenatal environment has the capacity to maximize healthy development or it can create biological and behavioural vulnerabilities in the brain of the child.

Epigenetic factors in these children should also be taken into account. "Epigenetics refers to the collective chemical and physical processes that program the genome to express its genes in a time- and cell-dependent manner" (Lutz & Turecki, 2014, p. 145). Epigenetic changes due to the stress of trauma in the parents have been shown to affect the epigenetic configuration of the foetus, which might cause the child to respond with less resilience in the face of traumatic and overwhelming experiences. Epigenetic factors might also have caused this group of children to be more vulnerable in their intra-utero experiences. Verny and Kelly (2004) referred to Sonntag who stated that exposure to distress in the uterus will alter the neuro-chemicals in the child and will leave the child with a heightened biological susceptibility to emotional distress after birth.

MacKinnon et al. (2018) refer to nonhuman primates where the offspring of stressed mothers showed higher cortisol, both at baseline and in a response to external stressful events. During these external stressful events, for example, in the case of domestic violence, the pregnant mother will endure significant stress. Her body will release cortisol that will cross the placental barrier to the foetus (Bergman, Sarkar, Glover & O'Connor, 2010). The impact on the foetus will be similar to that of the mother, with a raised heartbeat and possible fear/anxiety due to the altered physical changes in the body. The accompanying sounds, punches and verbal abuse could also have some impact on the foetus, who at a later stage during pregnancy will be able to hear and feel what is happening around him. What is the impact on the foetus if these experiences are happening regularly or relentlessly?

Case Vignette B

Lily, a six-year-old girl, drew herself inside her "mummy's tummy". She drew the fist that was "punching the baby", referring to herself in utero. Lily then continued to draw the fist bigger, and bigger and bigger, until it finally filled a full A4 page. At that stage, Lily filled seven pages with the fist, explaining how the punching continued, relentlessly. According to Lily, the baby inside was "crying" and finally, although she was born, there was a "Sad baby" and an "Angry baby" who were still not born. Neither of them could be born because they were "too scared". Further exploration indicated that Lily was adamant that "Angry" was hitting the foster carers because she got "confused" and thought they were the birth parents. It took persistent therapy and very hard work from the foster carers over a period of six months before "Angry" was finally able to accept that the foster carers were "safe" and would not hurt anybody before "Angry" agreed to be born. At that stage the external assaults on the foster carers started to slowly dissipate.

Kohler (2013, p. 10) states that the

> emotional life of the mother deeply influences the life of the foetus, which is connected to the mother with the umbilical court. Since feelings in the mother have a psychological basis and counterpart, any change in the mother's feelings state is immediately and automatically transmitted to the foetus.

We can accept that the fear, anxiety, emotional upset during severe conflict and domestic violence will also be soaked up by the foetus who somehow has to 'feel' and 'manage' these in the best possible way.

"Raised maternal anxiety during pregnancy is associated with increased risk of adverse neurodevelopmental outcomes for her child. The mechanisms underlying this are not known but animal studies suggest prenatal stress may alter the function of the placenta" (O'Donnell, Bugge, Freeman, Khalife, O'Connor & Glover, 2012). It is possible that the raised maternal anxiety might specifically negatively impact the neurodevelopment of the child's capacity for future emotional regulation. It presently appears from the clinical population that the children who experienced extreme anxiety in utero externalize the worst levels of emotional regulation.

MacKinnon et al. (2018, p. 106) state that "recognizing and validating the consequences of prenatal stress on externalizing disorders is a crucial first step to developing interventions for highly stressed pregnant women". They also refer to the research of Bergman et al. (2010) who found that attachment moderates the association between prenatal stress and offspring neurodevelopment. But what happens if the attachment is inhibited as the mother is the victim of the child's aggression and anger on a daily basis?

Conclusion

The fields of prenatal trauma, memory recall and dissociation are mainly uncharted territory in the field of child psychotherapy. Over a period of 24 years, the number of traumatized children who disclosed and recalled events regarding prenatal trauma became significant enough for child and adolescent therapists to start looking into this as a potential key to unlock a door that has previously had no right to exist in our minds.

It appears that once the door of prenatal trauma is unlocked, and the trauma had been processed and 'stuck dissociative states' are freed to be born and integrated, there is a significant change in the behaviour of the child. Could this be an important factor to free children and adolescents from dangerous looping in trauma, aggression, violence, control, hopelessness, self-harm and suicidal thoughts? While therapists are often trying to 'stop' or 'minimize' negative behaviours, it might be possible that we need to move one step further to the exploration of prenatal experiences. It might be imperative to explore the clues that children provide during therapy referring to prenatal experiences. Presently these appear to be important, but still undervalued and underexplored factors.

In the multiple trainings that I have delivered on this topic, it appears that fear is prevalent in the therapists to move into this unchartered territory. On the other hand, the multiple therapists who have started to explore the prenatal world of the child have seen the presence of a prenatal self-state that moved from 'stuckness' to development, from a sense of dying to embracing life, from hating to loving, while realizing the importance of this information.

And finally, in the words of Chamberlain (2018, p. 261), "The womb is a school, and all babies attend. It is a fact of life. The practical questions to ask are "How bad or how good is the school?" and, perhaps more important, "Do you learn to love the teacher?".

Notes

1 An electronic device with two sensors which provides alternative pulses to deliver bilateral stimulation.
2 EMDR: Eye Movement Desensitization and Reprocessing is a technique to process trauma.
3 Bilateral stimulation in this instance is used for some children to process trauma due to poor eye movements.

References

Babenko, O., Kovalchuk, I., & Metz, G.A.S. (2015). Stress-induced perinatal and transgenerational epigenetic programming of brain development and mental health. *Neuroscience and Biobehavioral Reviews* 48, pp. 70–91.

Barker, E. D. & Maughan, B. (2009). Differentiating early-onset persistent versus childhood – limited conduct problem youth. *The American Journal of Psychiatry*, 166(8), pp. 900–908.

Bergman, K., Sarkar, P., Glover, V., & O'Connor, T.G. (2010). Maternal prenatal cortisol and infant cognitive development: Moderation by infant–mother attachment. *Biological Psychiatry* 67, pp. 1026–1032.

Chamberlain, D. B. (1987). The cognitive newborn: A scientific update. *British Journal of Psychotherapy* 4(1), Autumn, pp. 30–71.

Chamberlain, D. B. (2018). Pre- and perinatal psychology can transform the world. *Pre-and Perinatal Psychology Journal* 8(3), Spring 1994, pp. 187–199. Reprint *Journal of Prenatal and Perinatal Psychology and Health* 32(3), Spring 2018, pp. 259–270.

Class, Q. A., Abel, K. M., Khashan, A. S., Rickert, M. E., Dalman, C., Larsson, H., et al. (2014). Offspring psychopathology following preconception, prenatal and postnatal maternal bereavement stress. *Psychological Medicine* 44, pp. 71–84.

DiPietro, Janet A. (2004). The role of prenatal maternal stress in child development. *American Psychological Society* 13(2), pp. 71–74.

Etzel, R. A., Balk, S. J., Bearer, C. F., Miller, M. D., Shea, K. M., Simon, P. R., & Schell, L. (1997). Noise: A hazard for the foetus and newborn. *Pediatrics* 100(4), pp. 724–727.

Farmer, E. M. Z., Compton, S. N., Burns, B. J., & Robertson, E. (1998). Review of the evidence base for treatment of childhood psychopathology: Externalizing disorders. *Journal of Consulting and Clinical Psychology* 70, pp. 1267–1302.

Grizenko, N., Shayan, Y. R., Polotskaia, A., Ter-Stepanian, M., & Joober, R. (2008). Relation of maternal stress during pregnancy to symptom severity and response to treatment in children with ADHD. *The Journal of Psychiatry & Neuroscience* 33, pp. 10–16.

Grizenko, N., Fortier, M. E., Zadorozny, C., Thakur, G., Schmitz, N., Duval, R., & Joober, R. (2012). Maternal stress during pregnancy, ADHD symptomatology in children and genotype: Gene-environment interaction. *Journal of the Canadian Academy of Child and Adolescent Psychiatry* 21, pp. 9–15.

Jones, N. (2001). Babies musical memories formed in the womb. *Daily News*, 11 July, 2001. https://www.newscientist.com/article/ dn994-babies-musical-memories-formed-in-womb/.

Karr-Morse, R., & Wiley, M. S. (1997). *Ghosts from the Nursery: Tracing the Roots of Violence.* New York: Atlantic Monthly Press.

Kohler, R. M. (2013). Archetypes and complexes in the womb. The Jung Page, reflections on *psychology, culture and life.* Houston, TX: The Jung Centre. http://www.cjungpage.org/learn/articles/analytical-psychology/870-archetypes-and-complexes-in-the-womb.

Korhonen, M., Luoma, I., Salmelin, R., & Tamminen, T. (2014). Maternal depressive symptoms: Associations with adolescents' internalizing and externalizing problems and social competence. *Nordic Journal of Psychiatry* 68, pp. 323–332.

Lahti, M., Savolainen, K., Tuovinen, S., Pesonen, A. K., Lahti, J., Heinonen, K., et al. (2017). Maternal depressive symptoms during and after pregnancy and psychiatric problems in children. *Journal of the American Academy of Child & Adolescent Psychiatry* 56, Edition 7, pp. 30–39.

LaPrairie, J. L., Heim, C., & Memeroff, C. B. (2010). The neuroendocrine effects of early life trauma. In R.A.Lanius, E. Vermetten & C. Pain (Eds), *The Impact of Early Life Trauma on Health and Disease,* pp. 157–165. Cambridge: Cambridge University Press.

LeDoux, J. (2015). *Anxious: The Modern Mind in the Age of Anxiety.* London: Oneworld Publications.

Li, J., Olsen, J., Vestergaard, M., & Obel, C. (2010). Attention-deficit/hyper- activity disorder in the offspring following prenatal maternal bereavement: A nationwide follow-up study in Denmark. *European Child and Adolescent Psychiatry* 19, pp. 747–753.

Liu, J. (2004). Childhood externalizing behavior: Theory and implications. *Journal of Child and Adolescent Psychiatric Nursing* 17, pp. 93–103.

Lutz, P. E., & Turecki, G. (2014). DNA methylation and childhood maltreatment: From animal models to human studies. *Neuroscience* 264, pp. 142–156.

MacKinnon, N., Kingsbury, M., Mahedy, L., Evans, J., & Colman, I. (2018). The association between prenatal stress and externalizing symptoms in childhood: Evidence from the avon longitudinal study of parents and children. *Biological Psychiatry* 83, 15 January 2018, pp. 100–108. Source: www.sobp.org/journal.

Mariette, M. M., & Buchanan, K. L. (2016). Prenatal acoustic communication programs offspring for high post hatchling temperatures in a songbird. *Science,* 353(6301), pp. 812–814.

Nazzi, T., Bertoncini, J., Mehler, J. (1998). Language discrimination by newborns: Toward an understanding of the role of rhythm. *Journal of Experimental Psychology: Human Perception and Performance,* 24(3), June 1998, pp. 756–766.

Ninio, A., & Snow, C. (1996). *Pragmatic Development.* Boulder, CO: Westview Press.

O' Donnell, K. J., Bugge Jensen, A., Freeman, L, Khalife, N., O' Connor, T. G., & Glover, V. (2012). Maternal prenatal anxiety and downregulation of placental 11β-HSD2. *Psychoneuroendocrinology* 37(6), 2012 June, pp. 818–826. doi: 10.1016/j.psyneuen.2011.09.014. Epub 2011 October 15.

Piontelli, A. (1992). *From Fetus to Child: Observational and Psychoanalytical Study.* London: Routledge.

Schore, A. (2012). *The Science of the Art of Psychotherapy, Norton Series on Interpersonal Neurobiology,* New York: Norton & Company.

Stern, D. N. (1998) *The Interpersonal World of the Infant: A view from psychoanalysis and Developmental Psychology*. New York: Karnac.

Tasker, R. C., McClure, R. J., & Acerini, C. L. (Eds.). (2013). *Oxford Handbook of Paediatrics*. Oxford: Oxford University Press.

Van Batenburg-Eddes, T., Brion, M. J., Henrichs, J., Jaddoe, V.W.V., Hofman, A., Verhulst, F.C., et al. (2013). Parental depressive and anxiety symptoms during pregnancy and attention problems in children: A cross-cohort consistency study. *Journal of Child Psychology and Psychiatry* 54, pp. 591–600.

Van der Kolk, B. (2014). *The Body Keeps the Score: Mind, Brain and Body in the Transformation of Trauma*. London: Penguin Publishing Group.

Verny, T., & Kelly, J. (2004). *The Secret Life of the Unborn Child*. London: Time Warner Book Group UK.

Yao, Y., Robinson, A. M., Zucchi, F. C. R., Robbins, J. C., Babenko, O., Kovalchuk, O., et al. (2014). Ancestral exposure to stress epigenetically programs preterm birth risk and adverse maternal and newborn outcomes. *BMC Medicine* 12, pp. 121. Source: http://www.biomedcentral.com/1741-7015/12/121.

Yehuda, N. A. (2016). *Communicating Trauma: Clinical Presentations and Interventions with Traumatized Children*. London: Routledge.

Chapter 5

A case series of 70 victims of exploitation from child sexual abuse imagery

Joyanna Silberg

Introduction

The creation of child sexual abuse imagery (CSAI, previously termed child pornography) is a billion-dollar industry. Since the early 1990s, individuals with a motivation to exploit children sexually have found ways to profit from their proclivities through the creation of private chat rooms and websites, where members are charged to view images of children engaged in sexual activity or in provocative poses. These photographs are often brutally sadistic. Once a picture is distributed on the Internet, it is virtually impossible to remove it. Pictures get traded and reproduced simultaneously in multiple locations and so the proliferation of images is astronomical. Even pictures taken in the early 1990s when the Internet first came on the scene are routinely found when child pornography criminals are arrested (Finkelhor & Ormrod, 2004).

Organized rings involving the creation of child sexual abuse imagery have been exposed all over the world (Gilad, 2013). Few assessment tools include questions regarding online exploitation and many practitioners familiar with sexual abuse have no familiarity with this topic (Martin, 2014). Gilad (2013) defined *Cyber Child Pornography Rings* (*CCPRs*) as "organized communities dedicated to the illegal depiction of minors engaged in sexually explicit acts, and utilize the Internet in one way or another to further their criminal activity." In 2016, a child sexual abuse imagery bust in Scotland revealed over 500 child victims and over 70 perpetrators (Press Association, 2016). People are often surprised that respected professionals—doctors, lawyers, policeman, executives, and government officials—are involved in this industry. In 2013, an international child pornography ring was busted in Toronto called the SPADE Project. Investigators uncovered 400 victims and over 300 perpetrators including teachers, priests, and other community leaders (Silva, 2013). In a child pornography ring called "The Club" uncovered in 2001 by the FBI, members requested "custom-made pictures" of specific activities involving 45 children (Gilad, 2013).

DOI: 10.4324/9781003246541-6

These recent criminal investigations have revealed that current exploiters of CSAI are using younger images, and children of Caucasian race are more desirable for trading or commercial benefit. In a recent study of young adults whose pictures were found online after being abused for the creation of CSAI, the symptoms displayed were very severe, including a high percentage of dissociative disorders (Canadian Centre for Child Protection). Of this group of survivors, 53% indicated that their sexual abuse occurred with multiple perpetrators in an organized way (Canadian Centre for Child Protection, 2017, Jan 17). These survivors, whose pictures were posted online when they were children, displayed symptoms of dissociation, depression, nightmares, and self-harm, which are expected correlates of extreme trauma.

Organized rings are particularly difficult to infiltrate and expose. This is because the perpetrators are often extremely technically savvy and therefore are able to cover their tracks with sophisticated encrypting. In addition, the high positions of many of the members of these rings allow them to counter law enforcement efforts and divert them.

As cybercrime has continued to proliferate on the Darknet (an encrypted place on the Internet difficult to access), the level of torture shown has increased, victims may be of younger ages including infants, and the extremity of the criminal behavior has increased. The most severe sexual abuse imagery has been termed "Hurtcore" and may include severe torture and even death of young children being sexually tormented (Maxim, Orlando, Skinner, & Broadhurst, 2016). Recent arrests of individuals engaged in this severe criminal activity in Australia have revealed the high level of torture these individuals are willing to engage in with younger and younger victims.

It is difficult to depend on the children for disclosures that lead to arrests in many online sex rings. Children often delay disclosure because they are ashamed, confused, afraid to not be believed and terrorized by threats of death or death of family members. Even when pictured evidence is found, children often deny their participation in the experience (Sjöberg & Lindblad, 2002a, 2002b). In addition, the children chosen may have vulnerabilities which make it difficult for them to report on their experiences such as a very young age, developmental delays or autism, or having been drugged. As child services organizations have become increasingly careful about multiple interviews of children, many children receive only one interview in which they don't disclose due to fear and unfamiliarity with the examiner. The process of dissociation, a coping tool that allows the mind to forget unpleasant information, is often used by these children making it difficult for them to report on their experiences (Putnam, 1997; Silberg, 2022; Waters, 2016). In addition, dazed states and frantic avoidance behavior may be mistaken for other more common childhood conditions such as seizures or hyperactivity disorder.

In the cases described here occurring in the religiously devout community in Jerusalem, aspects of the community made the children more accessible to this kind of illegal industry. The religiously devout community has a belief in the goodness of their own community. As Salter (2003) has described, good people tend to be trusting and have a low index of suspicion that others are meaning to harm them, particularly members of their own community who share their values. Children who are abused in the context of tight knit religious communities may find it particularly difficult to report the abuse as they have little context to understand their traumatic experiences and tend to be compliant to authority (The American Interest, 2012). The belief system of the community makes modesty a very high value and discussion of sexuality is very limited. This may make it difficult for children to find language to describe their experiences of sexual abuse, and they feel shame about what they have been exposed to. This shame presents a barrier to opening up readily to their parents regarding what they have experienced and promotes compartmentalization of their experiences (dissociation), making the information harder for them to access (Silberg, 2017).

Methodology

The author had been contacted for supervision from therapists in Israel and the United States due to her expertise in treating severe child abuse and dissociation. These therapists described seeing multiple children with similar symptoms, reporting abduction and abuse by strangers in religious neighborhoods in Jerusalem. The therapists in the United States were treating children whose families had recently relocated from Jerusalem. The extreme nature of the symptoms presented and commonalities across cases suggested the possibility that there was a common source of the abuse, resembling what is known internationally about organized abuse with multiple perpetrators and multiple victims.

The author undertook the task of organizing case histories for the purpose of alerting community members and law enforcement in a time sensitive manner due to the extreme risk of widespread harm to children. The author developed a data entry form after interviewing 15 families and children. This form was developed to track the major trauma symptoms described by the families, to categorize the forms of abuse and abduction described by the children, and to provide information about whether the case was reported to local authorities. Existing checklists like the Child Dissociation Checklist, the Trauma Symptom Inventory, and symptoms described by Silberg (2013) in *The Child Survivor* and Waters (2016) in *Healing the Fractured Child* were reviewed so as to include all symptoms relevant to severe trauma. Definitions of the symptoms and disclosure categories are contained in Appendix.

Permission was obtained by each family to include their child's information in the group data with an assurance of confidentiality in the reporting. These data entry forms were distributed to ten therapists who were asked to submit the completed forms on their patients, without names, to maintain the children's anonymity. In cases where the therapists did not have the relevant information or time to complete the forms, the families agreed to interviews with the author, who filled out the data entry form.

Two research assistants and the author coded each data entry sheet based on shared definitions of the variables. If questions arose about how to code a disclosure or symptom, consensus was reached through discussion among the research assistants and author (see Appendix for definitions of variables).

Reliability was enhanced through discussion and clarification of definitions during the coding process. The symptoms were written in language easily understood by professionals, and the definitions explained to the research assistants who did the coding. In some instances, children were seen by multiple professionals, and in some cases a collateral professional or consultant filled out the data sheet.

Criteria for inclusion of the case in this series were the following:

1. *Parent was concerned about a child's behavior and functioning, sought therapy for their child's symptoms, and was living or had recently lived in Jerusalem or surrounding areas. Children were either in therapy or waiting for a therapist's availability.*
2. *Disclosure from the child involving some form of "abduction" (abduction content could be reported as a "dream" or "bad thought") or a disclosure of abuse or a traumatic reenactment of abuse from a perpetrator outside the family*
3. *Exclusion criteria included families who reached out for therapy, but had no symptoms to report; families whose children reported interfamilial abuse; and families who lived in other areas when the children began to be symptomatic and had not lived in Jerusalem.*

These criteria resulted in 70 children who were being seen by a therapist or waiting for therapist availability. Case histories and symptoms profiles were collected from the practices of 14 practitioners of child psychotherapy in the United States—in Maryland, New Jersey, New York, and Israel—who got permission from the parents to report anonymously about the children's symptoms on a form created by the author (see Appendix A). The author filled out the form for children seen by three American therapists through interviews with the family. Collateral therapists filled out forms for two shared clients in Israel. The data was entered into an excel data sheet and statistical summaries were tabulated and graphed. All therapists had attended training in severe child trauma and in childhood dissociation and have experience working with traumatized children.

Because of the urgent need for information to be provided, this research represents a preliminary analysis of the information available. Currently, an additional cohort of children is being collected for analysis including children from the practices of some additional therapists. In addition, some new variables will be analyzed in the future including physical signs presented by the children, and disclosures of observations of violence. Finally, further analysis will be done of eating disorder and self-harm issues, along with more detailed examination regarding content and timing of abuse disclosures.

Results

Demographics

Most of the families reaching out for help were American born who had moved to Israel for a variety of economic or familial reasons. Upon learning of the harm their children were suffering, some moved back to the United States to get care for their children and support from their extended families. All the children were Caucasian and ranged in age from three to 13. Most children (31) were between the ages of six and eight, but 22 children were preschoolers between the ages of three and five. Sixty percent of the children were male. Table 5.1 shows the age and gender of the children.

Symptomatic presentations

Table 5.2 displays the primary symptoms of the children. The most common symptoms were nightmares and other sleep disorders, rages, and sexualized behaviors. Sleep problems included inability to sleep in one's own bed, not being able to fall asleep due to "bad memories," repeated night waking, and refusing to sleep without a parent in the room.

One of the most problematic symptoms was the spontaneous rages that many of the children experienced. During these episodes, children often displayed violent behaviors such as chasing siblings and attempting to stab or choke them. This behavior cannot be blamed on exposure to movies or television as these were not allowed in the children's community. The children's

Table 5.1 Age and gender of children

Age	Male	Female	Total
3–5	13	9	22
6–8	16	15	31
9+	13	4	17
Total	42	28	70

Table 5.2 Symptom categorization

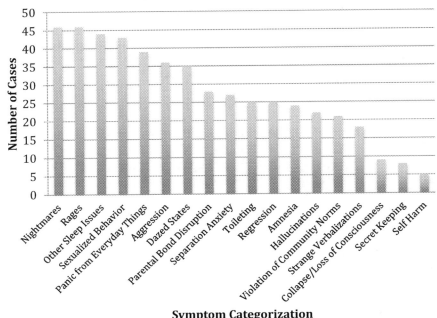

Symptom Categorization

violent outbursts suggest that they may have been victims of or witnessed aggression.

Another frequent finding was sexualized behavior. It is important to keep in mind that these children have had no exposure to television or Internet materials and so any sexualized behavior they have learned would be from direct observation or experience. These behaviors included sexual acts between siblings, attempting to touch a parent's private areas, taking off clothes and posing provocatively, playing out sexual themes with dolls, masturbating in public or to the point of injury, and drawing pictures with explicit sexual content.

Dissociative symptoms were prominent such as dazed states, forgetfulness, and hearing internal voices. Some of the children reported multiple voices of perpetrators that continue to direct them, coded below as "hallucinations." These internal voices continue to command them to do negative behaviors even after they have moved to other countries or cities. According to the children, some of the internal voices had the name of the child's perpetrators. This phenomenon has previously been described in the literature and childhood dissociative disorders (Silberg, 2013; Waters, 2016; Wieland, 2015). Amnesia is generally a rare symptom in children. However, many of these children reported forgetting their own recent experiences like accompanying a parent to work, going to school, going on an outing, as well as spotty memory for the abusive activities. The type of amnesia is consistent with dissociative disorders in children (Silberg, 2013; Waters, 2016).

The most severe dissociative symptom involved a complete physical collapse, also termed "collapsed immobility" (Koslowska, 2013 or "dissociative shutdown" (Silberg, 2022). Physical collapse was displayed by nine of the children. This reaction is a rare phenomenon and a sign that the brain's fear system has been activated to such an extreme degree that the child reverts to a very primitive avoidance response (Perry et al., 1995). Some children may simply freeze in the middle of a sentence and remain frozen for 20 minutes or more. Others may collapse on the ground and remain unresponsive for several minutes or longer. The "dazed states" of these children are consistent with dissociation (Putnam, 1997; Silberg, 2022; Waters, 2016). The children appear to be in another world, their eyes may go blank, and they may twirl looking at their hands in stereotyped movements that resemble autistic behaviors. Because of this, some of the children had been labeled with developmental disorders; however, the rapidity of progress after treatment and the uneven developmental presentation made it clear that the behavior was trauma-based (Silberg & Lapin, 2017).

Regression and other changes of state involve children acting younger than their age, suddenly talking with strange voice or different accents, or changing mood quickly and without warning. One five-year-old boy, with no apparent familiarity with people from Britain, suddenly began to speak with a British accent. Many started speaking in baby talk, particularly at night, and acted very regressed. Others seemed to enter a different state when they were sad, with tears rolling down their face but impervious to questions or comforting from a parent. This type of unpredictable affect and state change is a familiar symptom among dissociative children. Their changes of state can be triggered reactions to overwhelming stimuli or memories, and the triggering events are often subtle and invisible to observing adults (Putnam, 1997; Silberg, 2022, Waters, 2016; Wieland, 2015).

Ongoing panic and fear triggered by multiple environmental stimuli was described by 37 of the children. This included fear of certain colors, certain cars, being alone in a room, being alone in their own bed, being near a window, going past certain buildings, and certain foods and drinks. The fear of food and drink resulted in dietary restrictions that could be very unhealthy, such as a child eating only bread. This panic, often not understood by the family, could lead a child to have extreme crying fits in public when the parent, for example, parked on the wrong street (according to the child), won't enter a building using a certain door, or gave the child the "wrong" drink.

Disruption of attachment is a known consequence of early trauma (Perry & Szalavitz, 2007; Silberg, 2022; Waters, 2016). Whether or not the parent was responsible or knew about the abuse, children felt alienated from their parents for not having "saved them" when they were frightened and alone and being hurt. This often translates into rage at the parents and refusal of physical contact or eye contact. Many of the children verbalized, "You are not my Mommy," and rejected soothing. Some children describe direct manipulation of their attachment, having been told that they were not the "real" children of their parents, or that they have other parents. This becomes a main target of intervention as it is impossible for the child to heal without accepting the soothing efforts of a loving parent or other primary caregiver.

However, this difficulty with attachment is often accompanied by extreme anxiety during separation. Separation anxiety displayed is way beyond the normal anxiety displayed by young children. Children ask to go into the bathroom with their parent, and even seven-year-old often cannot tolerate a parent entering another room, so the children with this symptom follow parents from room to room. This interferes with the children's ability to play or entertain themselves, as fear appears to be the overriding affect driving their behavior even when there is no overt threat present.

Toileting issues involve accidents during the day and/or night after successful toilet training. Some of the children, even while feeling the need to go, refused to go to the bathroom and then ended up having an accident. Others reported no longer having the sensation to void or defecate. Direct work on enhancing sensitivity to these bodily states is recommended in treatment. Some children described forced ingestion of urine and feces. Some of the children would urinate or defecate only in cups or bathtubs, but not in the toilet. Some children would dangerously retain feces for fear of using toilets with which they were unfamiliar. Many refused to go to bathrooms unaccompanied, even at older ages, when privacy is usually preferred.

Violation of community norms involved the children refusing to attend celebrative family events, throwing chairs from the table, running out of the room during prayers, and throwing religious books on the ground. While rebellious children when angry may show this kind of disregard for the religious values of the community, these behaviors far exceeded this kind of rebelliousness. This occurred in children typically too young to show this kind of rebelliousness. In addition, the children described a struggle between wanting to follow the norm but feeling unable to, or hearing a voice telling them not to. This kind of conflict is not typically seen in teen or preteen rebelliousness.

Strange verbalizations included nonsensical statements from the children often involving themes of death or identity like "I'm already dead...they killed me yesterday," or "I am not your child." Also included were assertions of opposites such as "Did you know that hot is really cold?" These statements appear to represent ways of disclosing information without directly disclosing due to fear of harm, or as the result of cognitive confusion instilled by the perpetrators.

Secret-keeping involves children responding to questions by saying, "that is a secret" or "I am not allowed to tell you." Self-harm behavior involves skin picking, hitting the head with hands, or banging the head against objects. Self-harm of this type may be a symptom of physical abuse and can be a way to call for help in young children. Self-stimulating or repetitive self-harm can also be a self-soothing strategy for children with impaired attachment as is seen in late adopted children from orphanages.

The extreme severity of the symptom presentation cannot be overemphasized. These families were in painful disarray, getting little sleep as their children often had nightmares and sleep terrors throughout the night. During the day, many children displayed panic, and disrupted the family by refusal to sit at the table, refusal of foods, and sudden meltdowns where the triggering events could not even be discerned. The children were often aggressive and went into states where they seemed unreachable. The normal emotional responses that allow parents to interact with children and provide consequences were often missing in these children. Thus, they ignored parent direction, acted impervious to punishment or reward, entered into states of unawareness, and struggled to follow normal daily routines that other children easily do such as going to school or playing with friends. While there was huge improvement after safety and the initiation of therapy, nightmares and sleep disorders often remained, and special school programs were often necessary to address problematic behaviors displayed in school. The families, by and large, were very receptive to therapy, utilized techniques that they learned and are trying hard to move on with their lives despite the severe disruption these events have caused to their family life.

Abduction

Table 5.3 shows methods of abduction reported by the children. Children reported abduction during the school day from people known to them (14) and unknown to them (34). They reported being abducted by being taken out of school (34), while being driven on vans or buses (usually to or from school by the bus driver) (22), taken while playing outside (13), or taken by babysitter (12). Several children reported multiple methods of abduction.

Parents report that security at some of the schools remains lax, with breaches in walls or fences, no system for checking attendance, security guards waving people through without checking them, and low teacher to student ratio on the playground. The children report that often they leave the school with older students, who presumably have already been exposed to the abuse and threatened, which would attract little attention.

Table 5.3 Abduction disclosures

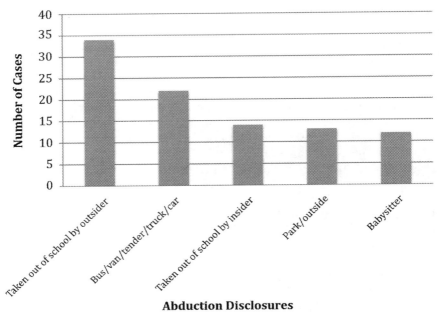

The types of abuse disclosed are displayed in Table 5.4. While some of the children disclosed full narrative details of their abuse and others provided only sketchy information, there were clear commonalities in the reports. The most common descriptions involved physical abuse and/or sexual abuse. The nature of the physical abuse included being hit, hurt with knives, being put in hot or cold water, being burned or threatened with being burned, and pain induced under the fingernails. Many of the descriptions of abuse included acts which would be considered torture, such as being hung upside down nude, pushed underwater with fear of drowning, and induction of severe pain under the fingernails. This type of intense physical abuse is associated with dissociative symptomatology, as when there is no escape from overwhelming pain; the body's own anesthesia through dissociation may take over (Nijenhuis, VanderLinden, & Spinhoven, 1998). The level of abuse described by these children would be sufficient for spontaneous dissociation from fear and overwhelming affect, but of course it is possible that perpetrators aware of children's propensity to dissociate may exploit this vulnerability and enhance it (Noblitt & Perskin, 2014).

Abuse disclosures

The nature of the sexual abuse appeared both voyeuristic ("We had to dance around without clothes on") and penetrative ("Boy's x's go in the girl's x's [colloquial word for privates or bottom]). The children who disclosed sexual abuse disclosed forced child-on-child sex, adult-on-child sex including both men and women, along with both oral and genital contact. Shame about these behaviors often resulted in sexual abuse disclosures being the last ones to emerge. The shame and fear about sexual abuse often led therapists and children not to talk about this aspect of the abuse as much emotional abuse such as trickery and threats.

Threats involved children being told that they would be put in jail or they or their parents would be killed if they disclosed the abuse. Some children

Table 5.4 Abuse disclosures

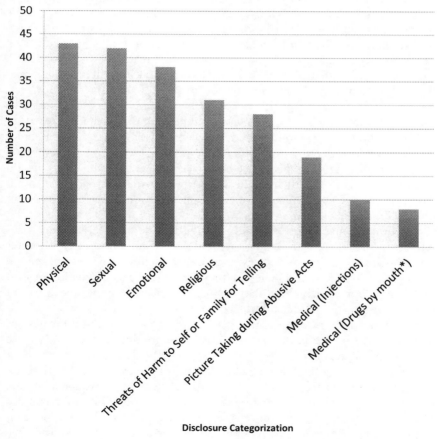

described being forced to watch videos in which children and parents were killed or tortured when a child disclosed. According to the children interviewed, the threat of harm to siblings was a particularly powerful motivation to keep quiet.

Ten children reported being medicated by injections between their toes, while eight children reported ingesting foods that made them "sleepy." Substances known to be used by those involved in sexual abuse to subdue child victims can include ketamine or rohypnol, GHB (Gamma Hydroxy Butyrate), as well as prescription and over-the-counter medications such as antihistamines, anticholinergics, and antitussives (Bechtel & Holstege, 2007).

While the children described some fantastical or bizarre elements in their reports, it is well known that perpetrators may mislead children and work to affect their credibility by presenting improbable events to lead children to not be believed (Dalenberg, 1996; Everson, 1997). For example, various animals have been described that frightened them, which may have been people in costumes confusing younger children, images on videos, or even robotic toys. In addition, drugs administered during the abuse may have confused perception and made virtual images appear more real.

Eighteen children explicitly described cameras taking still or moving pictures of them during abusive acts or performing for the cameras. However, most children did not explicitly describe the use of cameras but alluded to these activities in their behaviors. For example, some children showed traumatic reactions of fear and shutdown when they saw cameras (one child refused to return to a therapy session after a video recorder was used in the session), or engaged in provocative poses asking their parents if they would like to take pictures of them. Others reported having seen videos of other children engaged in sexual acts—a grooming technique often used by pedophiles (Salter, 2003).

Emotional abuse involves children being belittled or criticized such as telling them that they are "ugly," "stupid," or "bad." Several children reported being forced to touch or even taste excrement which led to perpetual feelings of "dirtiness" and believing they were viewed as disgusting by others. Some reported being told that they can never learn, and some apparent learning disabilities in the children could be traumatic reactions.

Religious abuse involves taking a child's religion and using it for manipulation or the infliction of emotional harm by forcing children to violate religious precepts, or to endure humiliating and belittling comments about their religion. In these cases, the children reported being told that they are really a different faith, or that they must break certain rules such as saying prayers. Many reported having been instructed to desecrate religious objects. This kind of religious abuse is very traumatic in a religious child, as it causes intense shame and confusion about their attachment relationships. These messages were most likely conveyed to disrupt the bond between the child and the parent along with isolating the child from their religious community. The religious confusion of these children should not be confused with attempts at conversion to any mainstream faith, as the children reported being taught that their own religion was not good yet they were not provided with any coherent set of other beliefs. The attempt at interfering with children's religious beliefs was most likely done to induce shame and ensure secrecy. For example, making children desecrate holy objects leads to feelings of innate badness and guilt which further isolated children from their parents and community. This helps ensure secrecy as children may believe that they will be punished by their parents or by a divine force, if they are discovered.

As data is collected for the second cohort, additional variables are being collected including more detailed information about "observation of violence" and physical manifestations on the body including genital bruising, pinprick marks, and other unusual injuries.

Discussion

The purpose of this study was to describe the presentation of a cohort of children from an insulated religious community who all described similar forms of abuse. These data suggest that multiple children in a particular Jerusalem in several neighborhoods are experiencing severe symptoms indicative of systematic abuse, and the pattern of reports resembles those found when child pornography crime rings are exposed (Canadian Centre for Child Protection, 2017). This finding is supported by the number of cases with similar and extreme symptoms, and the fact that similar reports emerged from children who had no contact with one another and who were seen by a number of different therapists who, for the most part, also did not have contact with one another. In fact, some therapists were located in Israel while others were located in the United States. This is because, many families have moved or were in the process of moving to America to find safety for themselves and their children. Others have stayed in Israel but moved to a different city, hired aides to accompany their children all day at school, put GPS monitors on their children's wrists, did spot checks at the school, or tutored their children at home.

However, the community has been slow to recognize the significant abuse the children disclosed. The community places a high value on modesty, television is not allowed, and discussion of sexuality is very limited. This may make it difficult for children to find language to describe sexual abuse and enhances feelings of shame about their experiences. The illusion of the protected safe community leads to lax supervision by parents. Young children often walk alone and travel to and from school without significant adult supervision. Parents tend to have large numbers of children and have not been hypervigilant about when children return home or whom they may be visiting during lunch or after school, as they trust their community. (These community norms are beginning to change.) Some classrooms do not have a clear-cut methodology of noting who is absent for a period of time during the day, and some of the playgrounds are not well supervised. Thus, children could be missing from playgrounds or from school for hours at a time without parents being aware that their child was gone.

Although law enforcement was contacted when the abuse pattern was discovered, they initially resisted taking reports at face value. Instead, multiple alternate theories have surfaced. The Israel Police put out a press release on August 12, 2016 stating that the explanation for multiple children reporting similar abuse was malfeasance on the part of the therapists involved. The police suggested that the reports were part of a calculated scheme by some local therapists to bilk money out of the community. The therapists were eventually released due to a lack of evidence. Given the number of trained therapists, both in America and in Israel seeing this cohort of 70 children, and the severity of enduring symptoms, it is hard to accept this explanation as plausible. In addition, the parents reported having seen multiple physical signs such as bruises on thighs, legs, or buttocks, rashes, cuts, eye discoloration, and unusual skin eruptions. Newer law enforcement efforts have taken newer information into account.

Some have attributed the children's symptomatology to "mass hysteria," particularly members of the community who do not have children directly affected (personal communication with community leaders). This view is comforting and plays into the instinctive denial that many have when faced with crimes against children of this magnitude. Some have argued that abuse found in preschools or young children is likely mass hysteria or "witch hunts" such as the McMartin Day Care scandal, in which the alleged perpetrators were eventually freed when the interviewing of the children was deemed suggestive. However, Cheit (2014) conducted an exhaustive examination of original data from dozens of cases bearing the *witch hunt* label and found that almost all cases began with children who had significant physical evidence of abuse and that it is highly likely that some real perpetrators were freed in the reversal of these convictions. Thus, "the baby was thrown out with the bath water" as attention was focused solely on the flaws in the investigative process, and not on the children's symptoms and the physical evidence.

The field of suggestibility is controversial and most child sexual abuse experts believe that suggestibility has been overstated (Faller, 2007; Lyon, 2001). In fact, it is way more likely that the forces of coercive influence work in the direction of leading children not to disclose real abuse that has happened (Faller, 2017). Even children whose abuse was videotaped often deny that the abuse occurred (Sjoberg & Lindblad, 2002a, 2002b). Cheit argues that the ease with which people can be led to deny the reality of abuse may result in overlooking cases that are difficult to prove due to the age of the children and lack of clarity in reports. Yet, the newest trends in online exploitation clearly reveal that young preschool children are the preferred target group (Gilad, 2013).

In my own caseload, I have seen cohorts of children who have reported organized abuse in preschools and in schools for disabled children. In another neighboring country, there is a report of children displaying similar symptoms to these children (regressed behavior, toileting accidents, denial that parent is their parent) after organized abuse through a babysitting ring which led to an arrest (personal communication, James Marsh). Yet, when people hear stories of extreme abuse of young children, there is a tendency for people to reflexively claim that these are false allegations made by highly suggestible children. These claims are often made with strong confidence by people who have not viewed the evidence or conducted even a rudimentary investigation as if claims of suggestibility have equal weight to evaluation of existing evidence.

While something was learned from these cases in the 80s and investigative and therapeutic techniques have become more rigorous as a result, many would argue the pendulum has swung too far. Social service departments in the United States will often not interview children more than once, and thus children whose initial abuse is reported when they are three or four will often never be interviewed again even when they are six or seven and can disclose more clearly. This has led to the continued abuse of children particularly in families (Silberg & Dallam, 2019) where the reports of abuse are often dismissed as a strategy to gain custody. In the cases in Jerusalem included in this sample of children, there is little evidence of any suggestive interviewing. Many of the parents were too fearful to talk to their children about the possibility of abuse and didn't even know what to ask. While some parents have asked direct questions, this has most often led to denials rather than disclosures. In one case in this sample, a mother offered ice cream and cookies for the child to talk, but nothing was told. Then all of the information emerged during a nighttime fever six months later. It would be hard to connect this inappropriate bribing with the spontaneous emergence of the material months later. If some children have been victims of inappropriate questioning, they would not show the extreme posttraumatic stress and behavior changes these children display.

The therapists the author has supervised have used an indirect play therapy approach waiting for the children to play out or spontaneously disclose abuse. Four of the therapists have PhDs and the other ten have master's degrees. In early cases, no one knew abuse was occurring so it was not discussed. Once word of the abductions got out, some children have talked with each other about whether they heard about some children being "kidnapped"; however, children are not sharing between families the details of sexual abuse and sadistic harm. They are sharing in play and talk that there are "thieves" in the neighborhood, and that people could go to jail. Still, the abuse details from children who do not know each other and families that have never met are shockingly similar. Within families, it is possible some younger children have joined in the posttraumatic play of older children, but these younger children don't develop the extensive symptoms that the affected children have.

In formal forensic interviews, some affected children have disclosed but the details were presented through the lens of a child and were misinterpreted and thus not understood by the interviewers, or viewed as fantasy. For example, the child might say, "There was a lion that was going to eat us." While this would appear to be fantasy, the child could have been referring to a costumed person, a dog groomed to resemble a lion, a robotic toy, or even a movie, and the young child could not discern this. In other cases, details of the abuse are dissociated from central awareness or threats and fear have coerced the children into silence. While some children have been surprisingly candid in therapy, others are filled with shame and can barely talk to their therapists without avoidant behaviors, dissociative shutdown, or rage attacks. These children do not discuss abuse easily. Discussing abuse brings up painful feelings and children do not readily open up about these experiences.

While some have argued that the children have been influenced by each other, developed false memories after being coached by adults, or developed mass hysteria, these are common defense strategies in abuse scandals. For example, Paul Shanley, a priest in Boston was convicted of abusing numerous children, and Jerry Sandusky, a Pennsylvania football coach, was convicted of abusing multiple young boys despite the defense assertions that the children were lying, influencing each other, were suggestible, or had false memories The families of the children in the current study are struggling daily with aggressive, sometimes sexualized, out-of-control children reporting horrific abuse. These are not minor cases where it is unclear if anything occurred. These are families desperate for help, finding their children suddenly severely changed, and desperate for help from psychological professionals and law enforcement.

The mass hysteria hypothesis cannot explain the physical symptoms seen by several doctors, parents, and therapists (bruising on genitals, needle marks, pressure point bruising, unexplained cuts, or other injuries); the independent appearance of phenomenon with families who do not know each other; or the severity of symptoms like "collapsed immobility" which only occur from severe exposure to trauma. This hypothesis cannot easily account for the eruption of severe symptoms associated with the disclosure of exposure to abuse, and reduction of symptoms with therapy and removal from the reportedly unsafe environment. Furthermore, allegations have tended to cease once the families relocated to America. If these were cases of panic and hysteria instigated by frightened children, similar outbreaks would be occurring in the United States, with groups of children reporting similar events in the United States. The "mass hysteria" idea may feel comfortable to the community as accepting the existence of these horrific crimes is abhorrent to most civilized people.

In a recent journalistic investigation into these crimes television journalist Haim Rivlin, Channel 13, Israel, presented powerful evidence of the severity and prevalence of affected victims, and denial of authorities including the police. The two-part series called "HaMakor" presented in December 2019 and January 2020 led to meetings of the Israeli Knesset, some renewed police interest, and general public outrage (personal communication, Haim Rivlin, January 15, 2020). This series highlighted the difficulties inherent in investigation of a crime involving young children, reporting seemingly bizarre information, within an insular community.

Treatment approach

The treatment approach that appears effective for these children follows the important principles identified for the treatment of children with complex trauma (Ford & Cloitre, 2009) with attention to dissociative states and behaviors (Putnam, 1997; Silberg, 2022; Waters, 2016; Perry, 2006; Silberg & Lapin, 2017; Wieland, 2015).

1 Achieving safety is the primary goal. Children must be removed from schools where they report being abused or from which they report they are being abducted. However, this alone may be insufficient as these children now have a fear of being in any school and are easily triggered by stimuli in their environments that remind them of traumatic events. Moving out of the country, or moving to different neighborhoods or cities has been very healing for many of the children.
2 Because of the early onset of abuse for many of these children, basic developmental functions may be impaired. Therapists must have a developmentally sensitive approach to interventions, as some of the children have experienced delays in language, and motor function that may be trauma-based. Interventions involving play, rhythmic activities, and strengthening the child's ability to achieve a calm state are important for children whose trauma may have occurred pre-verbally (Perry & Pollard, 1998).
3 Psycho-education is a high priority as it educates the children and their families about the symptoms they are experiencing. It is important to emphasize to the children that the voice of perpetrators they may hear in their mind is not really the voice of the person that hurt them. This is very confusing to children. They need to make the distinction between what is just an internal reminder and what was actually experienced. Other important psycho-educational principles are that their mind coped in the best way it could and they are not at fault for what occurred.

4. Solidifying attachment is the next main focus of therapeutic work. These children often feel alienated from their parents and may believe that their parents wanted them to be abused or allowed it to occur. The parents must convince the children that they did not know about the abuse and would have rescued the child sooner if they had. Playing out rescue scenes becomes a very powerful "undoing" of the traumatic memories. Parents must emphasize again and again that whatever the child was forced to do, the child is not to blame and not in "trouble" for this. This includes bad behavior that the child may have displayed after the abuse such as attacking a sibling. This was simply their only way to cope. This helps break the extreme shame that these children feel. The parents must also reassure the child that he is safe now, that they will be there for him, and there is nothing inside them that is a cause for rejection. The parents must also make a connection with parts of the children who may feel some loyalty to the perpetrators. This becomes a very big challenge. Some children become overly fearful of any separation when they are reconnected to their parents and can't tolerate being alone. Helping the children hold on to transitional objects that remind them of the parent whenever the parent leaves the room is one intervention that has been successful. However, this symptom has to be approached slowly, with gradual desensitization to the feeling of terror when left alone.
5. These children need opportunities to experience mastery and self-efficacy to overcome their feelings of helplessness. A variety of psychomotor play interventions may be used to practice running, breaking away, saving other children, or in other ways learning to master the trauma.
6. Grieving with the family about the pain and sadness of what they experienced is an important element of treatment that provides validation and further strengthening of the attachment.
7. The children retain a variety of posttraumatic problems including bad dreams and difficulty with sleep. Pragmatic approaches of helping children "change the nightmares," getting night-time reassurance, developing safe places in imagination, and drawing pictures of them can all be effective interventions.
8. These children must learn a variety of alternate self-regulating techniques for calming down, expressing anger, and substituting direct communication when they feel triggered by a frightening thought, or are triggered into overwhelming memories.
9. A pragmatic approach to sexualized symptoms involves guiding the parents to explain that exposure to these things is not meant for children and that they are very sorry that adults without modesty got them involved in these things. Children can be distracted from sexual feelings with other nonsexual sensory stimuli and encouraged to find other ways to self-soothe other than masturbation.

10 Dissociative symptoms can be addressed directly by re-framing voices in the mind as "memory voices" and talking about the importance of the whole self working together and urging the child to take responsibility for the child's own behavior (Silberg, 2022; Waters, 2016). Sudden shutdown or frozen states can be addressed by analyzing the triggering moment before the onset of the "freeze" and finding a method for calming and self-soothing at the onset of a bad memory or negative cognition such as "I am dirty" and "I can never be loved" (Silberg, 2017). Many of these negative cognitions are shame-based such as having been forced to engage in humiliating behaviors.

11 There are a variety of books the practitioner can refer to on dealing with severe trauma in children including Silberg (2022), Wieland (2015), Waters (2016), Struik (2014), Blaustein and Kinniburg (2010), Perry and Szalavitz (2007). For a comprehensive review of the treatment of children in this cohort see Silberg (2022).

Conclusion

This is a very unusual situation in which a group of parents and therapists are working to help very severely disturbed abused children, apparently abused through organized criminal activity, where law enforcement intervention and mental health intervention have been slow to catch up with the severity and extensiveness of the abuse reports. At the time of this report, new cases continue to emerge and a second cohort of children's case histories is being documented to further activate all community resources for the help of these families. The newer cohort of children is eliciting a more serious response from some law enforcement agencies. The families who have been already identified are grateful for the opportunity to receive treatment that addresses the children's symptoms, and are receptive to therapeutic recommendations, devoted to their children, and the majority of children have responded extremely well to therapy provided when they are removed from the settings in which they report abduction and abuse.

This case series also illustrates some of the huge obstacles facing therapists who work with children who have been exploited in organized ways by multiple perpetrators in the community. The need for treatment of these children is urgent and immediate, as some are engaging in life-threatening behavior, and cannot wait for law enforcement to first find proof. In addition, there are huge barriers to community acceptance and understanding of the scope of this kind of trauma, which adds to the isolation of both therapists and families.

The author is hopeful that this chapter sheds some light on the presentation of young children with extreme symptoms and the possibility that severe trauma may be a precipitating factor. This case series should help alert the reader to recognize that children are increasingly being used in child pornography and this may lead to a variety of symptoms including apparent developmental delays, sleep irregularities, separation anxiety, night terrors, rapid behavioral changes and multiple unexplained phobias.

It is also important that all disciplines working with young children become familiar with these patterns of behavior as these children may present first to pediatricians and other developmental specialists. As we become alert to the new dangers of technological advances aiding the abuse of young children, it is important that we become more adept at safeguarding children from sexual exploitation and more proficient in recognizing and prosecuting the criminals involved.

References

The American Interest. (2012, Mar, 20). Sexual abuse is not just a Catholic problem. Available at: https://www.the-american-interest.com/2012/03/20/sexual-abuse-is-not-a-religious-problem/.

Bechtel, L. K. & Holstege, C. P. (2007). Criminal poisoning: Drug facilitated sexual assault. *Emergency Medical Clinics of North America*, 25(2), 499–525. doi:10.1016/j.emc.2007.02.008.

Blaustein, M. E. & Kinniburg, K. M. (2010). *Treating Traumatic Stress in Children and Adolescents: How to Foster Resilience through Attachment, Self-Regulation, and Competency*. New York: Guilford.

Canadian Centre for Child Protection. (2017, Jan, 17). Press release: Groundbreaking tool to remove online child sexual abuse material. Author. Available at: http://childvictims.us/groundbreaking-new-tool-to-remove-onlin:e-child-sexual-abuse-material/#.WWbB1meWymQ.

Ceci, S. J. & Bruck, M. (1995). *Jeopardy in the Courtroom: Scientific Analysis of Children's Testimony*. Washington, DC: American Psychological Association.

Cheit, R. (2014). *Witch-Hunt Narrative: Politics, Psychology, and the Sexual Abuse of Children*. London: Oxford University Press.

Dalenberg, C. J. (1996). Fantastic elements in child disclosures of abuse. *APSAC Advisor*, 9(2), pp. 1–10.

Everson, M. D. (1997). Understanding bizarre, improbable, and fantastic elements in children's accounts of abuse. *Child Maltreatment*, 2(2), pp. 134–149.

Faller, K. C. (2007). Coaching children about sexual abuse: A pilot study of professionals' perceptions. *Child Abuse & Neglect*, 31, pp. 947–959.

Faller, K. C. (2017). The witch-hunt narrative: Introduction and overview. *Journal of Interpersonal Violence*, 32, pp. 784–804.

Finkelhor, D. & Ormrod, R. (2004, December). Child pornography: Patterns from NIBRS. *Juvenile Justice Bulletin*. Washington, DC: US Government Printing Office. Available at: https://www.ncjrs.gov/pdffiles1/ojjdp/204911.pdf.

Ford, J. D. & Cloitre, M. (2009). Best practices in psychotherapy for children and adolescents. In C. A. Courtois, Ford, J. D., & J. L. Herman (Eds.), *Treating Complex Traumatic Stress Disorders: An Evidence-Based Guide*, pp. 59–81. New York: Guilford Press.

Gilad, M. (2013). Virtual or reality: Prosecutorial practices in cyber child pornography ring cases. *Richmond Journal of Law & Technology*, 18(2), pp. 1–66.

Koslowska, K. (2013). Stress, distress and bodytalk: Co-constructing formulations with patients who present with somatic symptoms. *Harvard Review of Psychiatry, 21*(6), pp. 1–20.
Lyon, T. D. (2001). Let's not exaggerate the suggestibility of children. *Court Review, 38*(3), pp. 12–14.
Martin, J. (2014). Child sexual abuse images online: Implications for social work training and practice. *British Journal of Social Work, 46*(2), pp. 372–388.
Maxim, D. J. A., Orlando, S. M., Skinner, K. L, & Broadhurst, R. G. (2016). Online child exploitation material – Trends and emerging issues, Australian National University, Cybercrime Observatory with the Australian Office of the Children's e-Safety Commissioner, Canberra.
Nijenhuis, E. R. S., Vanderlinden, J., & Spinhoven, P. (1998). Animal defensive reaction as a model for trauma-induced dissociative processes. *Journal of Traumatic Stress, 11*, pp. 243–260.
Noblitt, R. & Perskin, P. (2014). *Cult and Ritual Abuse: Narratives, Evidence, and Healing Approaches* (3rd ed.). Santa Barbara, CA: Prager.
Perry, B. D. (2006). The neurosequential model of therapeutics: Applying principles of neuroscience to clinical work with traumatized and maltreated children. In N. B. Webb (Ed.), *Working with Traumatized Youth in Child Welfare*, pp. 27–52. New York: Guilford Press.
Perry, B. D., Pollard, R., Blakely, T., Baker, W. & Vigilante, D. (1995). Childhood trauma, the neurobiology of adaptation and use-dependent development of the brain: How states become traits. *Infant Mental Health Journal, 16*, pp. 271–291.
Perry, B. D. & Pollard, K. (1998). Homeostasis, stress, trauma, and adaptation: A neurodevelopmental view of childhood trauma. *Child and Adolescent Psychiatric Clinics of North America, 7*(1), pp. 333–351.
Perry, B. D., & Szalavitz, M. (2007). *The Boy Who Was Raised As a Dog: And Other Stories from a Child Psychiatrist's Notebook – What Traumatized Children Can Teach Us About Loss, Love, and Healing.* New York: Basic Books.
Press Association. (2016, July 29). Child abuse probe leads to 77 arrests as police identify over 500 potential online victims. *Daily Record.* Available at: http://www.dailyrecord.co.uk/news/child-abuse-probe-leads-77-8521410.
Putnam, F. W. (1997). *Dissociation in Children and Adolescents: A Developmental Approach.* New York: Guilford.
Rivlin, H. (Dec 2019, Jan 2020). Two-part TV series, HaMakor. Channel 13, Israel. Available at: https://13tv.co.il/item/news/hamakor/season-17/episodes/ze-p8-1975402/?fbclid=IwAR2EUBScpYDNAI2OhoyD71g_dnFJD7KVCvfZx-4JY0b0-s8KXS3y1BUnWosk.
Salter, A. C. (2003). *Predators: Pedophiles, Rapists and Other Sex Offenders: Who They Are, How They Operate, and How We Can Protect Ourselves and Our Children.* New York: Basic Books.
Silberg, J. L. (2013). *The Child Survivor: Healing Developmental Trauma and Dissociation.* New York: Routledge.
Silberg, J. L. (2022). *The Child Survivor: Healing Developmental Trauma and Dissociation.* 2nd Edition. New York: Routledge.
Silberg, J. L. (2017). Trauma-informed dissociative interventions. In S. N. Gold (Ed.), *APA Handbook of Trauma Psychology: Trauma Practice, Vol. 2*, pp. 411–427. Washington, DC: American Psychological Association.

Silberg, J. L. & Dallam, S. J. (2019). Abusers gaining custody in family court: A case series of overturned decisions. *Journal of Child Custody*, 16(2), pp. 140–169.

Silberg, J. L. & Lapin, C. L. (2017). Expanding your toolkit through collaboration: DIR/Floortime and dissociation-informed trauma therapy for children. *Frontiers in Psychotherapy for Trauma and Dissociation*, 1(1), pp. 45–64.

Sjoberg, R. L. & Lindblad, F. (2002a). Limited disclosure of sexual abuse in children whose experiences were documented by videotape. *American Journal of Psychiatry*, 159, pp. 312–314.

Sjoberg, R. L., & Lindblad, F. (2002b). Delayed disclosure and disrupted communication during forensic investigation of child sexual abuse: A study of 47 corroborated cases. *Acta Pædiatrica*, 91, pp. 1391–1396. doi:10.1111/j.1651-2227.2002.tb02839.

Struik, A. (2014). *Treating Chronically Traumatized Children*. New York: Routledge.

Waters, F. S. (2016). *Healing the Fractured Child*. New York: Springer.

Wieland, F. S. (2015). *Dissociation in Traumatized Children and Adolescents: Theory and Clinical Intervention* (2nd ed.). New York: Routledge.

Appendix: Definitions

Physical Abuse: Child describes harm inflicted to body or pain (e.g., "He put me in Hot water and I could not breathe"; "He put things under my fingernails").

Sexual Abuse: Child described children having clothes taken off, private parts touched, or forced to do sexual acts on children, men, or women (e.g., "Our x's were touching"; "Boy x's were in girl x"; "Dancing without our clothes on").

Emotional Abuse: Child described being criticized or belittled (e.g., being called stupid or bad; being told, "You will never learn anything").

Religious Abuse: Child made to feel his religion was wrong or invalid or was forced to violate key precepts of their faith.

Threats of Harm: Child and/or child's family was threatened with harm (e.g., "I will kill you and your family if you tell").

Medical Abuse: Some kind of drug was administered (e.g., "Needles in my toes made me sleepy"; "Bad food that makes you fall asleep").

Pictures: Any descriptions of pictures or video being taken, or watching videos or pictures of others.

Abduction

School People Known: Teachers or other school workers child is familiar with (e.g., "Adon X took me and my friends to a different room").

School People Unknown: Unfamiliar people who took children from school or buses.

Outside: Abduction from yards or playground.

Buses, Vans, Other Vehicles: Children describe that the bus to or from school does not go directly to school but they are taken to places where they are abused. Sometimes this disclosure was associated with a "substitute" bus driver. Some children reported only this form of abduction, while others described this form as well as others.

Babysitters: People who the parent placed in charge of the child's care. In this category are also suspicions of babysitters by parents when babysitter behavior was very odd: parent reported when they came home, children and babysitter were disheveled and not the way the children were left.

Symptoms

Rages: Child destroys things, screams, uses threatening language, or is hard to calm down.

Sleep Issues: Trouble going to sleep, fear of being in bed, waking up multiple times.

Nightmares: Waking up screaming or crying due to nightmares.

Sexualized Behavior: Public or vigorous masturbation, attempts to touch genitals of adults or other children, parading naked in home, sexual abuse of sibling, posing provocatively, inserting objects in anus or vagina.

Aggression: Child attacks members of the family causing injury (e.g., banging sibling's heads, kicking, using weapons).

Violation of Community Norms: Child causes disruptions by refusing to adhere to important norms of the community.

Attachment Difficulties: Problems in emotional attachments to parents (e.g., stating mother is not really their mother; refusing to go home with parent on pick up; rejecting hugs or soothing from parent).

Separation Anxiety: Child experiences excessive anxiety regarding separation from parent (e.g., child insists on sleeping with parent; refuses to be alone in a room without parent present, refuses to use the bathroom without parent present).

Regression or State Changes: Child acts significantly younger than age or at times acts like a very different person (e.g., at times, speaks with a different accent or displays different knowledge).

Dazed States: Child has spaced out look, parents can't get his attention, child engages in repetitive activities such as twirling or staring at hands.

Amnesia: Loss of memories for facts, information, and/or experiences (e.g., child cannot remember recent events, places he has been, or recent things that he has done with his family).

Collapse: Child appears to lose consciousness or suddenly fall asleep after encountering something stressful or fear inducing.

Toileting Problems: Child has regression in toileting, wets bed, defecates in pants when fearful. Child seems unable to learn regular toileting skills.

Hallucinations: Sensory distortion in which child appears to hear or see something that isn't actually there (e.g., child hears things such as voices of people that hurt him in his mind, or sees them through his window).

Strange Verbalizations: Child things that don't make sense or uses backward language (e.g., "Isn't it true Mommy, I am already Dead?"; "Up means down").

Secret Keeping: Child states he can't answer parent's questions because it is a secret.

Self-Harm: Child appears to hurt himself on purpose (e.g., skin picking or scratching, head banging, hitting head with hands).

Panic about Everyday Things: Unusual fear of buses, cars, buildings, foods, taking a bath, toys, etc.

Chapter 6

The Star Theoretical Model

An integrative model for assessing and treating childhood dissociation

Fran Waters

Introduction

In the mid-1990s, after a decade of working with dissociative children, I began to ask these questions to gain more clarity on dissociative children's pathways towards developing dissociation: at what age(s) did the trauma occur and what impact did it have on their development? Were there self-states that were formed at that time of their trauma to manage it? Were their self-states stuck at the development stage when they were formed? What attachment style did they exhibit with their parents? Did the self-states assume different attachment styles? How did the trauma impact their attachment behaviour to other caregivers and peers? Did the children or their self-states mirror their parents, abusers, hero figures? What were the communication patterns between their parents and the child and between family members who impaired the traumatised child's openness and therefore contributed to their dissociation? Were there threats, abuse, and rigidity that could result in dissociation? How did the children relate to others consequently? How were traumatised children's brains impacted in utero as a result of pregnant mothers who were drug addicted, stressed from a domestic violent environment, or experiencing some medical condition? How does trauma impact the developing brain of young children during sensitive periods of neurodevelopment? What does chronic trauma do to a child's brain?

I realised that one theory was insufficient to fully encompass the development of dissociation and that there are multiple pathways that provide a more thorough understanding to this complex issue. A comprehensive theoretical model was needed to understand the complexities and nuances that influence traumatised children's reliance on dissociation. I therefore developed the Quadri-Theoretical Model (Waters, 1996) that interlinked four prominent theories—attachment, child development, family systems, and dissociation for assessment and treatment of traumatised children with dissociation. This model was recently revised to include neurobiology as the fifth theory and is now called the "Star Theoretical Model" (STM) (Waters, 2016). See Figure 6.1. The STM's star shape represents the child exposed to

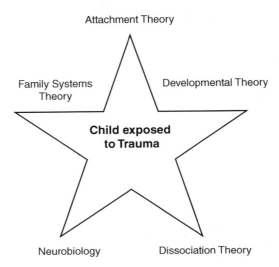

Figure 6.1 Star Theoretical Model for Assessment and Treatment of Childhood Dissociation.

trauma. Attachment theory is intentionally placed at the top of the star to signify the paramount role that a parent-child attachment relationship plays in contributing to the child's development and ongoing reliance on dissociative coping mechanisms. Also, a healthy attachment is an anchor for the child's ability to heal.

This integrative model that combines each theory—dissociation, attachment, neurobiology, child development, and family systems—offers a unique perspective that furthers our understanding of the development of dissociation. The overlap and interrelationship between all five theories strengthens the assessment process for children suspected of dissociation. It is such interconnectedness that provides a comprehensive evaluation and lays the groundwork for a multifaceted treatment plan. Treatment interventions that take into consideration these five theories can more often lead to a positive outcome when the child is in a secure and safe environment.

Let's examine the relevant factors of each of these theories to understand the child's reliance on dissociation.

Dissociative theory of the STM

Relationship between trauma and dissociation

It is recognised in research and clinical cases that multiple forms of trauma can lead to childhood dissociation (Chu & Dill, 1990; Chu, Frey, Ganzel, &

Matthews, 1999; Diseth, 2006; Hulette, Fisher, Kim, Ganger, & Landsverk, 2008; Kisiel & Lyons, 2001; Kisiel, McClelland, & Torgersen, 2013; Milot et al., 2013; Silberg, 2013; Teicher, Samson, Polcari, & McGreenery, 2006; Vásquez et al., 2012; Waters, 2016; Wieland, ed., 2015). There is a direct relationship between children reporting multiple types of trauma and increased complex symptoms (Cloitre et al., 2009; Hulette et al., 2008; Kisiel & Lyons, 2001). The relationship between trauma and dissociation has been demonstrated cross culturally in many different countries (Farrington, Waller, Smerden, & Faupel, 2001; Muris, Merckelbach, & Peeters, 2003; Nilsson & Svedin, 2006; Sar, Onder, Killicaslan, Zoroglu, & Alyanak, 2014; Tolmunen et al., 2007; Yoshizumi, Hamada, Kaida, Gotow, & Murase, 2010; Zoroglu, Sar, Tuzun, Tutkun, & Savas, 2002).

Infant trauma and dissociation

A particularly pernicious form of trauma that has been less recognised is infant trauma. Infants can be negatively impacted by a number of experiences such as birth trauma; painful medical procedures; early deprivation; physical, sexual, and emotional abuse; and disruption in attachment (Waters, Marks, & Parker, 2018). Traditional definitions of trauma may fail to recognise that infants' symptoms relate to traumatic experiences. This may be due to the myth that infants and toddlers are either "resilient" or unaffected by traumatic events. In reality, the younger the children are when they experience trauma, the more likely they are to suffer enduring and pervasive problems (Perry, 2006).

The implicit memory system is always operating—calculating and tabulating sensory experiences, and although infants' physical and emotional pain may be discounted or unrecognised as causing disturbance, Gaensbauer (2002) noted that newborns manifest all of the cardinal physiologic stress responses to pain. Fraiberg (1982) succinctly states that it is not possible to say that infants do not experience trauma and are "too young to feel or remember" (p. 612). Bowlby (1980) and Fraiberg (1982) who observed infants who experienced maternal separation and deprivation found that they demonstrated freezing behaviours, trance states, and memory problems resulting in total disorganisation. Research described infants with a disorganised attachment style demonstrating dissociative behaviour (Main & Hesse, 1990; Ogawa, Sroufe, Weinfield, Carlson, & Egeland, 1997). Yet, today, many clinicians fail to recognise these as dissociative behaviours related to traumatic experiences and instead ascribe them to other diagnoses, i.e. an attachment disorder, attention problems, oppositional defiant disorder.

In summary, these studies point to the need to conduct a comprehensive trauma history and assess all children including infants for dissociation, at whatever age they come to the attention of mental health professionals.

Conceptual models of dissociation

Since the early 19th century, a number of theoretical concepts have emerged that has formed our understanding of the development of dissociation, i.e. hysteria (Ferenczi, 1933; Freud, 1896; Janet, 1907), structural dissociation (van der Hart, Nijenhuis, & Steele, 2006; van der Kolk, van der Hart & Marmar, 1996), Putnam's defence model and discrete behavioural states (1997), Watkins and Watkins' Ego State Theory (1997), Affect Avoidance Theory (Silberg, 2013), and Betrayal Trauma Theory (Freyd, 1996). These models are all based on the premise that pathological dissociation derives from traumatic experiences causing disturbances in consciousness, memory, identity, somatic, affect, and behaviour. In extreme forms of dissociation, there is the presence of self-states that influence the child either internally or directly by taking executive control over their bodies. Treatment interventions include working with the child's self-states; facilitating modulation, cooperation, and teamwork between them; resolving traumatic memories; and integrating the child (Silberg, 2013; Waters, 2016).

Dissociation: a psychological escape hatch

Putnam (1997, pp. 67–75) views dissociation as a defence mechanism with three major tasks: (1) the automatisation of behaviour in the face of psychologically overwhelming circumstances; (2) compartmentalisation of painful affect and memories; and (3) estrangement from self in the face of potential annihilation. The mind becomes overwhelmed with fear and the child functions on automatic pilot—going through the experience without conscious thought or feeling. To hold the trauma in one's conscious memory would present a dangerous dilemma, particularly if a child depends on the abuser for care. It is safer for the child to not know or not to feel. The child can compartmentalise parts or all of the experience across affect, behaviour, sensation, and memory because facing it would overload the child's coping abilities. While this survival technique is adaptive at the time, it can later interfere in the child's effectiveness in navigating the world.

The ability to dissociate is an amazing feat when a child has no other way to escape life-threatening events. In many respects, dissociation is like a secret trap door, as performed by an escape artist, like Houdini, who was a master at devising illusions that made animals and people disappear through a trap door (Gibbons, 2014). Only dissociation is not a trick but a defensive, instinctive, biological survival mechanism (Porges, 2011) that is activated when the threat is so great, and fear is so overwhelming that the child feels imminent death (Putnam, 1997). Dissociation is a psychological escape hatch—the only getaway at the time of the trauma.

However, children can be plagued with persistent internal voices and images that the child cannot escape from. One five-year-old girl, Kaitlyn, powerfully described the voice of Charlie and how very hard she tried to ignore this voice, but eventually she succumbed. Kaitlyn held the puppet of the Alien representing Charlie and said, "...he gets louder, louder and louder, and then he shoves out!... and then my mind walks away and he's in my mind!" When I asked what happens next, she replies, "I don't know" (Waters, 2016). Yet, Charlie, the internalised state of her adolescent perpetrator, carried all of the rage and power over Kaitlyn who reports, "That mean Charlie makes me do bad things." Kaitlyn then has no control or no memory of what she does.

The existence of self-states with different genders, ages, and roles can seem hard to comprehend but Putnam (1997) succinctly captures the meaning of them by stating:

> Alter personalities are real. They do exist, not as separate individuals but as *discrete dissociative states of consciousness*. When considered from this perspective, they are not nearly so amazing to behold or so difficult to accept.
>
> (ibid., 1997, p. 90, italics added)

Putnam then quoted Coons (1984) who stated, "Only when taken together can all of the personality states be considered a whole personality" (ibid., p. 90). Understanding this important distinction can help many sceptics to better accept the existences of self-states.

Let's examine the relationship between trauma, dissociation, and neurobiology and how it furthers our understanding of dissociation and self-states.

Neurobiology in the STM

Memories and brain networks

Memories are usually stored in distributed brain networks through the process of state-dependent learning. When the conditions are similar, those memories are then activated and recalled. Furthermore, numerous researchers have recognised the impact of chronic traumatic stress on memory and brain structures (e.g. hippocampus, amygdala, prefrontal cortex, corpus callosum) (Bremner, 2005; DeBellis et al., 1999; Frewen & Lanius, 2006; Nijenhuis & den Boer, 2009; Reinders et al., 2003; Vermetten, Schmahl, Loewenstein, & Bremner2006) that impair in storing and recalling memories. Stress can lead to the deactivation of certain critical structures in the brain that encode and consolidate memories into the conscious memory system accounting for memory problems and dissociative responses (Bremner, 2005; Perry, 2001; Vermetten et al., 2006).

A recent study by Jovasevic and colleagues (2015) has confirmed a neurological pathway for inaccessible traumatic memories in their experiment with mice that were administered a chemical, gaboxadol, with extra-synaptic GABA receptors that induces a state similar to mild inebriation. The mice were then placed in a box and given a brief, mild shock. The next day, the mice were placed in the same box without the chemical administered beforehand. The mice moved about freely, unafraid, indicating they did not recall the shock. Later, the mice were given the chemical and again placed in the box. This time when they entered the box, they froze in fear anticipating another shock. Thus, when the mice were returned to the same brain state they were in when they received the shock, they remembered it. State-dependent learning is believed to contribute to the formation of memories and accessibility of those memories, as demonstrated in Jovasevic et al.'s study.

Further understanding of different brain systems and pathways that contain memories is illuminated by one of the colleagues in the above study, Jelena Radulovic, who stated, "The brain functions in different states, much like a radio operates at AM and FM frequency bands." She noted that it is as if the brain is normally tuned to FM stations to access memories but needs to be tuned to AM stations to access traumatic memories (Science Daily, 2015). The memory of the traumatic event cannot be accessed unless the same neural pathways are activated once again, essentially tuning the brain back into the AM stations. This research provides insight about how self-states can coexist with different memory systems that activate correlated emotions and responses.

Groundbreaking studies have demonstrated neurobiological differences in self-states of DID patients. Reinders, Willemsen, Vos, Den Boer, and Nijenhuis (2012) looked at self-states with brain imaging. They found striking neurobiological differences in authentic self-states in DID patients compared with a control group of healthy high and low fantasy-prone adults simulating self-states in role play. Frewen and Lanius (2006) reviewed brain-imaging studies finding that dissociation involves a disconnection in the neural pathways normally linking self-awareness with somatosensory awareness that could lead to the development of dissociative identities in traumatised individuals.

Polyvagal Theory, ANS, and dissociation

The autonomic nervous system (ANS) also plays a role in dissociation. This system works automatically without a person's conscious effort. Stephen Porges, originator of the Polyvagal Theory, has extensively studied the ANS, a neuro-endocrine-immune structure that enables survival. The ANS innervates the internal organs (e.g. the heart and digestive system) and regulates their functions. It was previously thought that the ANS had two main divisions, sympathetic and parasympathetic, but Porges (2011) discovered a third branch of the ANS, termed social engagement, that promotes connections to others through responding to interpersonal cues. According to Porges (2011), these three branches of the ANS are developed phylogenically with sequential ordered responses that are instinctual and unconscious. The most primitive branch of the ANS is the parasympathetic nervous system. It is associated with primal survival strategies of primitive vertebrates, reptiles, and amphibians and remains functional in humans. It encompasses the unmyelinated portion of the vagus nerve that regulates the digestive and reproductive systems and creates a metabolic baseline of operation to manage nutrients getting to the cells. When activated by fear, it initiates a shutdown response involving immobilisation, feigning death, and/or dissociation. Up the evolutionary chain is sympathetic system that enables mobility for finding food and defending against threats with development of limbs and arms. It is responsible for fight or flight behaviours. The most advanced branch of the ANS is the social engagement system that is mediated by the myelinated portion of the vagus nerve. This branch fosters social communication and maternal bonding via facial expressions, vocalisation, and listening.

Porges cites on Jackson's Theory of Dissolution (1958) that explains the hierarchical functioning of the nervous system, "The higher nervous system arrangements inhibit (or control) the lower, and thus, when the higher are suddenly rendered functionless, the lower rise in activity" (Porges, 2011, p. 162). For example, when a child is under threat by caregiver via a form of maltreatment, the most evolutionary function of the ANS, the social engagement system, shuts down. The social engagement between the child and the parent is severed. Then if the child cannot fight or flee from the caregiver, the sympathetic nervous system is further rendered helpless. The child's last resort of survival is the activation of the most primitive portion of the ANS, the parasympathetic nervous system—which initiates the freeze response—a general shut down of the body leading to immobilisation, feigning death, and/or dissociation.

Use-dependent development of the brain

Bruce Perry, developer of Nuerosequential Model of Therapeutics, has conducted extensive research on traumatised children and provides a conceptual framework for understanding how childhood trauma can result in long-term changes in the functioning of children's nervous systems. Perry's model explains how transitory states can over time become enduring traits. According to Perry, Pollard, Blakely, Baker, and Vigilante (1995), repetitive neural activation caused by repeated exposure to threatening stimuli causes sensitisation of the nervous system. The more a neural network is activated, the more there will be use-dependent internalisation of new information needed for survival. Perry and colleagues explained, "The more frequently a certain pattern of neural activation occurs, the more indelible the internal representation" (p. 275).

This use-dependent activation can be viewed as a template through which future input is filtered. Use-dependent internalisation of a state of anger or fear, for example, may explain how children can have certain self-states that they identify as "the fearful one," or "the angry one." Perhaps this may also explain self-states that identify with the perpetrator or with hero characters, as children may internalise representations of these figures when they are abused. Over time, these internal representations are reinforced and become self-states that are activated whenever trauma-related cues are present. Due to sensitisation, stress-induced activation of these internal representations can be elicited in response to minor stress resulting in the child developing hyperarousal or dissociative reactions (Perry et al., 1995).

Mirror neurons

An understanding of why traumatised children may mimic or take on certain characteristics of others, including the mirroring found in self-states, can be further explained by the discovery of mirror neurons in the brain (Gallese, Fadiga, Fogassi, & Rizzolatti, 1996; Rizzolatti, Fadiga, Gallese, & Fogassi, 1996). While studying macaque monkeys, researchers found that when one monkey was grasping for food and another monkey was observing with the intention to grab for food, the identical neurons fired in both monkeys. Iacoboni (2009) noted that core circuitry in mirroring is the superior temporal cortex, inferior parietal lobule, and inferior frontal cortex.

This landmark discovery has increased our understanding of human interactions including facial imitation, perception, and action (Casile, Caggiano, & Ferrari, 2011). Iacoboni (2009) found evidence to suggest that there are mirror neurons that code facial actions. This innate ability to imitate others may help us to better understand the people around us. According to Iacoboni, mirror neurons "provide a prereflective, automatic mechanism of mirroring what is going on in the brain of other people that seems compatible with our ability to understand others effortlessly and with our tendency to imitate others automatically..." (p. 658). Children who are dependent on others for survival, particularly their parents, often seek to mimic them. Iacoboni hypothesised that children may be prewired to imitate their parents in order to gain their favour.

Mirror neurons and children's desire to imitate and please caregivers who may also be abusive have implications for dissociation. When parents vacillate from being nice to being abusive, the child who is prewired to mirror is in a double bind. The child may deal with this bind by developing self-states that mimic the different representations of their parents to manage contradictory working models of attachment (see Blizard, 2003). The presence of a prewired system to mirror others may also explain why traumatised children internalise self-states that mimic their favourite cartoon heroes or pet animals from whom they receive comfort. I have had a number of children who had self-states that were hero figures or beloved pet animals that were either killed by the child's abuser or had comforted the child when abused.

Attachment theory of the STM

> [M]other-love in infancy and childhood is as important for mental health as are vitamins and proteins for physical health.
>
> John Bowlby (1953, p. 182)

The attachment portion of my model is primarily derived from the works of Bowlby, the father of attachment theory, along with the findings of other researchers that have built on his work (e.g. Main & Hesse, 1990). Bowlby (1969) indicated that attachment is a "lasting psychological connectedness between human beings" (p. 194) and defined attachment behaviour as an instinctual drive of the infant to connect to the parent for survival. It is any behaviour that the person engages in from time to time to obtain or maintain a desired proximity, particularly during times when security and closeness are needed to cope with challenges (Bowlby, 1982a). Attachment and attachment behaviour is a dynamic operating within the life span of the individual. Knowing that the attachment figure is available and responsive provides security for the individual.

A secure attachment is formed through a repetitive interplay between mother and child in which the mother is in attunement with her child and the child's needs are met with consistent nurturing responses. Bowlby (1980) believed that the formation of a secure attachment with the mother in a child's early years provides the capacity and confidence for managing stress, managing transitions, and developing intimacy with others. Thus, the mother lays the foundation for the child's ability to form other relationships and becomes the regulatory mechanism for child's own expressions and to manage transitions. Bowlby's viewpoint is supported by Shore who stated, "Attachment theory is essentially a regulatory theory, and attachment can be defined as the interactive regulation of biological synchronicity between organisms" (p. 23). It is through this interplay (whether positive or aversive) that the child develops internal working models of representation of the self and attachment figure (Bowlby, 1973), which is further described below.

However, a lack of an enduring attachment or attachment bond can have a profound impact on the child's personality development.

Traumatic grief in children

Loss of a loved person is as traumatic psychologically as being severely wounded or burned is physiologically (Engle (1961) as cited by Bowlby (1980, p. 42).

Bowlby was particularly concerned with loss and mourning in young children who experienced separation from their mothers that lead to traumatic grief, which Bowlby termed "pathological mourning." According to Bowlby

(1961), pathological mourning results from the child's inability to overtly scold the parent for deserting him. The child's urges to recover and reproach the parent becomes "split off and ...continued as active systems within the personality..." influencing the child's feelings and behaviours "*in strange and distorted ways...*" (p. 485, italics added). Bowlby's description is analogous to current nosology of development of self-states as active systems containing traumatic elements.

Robertson and Bowlby (1952) observed children demonstrating profound detachment from their mothers who complained that their children treated them as strangers. Bowlby (1980) described three cases—Laura, Kate, and Owen, separated from their parents in their second year of life—who demonstrated signs of amnesia, identity disturbance, and loss of consciousness. Significantly, Bowlby ascribed such responses to a "splitting of the ego" in which one part recognised that the mother was lost and another part did not recognise that the mother was lost (1961, p. 486). He used the term "detachment," analogous to dissociative splitting to explain this phenomenon.

According to Bowlby (1982a), detached children did not seek comfort when hurt. He recognised that such signals that would ordinarily activate attachment behaviour were "failing ... blocked off" resulting in an immobilisation of affect and incapacity to be comforted (p. 673). Bowlby recognised

> this detached behaviour is derived from unconscious mental processes that selectively shut off specific information without the person being aware that it is happening. There is blocking off of the signals internally and externally that would allow the child to love and be loved. Bowlby called this phenomenon "defensive exclusion.
>
> (p. 674)

Bowlby's description of the faulty mechanisms is astonishingly synonymous to our current understanding of dissociative defences resulting in a signal failure due to amnestic barriers or impermeable boundaries between self-states that contain unwanted traumatic material that interferes in the activation of the attachment behaviour.

Self-states that were formed to hold the "contaminated material" were not "born" from their mother and instead were formed void of a relational context. They exist to defend or protect the child from further loss and grief. Moreover, because these systems were created in the absence of any nurturing figure, such a self-state did not know to seek comfort when hurt. Instead, this state was developed to fight or flee from a perceived threat. I have treated many children who would shift into a defensive state in a matter of seconds and attack the parent who attempts to comfort the child. When the parent retreats, the child switches into the state that fears abandonment, and panics and runs after the parent. When the parent attempts to comfort the child again, the other state is reactivated that then attacks the parent resulting in a vicious cycle until both parent and child are despondent and rendered helpless to resolve the conflict of fear of closeness and fear of abandonment.

Bowlby's internal working models and development of dissociated self-states

Bowlby (1973) defined what he called segregated states as "states of the mind" (p. 203). According to Bowlby (1982b), within the first few years of life, the child develops internal working models from caretakers and significant others that become incorporated into the child's identity. The development of these working models is an unconscious process based on children's expectations about how the physical world operates, how their mother and other significant persons may be expected to behave, and how they all interact with each other. Children respond to their parents (including attachment behaviour) based on perceptions of how accessible, responsible, and acceptable they are to them (Bowlby, 1973).

Children can develop different and incompatible internal working models based on provocative situations with parents who are frightening, neglectful, or abusive. These internal models can represent different states, i.e. the good parent, the abusive parent, the victim, and one that van der Hart et al. (2006) terms "the apparently normal personality" that attends to daily functions. These incompatible internal working models can represent the shifting self-states that assume different roles, affect, behaviours, sensations, and memories. Because these incompatible models can contain distorted, biased, and contradictory perceptions, they can impair the development of future relationships. These internal working models have implications for psychological responses to grief and mourning and my Star Theoretical Model.

Psychological responses to grief and mourning

Robertson and Bowlby (1952) recognised three psychological stages to grief and morning of parental loss—protest, despair, and denial or detachment—that children experienced. Later Bowlby (1960) noted a similarity of responses between children's grief reaction and older adults who lost their spouse, or another loved one. Bowlby (1960) revised his model into five stages of psychological responses to grief and mourning. These stages are (1) thoughts and behaviours still directed towards lost object; (2) hostility, for whomsoever directed; (3) appeals for help; (4) despair, withdrawal, regression, and disorganisation; (5) reorganisation of behaviour directed towards a new object. Bowlby recognised that the child's intense and unresolved grief over the loss of a parent is the underlying dynamic in these stages.

Bowlby's five stages of psychological responses and Star Theoretical Model

Loss and grief are inherent in all traumatic experiences, particularly interpersonal violence. Because I have found similar patterns in Bowlby's five stages of psychological responses with dissociative children, and his concept of internal working models and segregated states to have significance to the development of self-states, I have incorporated and expanded these concepts into STM.

Suffice it to say, not all maltreated children may experience the five stages of psychological responses of grief and mourning, or experience them sequentially, or display segmented discrete states. Rather, the STM recognises these are psychological responses to consider when evaluating and treating traumatised children. I describe each of the stages to aid the clinician in understanding the underlying dynamics associated with the child who dissociates across the domains of affect, cognition, behaviours, sensations, and relationships and, in severe cases, lead to the development of self-states. Self-states can range from fragments of the self with limited roles, behaviours, and affect, to more developed states that take executive control over the child's body.

Stage one: thought and behaviour still directed towards the lost object

In Bowlby's (1960) stage one, the child protests loudly in the hopes of being reunited with the parent. All thoughts and behaviour are directed towards reunification with the parent. In my comparison model, the abused child experiences grief over the loss of the desired, idealised perception of the parent. The child blames himself and feels unworthy of love, which can lead to feelings of depression. (A similar dynamic can occur even if the abuser was not a primary caretaker.) These unbearable feelings and contradictory perceptions of still desiring the love of the caregiver while fearing him or her are too difficult for the child to manage. In order to maintain the child's attachment to the parent, the child has to segment off the abusive experience along with the feelings of abandonment, betrayal, rejection, and loss of safety. The child compensates by developing self-states representing the abuser and/or the unbearable affect, i.e. pain, fear, rage, associated with the abuse. By segmenting this traumatic material from the child's awareness, the child is able to maintain attachment to the abusive parent and avoids the intolerable affect of helplessness, rage, grief, and loss.

Stage two: hostility, to whomsoever directed

In stage two, Bowlby (1960) described children in residential care exhibiting hostility towards anyone who tried to nurture them. They would also vacillate between rejecting care and clinging to the nurses. This contradictory behaviour is frequently found in dissociative children who face a dilemma due to unresolved abandonment, as described above. They can quickly shift from seeking comfort to rejecting care of their abusive caretakers and others, with whom they are dependent. The child fears further rejection and retribution if she expresses hostility to the parent, while also desperately desires to be loved and comforted. The only recourse is to dissociate these contradictory emotions. Her hostility becomes segmented into a self-state that exhibits aggression, anger, distrust, and suspicion of others. The hostile state hates feeling afraid because it activates feelings of vulnerability. That fear then becomes segmented into a fearful state that feels impotent, dependent and wanting to please others to avoid rejection and harm. The fearful state seeks out comfort and is loyal to the perpetrating parent for fear of rejection, while the hostile state despises the fearful state for his weakness. Consequently, when the different states are activated, the child can vacillate between closeness, hostility, and aggression.

These responses can become generalised towards all caregivers—including foster and adoptive parents who try to nurture the child. As a result, the child's presentation can be very confusing with shifting states that display intense conflicting emotions and behaviours from seeking comfort to hitting, kicking, and swearing at the caregiver.

If it is too threatening for the child to express her hostility outwardly, she will turn it inwardly with self-harming behaviours such as head banging, cutting, burning, purging, or substance abuse that can be contained in a state, as well.

If these extreme shifts between desiring closeness and meeting it with hostility persist into adulthood, the person may be diagnosed with having borderline personality disorder.

Stage three: appeals for help

In Bowlby's (1960) third stage, the child appeals for help are unmet and the child becomes resigned to the fact that the absent parent is unavailable. When this reality sets in, the child feels much despair. He feels immobilised with fear and distrust and is thus unable to reach outwardly for help, as this seems too dangerous and unpredictable. However, his overwhelming need for nurturing and comfort propels him to seek internal ways to satisfy this need. In my model, the child develops an internalised self-state that is a helper, an idealised parent, a comforter, or a hero figure to rescue him. Reliance on an internal helper feels safer, particularly when outside help has not been consistently available. I have frequently found helper states in children who resided in orphanages during their infancy and toddlerhood that helped them with hunger, coldness, isolation, and loneliness.

Stage four: despair, withdrawal, regression, and disorganisation

In the fourth stage, Bowlby (1960) found that toddlers who were separated from their mothers exhibited despair, withdrawal, regression, and disorganisation. Bowlby stated:

> ...there is no experience to which a young child can be subjected more prone to elicit intense and violent hatred for the mother figure than that of separation.
>
> (ibid., p. 24)

Bowlby noted research by Heinicke (1956) who studied children between 16 and 26 months who were placed for short periods of time in a residential nursery with a limited number of nurses caring for them. Heinicke observed the children seeking their mothers throughout their stay with the majority of children exhibiting crying for their lost mothers, autoerotic activity, and intense aggression. In his research, Bowlby observed children swinging from withdrawal, apathy, regression, mourning, and aggression.

In my comparison model, the chaotic, disorganised responses often found in traumatised children can be attributed to rapidly switching self-states that may contain different affects (e.g. depression, hostility, fear, or anger), varied behaviours (e.g. detachment, aggression, or seeking support), and erratic skill performance in areas such as schoolwork, sports, and self-care. The self-states may also present at different levels of maturity and express different preferences regarding food, clothing, etc. These children are often highly sensitised to subtle traumatic cues, and therefore exhibit extreme dysregulation.

The underlying feeling that the child is trying to cope with is unmanageable despair, shame, and grief over his or her betrayal and the concomitant loss of safety, trust, and care. There is often a younger self-state that displays regressive behaviour that appears to be the original self or a self-state that was created at the time of the trauma. I recall a ten-year-old girl who had been severely abused from infancy until she was age eight with conflicting need for closeness and fear of closeness. She had a complex configuration of self-states that would rapidly switch in response to minor stressors. One moment she would be curled up in a foetal position sucking her thumb and in the next moment she would be standing up and shouting profanities at her adoptive mother. These mercurial self-states can wreak havoc on the child's ability to form attachments and caretaker's ability to manage them.

Because these self-states can be formed for particular survival tasks (e.g. such as going to school, comforting the child, defending against any perceived threat), and not created within a contextual relationship with others, they are purely operating in a survival task-oriented mode. They often exhibit separation anxiety, detachment, or disdain towards caregivers. These children's self-states can intrude spontaneously and unconsciously resulting in making contradictory statements in short succession such as, "My mom is always mean to me but she is nice to me." Because the origin of attachment disturbances is misunderstood and dissociative shifts are unrecognised, they are often misdiagnosed with a Reactive Attachment Disorder. However, these extreme fluctuating states of affect and attachment behaviour do not meet the criteria.

Stage five: reorganisation of behaviour directed towards a new object

In the last stage, Bowlby (1960) indicated that reorganisation takes place partly in connection with the image of the lost object, and partly in connection with a new object or objects. This is the final phase of mourning in which the lost object returns or a new object—another person—is found to which the child can attach. Bowlby indicated that if the child can attach to one adult, the mourning ceases; however, if the child is exposed to numerous adults (via placements or numerous caretakers), the child can become self-centred and will have shallow relationships over his lifetime.

This fifth stage corresponds to the later phases of treatment in my model-trauma processing and integration (Waters, 2016). This phase involves grieving the traumatic losses and pain across all parts of the child. The key for recovery is to access self-states that have served to protect the child and working with these self-states to let go of their defences so that grief work can occur across all parts of the self. Based on my clinical experience with children and adults, there can be a very young hidden child (original self perhaps) who must be uncovered, helped to process the painful grief and morning. This usually occurs in the latter stage of treatment after considerable reframing of defensive self-states into collaborators, much ego strengthening, and processing the traumatic events that have occurred.

In a safe, nurturing environment, once the pain of the traumatic experiences and grieving of attachment figures are processed, then trust in self and others can be established. This will enable the child to develop the capacity to form enduring attachments as an integrated individual.

Developmental theory of the STM

Erik Erikson, the father of developmental and ego psychology, focuses on the development of ego identity—the conscious sense of self that is developed through social interaction (Erikson, 1968). According to Erikson, ego identity is constantly changing due to interactions between the body (genetics), mind (psychological), and cultural influences. A person's identity is shaped by human experiences and interpersonal interactions, in which new experiences are continually being assimilated resulting in solidifying, modifying, or disrupting earlier patterns of beliefs, affect, and behaviour.

Erikson's (1963) eight stages of psychosocial development encompass the lifespan of the individual. New experiences and information are obtained from daily interactions with others and impact the ability to be competent in each stage of psychosocial development. These stages parallel biological maturation and cognitive development. They are mastered within the context of healthy relationships and therefore overlap with attachment and family theories.

Erikson's psychosocial eight stages are: (1) basic trust versus basic mistrust in infancy, (2) autonomy versus shame and doubt in toddlerhood, (3) initiative versus guilt in early childhood, (4) industry versus inferiority in preadolescence and late childhood, (5) identity versus role confusion for the adolescent period, (6) intimacy and solidarity versus isolation in young adulthood, (7) generativity versus self-absorption in adulthood, and (8) integrity versus despair in old age.

Erickson (1963) outlined an order and timing for these psychosocial stages with the parents playing a major role in the child's early stages of development. Each stage builds on the preceding stage and paves the way for accomplishing subsequent stages. An individual achieves a stage of development after dealing with a biological crisis. In order to move through each stage, the individual experiences tension and conflicts within the relational context that effect resolution and competency. Ideally, the crisis should be resolved in order for development in the next stage to proceed. By mastering each stage, a person develops ego strength. However, failure to master a stage can result in less ability to manage the next stage, thereby leading to an unhealthy personality and diminished sense of self. According to Erickson, if an earlier stage's crisis is not fully mastered, it will likely resurface later in life.

Table 6.1 shows the significant relationships that play a role in the individual's success in mastering each stage along with favourable and unfavourable outcomes.

Because early and chronic childhood trauma often thwarts the achievement of these stages, it is important to examine the timing of children's trauma and to explore how the trauma influenced their ability to master the stage they were in when the trauma occurred and how the trauma has affected their subsequent development.

The Star Theoretical Model 89

Table 6.1 Erikson's stages of development

Stage (age)	Psychosocial dialectic	Primary activity	Significant relationships	Favourable outcome	Unfavourable outcome
0–1	**Trust vs mistrust**	Consistent stable care from parents	Main caregivers	Trust and optimism	Suspicion, withdraw, fear of future events
2–3	**Autonomy vs shame and doubt**	Consistent stable care from parents	Main caregivers	Sense of autonomy and self-esteem	Feelings of shame and self-doubt
4–5	**Initiative vs guilt**	Environmental exploration	Family, social institutions	Self-direction and purpose	A sense of guilt, anxiety, and inhibition
6 to puberty	**Industry vs inferiority**	Knowledge acquisition	Family, neighbours, peers, school	Sense of competence and achievement	A sense of inferiority and inadequacy at doing things
Adolescence	**Identity vs role confusion**	Coherent vocation and personality	Peers, group affiliations	Integrated self-image	Confusion over who and what one really is
Early adulthood	**Intimacy vs isolation**	Deep and lasting relationships	Friends, lovers, partners, family	Ability to experience love and commitment	Inability to form affectionate relationships, tself-absorption, isolation
Middle adulthood	**Generativity vs stagnation**	Productive and creative engagement in society	Offspring, family	Concern for family, society, and future generations	Concern only for self—one's own well-being and prosperity
Late adulthood	**Ego integrity vs despair**	Life review and evaluation	Humankind, and extended family	Sense of satisfaction, acceptance of death	Dissatisfaction with life, fear over death

Adapted from Erikson (1963)

Comparing Erickson's model with the Star Theoretical Model

Both Erikson's theory and the Star Theoretical Model are primarily concerned with the construction of identity and how the relational dynamics impact the process. The STM analyses how traumatic experiences can disrupt the child's ability to develop a cohesive identity causing a fragmented identity, and therefore impairs a child's capacity to master developmental conflicts and stages. The developmental portion of the Star Model holds that when a child is traumatised, the child can develop internal states with specific characteristics across multiple domains: behavioural, affective, relational, cognitive, spiritual/beliefs, and neurobiological (see Figure 6.2).

The Star Theoretical Model contends that each self-state can have divergent thoughts, feelings, relational capacity, beliefs, along with neurobiological differences that can impair the child's ability to effectively achieve developmental stages. To add complexity, certain self-states can be at different levels of development further thwarting the child from performing age-related expectations. Therefore, when evaluating traumatised children, in addition to recognising the child's current age appropriate to the psychosocial stage, it is important to know the child's psychosocial stage when the self-state was developed because that self-state can be stuck at that stage. This self-state can then interfere with the child's ability to deal with current developmental crises. For example, a 12-year-old with early and chronic trauma can have multiple self-states stuck at different developmental levels that can have devastating impact on the child's ability to meet developmental expectations. These states can contain a myriad of affect, behaviour, sensory disturbances, roles, and varied attachment styles causing severe

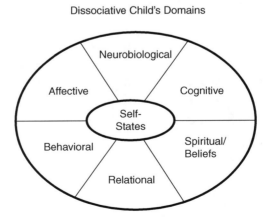

Figure 6.2 Developmental Model of Dissociative Child across Domains.

impairments. For successful treatment, each of the states within the child will need to master the developmental stages within the context of a positive relationship so that the child can eventually achieve a cohesive identity.

Family systems theory of the STM

> Feelings of worth can flourish only in an atmosphere where individual differences are appreciated, mistakes are tolerated, communication is open, and rules are flexible—the kind of atmosphere that is found in a nurturing family.
>
> Virginia Satir (n.d.)

Satir's profound words recognise that children's feelings of self-worth are primary to their health and the critical role that families play. We, in both big and small ways, must communicate this message to them and to their families.

Satir outlined three therapeutic beliefs about human nature: (1) every individual is geared to survival, growth, and obtaining closeness with others, no matter how distorted it may look; (2) what society calls sick, crazy, stupid, or bad behaviour is really the person's signal of distress and call for help; and (3) human beings are limited only by the extent of their knowledge, their ways of understanding themselves, and their ability to relate with others (1983, pp. 124–125).

Satir adhered to a growth model that is based on the notion that people change through interactions with other people and through an exploration of their inner life by exploring one's own thoughts, intentions, and perceptions of others. Satir's family systems theory coincides with Bowlby's and Erickson's models that recognise that family interactions play a significant role in the pathology of children—often the identified patient (1983). Satir understood that the openness, flexibility, clarity, and appropriateness of the family's rules will determine if developmental and life cycle changes of each family member will be successful, as supported by Erikson's theory.

Satir's guiding principles provide a foundation for our work with traumatised children and their families. I, therefore, largely base the family systems portion of the STM on her theories and approaches.

Because the identified child's symptoms reflect the distortions, pain, discomfort, and obstruction of growth present within the family system, she contends that the family needs to be treated as a unit. Accordingly, all family members at certain periods need to participate in family therapy sessions, as a symptom in any family member is a sign of a dysfunctional family system. I have found that due to their innocence, young children are more likely to reveal the family's secrets that open the door to explore hidden problems so that change can more likely occur.

In an open and safe environment, family rules and member's fears are discussed openly, directly, appropriately, and clearly. Conversely, in a closed family system characterised by maltreatment, distortions, and denial, maintaining the status quo is prominent. Such an abusive environment will promote a child's reliance on dissociation in order to conform to the distortions and denial. When confronted with change, an abusive family system will attempt to maintain past, ineffective ways of interacting, thus inhibiting effective management of the demands of relationship and life cycle changes. The resultant pathology is exhibited in the identified patient—often the child who suffers.

Satir (1965) recognises that each family member is unavoidably committed to the system of their family by the nature of their origin and dependency. Therefore, we need to recognise that we are working with three generations: the parents' history (including foster/adoptive parents), the current family, and the future family that the children will create when they become adults. An insightful task to help family members recognise transgenerational patterns is to create a genogram with notations on intergenerational histories of trauma, mental illness, separations, substance abuse, legal problems, etc. Exploring what each parent bring into their current family structure can help them become conscious of repetitive patterns that hinder growth.

With adoptive children, we can make educated guesses by their interactional patterns and behaviours what they bring from their biological families (and other placements) into their adoptive homes. Openly discussing messages, beliefs, and patterns that adoptive children exhibit can help them to discard traumatically based distorted beliefs and messages, and begin to overcome their fears, distrust, and reliance on dissociative responses and learn healthier communication patterns.

The therapist's role is to help family members clearly communicate their needs, wishes, and expectations and to examine any contradictory messages. Therapists observe verbal and nonverbal communication patterns and clarify any discrepancies between inferences and behaviours that can give mixed messages. It is important to document the relationship between patterns of communication and symptomatic behaviour, so that each family member can understand not only the power of words but tone of expression that can precipitate problematic behaviour. The therapist's task is to understand the family rules that govern and hinder each person's growth, and empathically and sensitively engage with them about how to transform to more effective ways of communicating and behaving for the good of them all. Moving the child out of the identified client to helping the parents recognise how their behaviours play a significant role on the child's healing can help parents to be motivated to engage in constructive ways of managing their traumatised child.

Nevertheless, it is particularly challenging to a parent of a dissociative child who can switch rapidly from one state to another displaying different attachment styles, myriad of affect, behaviour, and preferences. Suffice it to say, parents must accept all parts of their child even during these trying times and recognise that they are coregulators of their child. If parents demonstrate "calm in the midst of the storm," their child will deescalate quicker. Learning how to connect with the child with empathy and reflection before correcting her is a beginning step towards calming her. Because children's acting out behaviour can trigger parents unresolved traumatic past and attachment disturbances, they need to be aware of those triggers and ways to manage them effectively to avoid escalation. Recommending individual therapy for parents can give them the attention and support to work on their unresolved issues and learn healthy responses.

Summary

In the STM, I integrate solid theoretical models of attachment, development, dissociation, neurobiology, and family systems to provide a comprehensive approach to evaluating and treating children with dissociation. All of these theories interlock and contribute to a deeper understanding of the complexities and pathways involved in how a child develops dissociation. Each theory also provides guidance on treatment approaches to help traumatised children resolve their traumatic past, grieve their losses, develop healthy attachments, form a cohesive identity, and become productive members of society.

References

Blizard, R. A. (2003). Disorganized attachment, development of dissociated self-states, and a relational approach to treatment. *Journal of Trauma & Dissociation*, *4*(3), pp. 27–50. doi:10.1300/J229v04n03.

Bowlby, J. (1953). *Child care and the growth of love*. Baltimore, MD: Pelican Books.

Bowlby, J. (1960). Grief and mourning in infancy and early childhood. *Psychoanalytic Study of the Child*, *15*, pp. 9–52.

Bowlby, J. (1961). The Adolft Meyer Lecture: Childhood mourning and its implications for psychiatry. *American Journal of Psychiatry*, *118*, pp. 481–497.

Bowlby J. (1969). *Attachment. Attachment and Loss: Vol. 1. Loss*. New York: Basic Books.

Bowlby, J. (1973). *Attachment and loss, Vol. 2: Separation*. New York: Basic Books.

Bowlby, J. (1980). *Attachment and loss, Vol. 3: Loss, sadness and depression*. New York: Basic Books.

Bowlby, J. (1982a). Attachment and loss: Retrospect and prospect. *American Journal of Orthopsychiatry*, *52*(4), pp. 664–678.

Bowlby, J. (1982b). *Attachment and loss, Vol. 1: Attachment* (2nd ed.). New York: Basic Books.

Bremner, J. D. (2005). Effects of traumatic stress on brain structure and function: Relevance to early responses to trauma. *Journal of Trauma & Dissociation*, *6*(2), 51–68. doi:10.1300/J229v06n02.

Casile, A., Caggiano, V., & Ferrari, P. F. (2011). The mirror neuron system: A fresh view. *The Neuroscientist*, *17*(5), pp. 524–538. Retrieved from http://www.ncbi.nlm.nih.gov/pubmed/21467305.

Chu, J. A., & Dill, D. L. (1990). Dissociative symptoms in relation to childhood physical and sexual abuse. *The American Journal of Psychiatry*, *147*(7), pp. 887–892. Retrieved from http://www.ncbi.nlm.nih.gov/pubmed/2104510.

Chu, J. A., Frey, L. M., Ganzel, B. L., & Matthews, J. A. (1999). Memories of childhood abuse: Dissociation, amnesia, and corroboration. *American Journal of Psychiatry*, *156*(5), pp. 749–755.

Cloitre, M., Stolbach, B. C., Herman, J. L., Pynoos, R., Wang, J., & Petkova, E. (2009). A developmental approach to complex PTSD: Childhood and adult cumulative trauma as predictors of symptom complexity. *Journal of Traumatic Stress*, *22*(5), pp. 399–408.

Coons, P. M. (1984). The differential diagnosis of multiple personality: A comprehensive review. *Psychiatric Clinics of North America*, *7*(1), pp. 51–67.

DeBellis, M. D., Keshavan, M. S., Clark, D. B., Casey, B. J., Giedd, J. N., Boring, A. M., & Ryan, N. D. (1999). Developmental traumatology Part II: Brain development. *Biological Psychiatry*, *5*, pp. 1271–1284.

Diseth, T. H. (2006). Dissociation following traumatic medical treatment procedures in childhood: A longitudinal follow-up. *Development and Psychopathology*, *18*(1), pp. 233–251. Retrieved from http://www.ncbi.nlm.nih.gov/pubmed/16478561.

Engle, G. L. (1961). Is grief a disease? *Psychosomatic Medicine*, *23*(1), pp. 18–22.

Erikson, E. H. (1963). *Childhood and society* (2nd ed.). New York: W.W. Norton.

Erikson, E. H. (1968). *Identity: Youth and crisis.* New York: W.W. Norton.

Farrington, A., Waller, G. D., Smerden, J. D., & Faupel, A. W. (2001). The adolescent dissociative experiences scale: Psychometric properties and difference in scores across age groups. *Journal of Nervous and Mental Disease*, *189*, pp. 722–727.

Ferenczi, S. (1933/1949). Confusion of tongues between the adult and the child. *International Journal of Psychoanalysis*, 30, pp. 225–230.

Fraiberg, S. (1982). Pathological defenses in infancy. *Psychoanalytic Quarterly*, *51*(4), 612–635.

Freud, S. (1896). The aetiology of hysteria. *Standard Edition*, *3*, pp. 191–221.

Frewen, P. A, & Lanius, R. A. (2006). Neurobiology of dissociation: Unity and disunity in mind-body-brain. *The Psychiatric Clinics of North America*, *29*(1), pp. 113–128, ix–113–128, ix. Retrieved from http://www.ncbi.nlm.nih.gov/pubmed/16530589.

Freyd, J. (1996). *Betrayal Trauma: Logic of Forgetting Childhood Abuse.* Cambridge, MA: Harvard University Press.

Gaensbauer, T. J. (2002). Representation of trauma in infancy: Clinical and theoretical implications for the understanding of early memory. *Infant Mental Health Journal*, *23*(3), pp. 259–277.

Gallese, V., Fadiga, L., Fogassi, L., & Rizzolatti, G. (1996). Action recognition in the premotor cortex. *Brain*, *119*, pp. 593–609.

Gibbons, K. (2014). Houdini. *Multichannel News*, *35*(32), p. 23.

Heinicke, C. M. (1956). Some effects of separating two-year-old children from their parents: A comparative study. *Human Relations*, *9*, pp. 105–176.

Hulette, A. C., Fisher, P. A, Kim, H. K., Ganger, W., & Landsverk, J. L. (2008). Dissociation in foster preschoolers: A replication and assessment study. *Journal of Trauma & Dissociation*, *9*(2), pp. 173–190. doi:10.1080/15299730802045914.

Iacoboni, M. (2009). Imitation, empathy, and mirror neurons. *Annual Review of Psychology, 60*, pp. 653–670. doi:10.1146/annurev.psych.60.110707.163604.

Janet, P. (1907). *The major symptoms of hysteria*. London and New York: Macmillan.

Jovasevic, V., Corcoran, K. A., Leaderbrand, K., Yamawaki, N., Guedea, A. L., Chen, H. J., & Radulovic, J. (2015). GABAergic mechanisms regulated by miR-33 encode state-dependent fear. *Nature Neuroscience, 18*, pp. 1265–1271. doi: 10.1038/nn.4084.

Kisiel, C. L., & Lyons, J. S. (2001). Dissociation as a mediator of psychopathology among sexually abused children and adolescents. *The American Journal of Psychiatry, 158*(7), pp. 1034–1039. Retrieved from http://www.ncbi.nlm.nih.gov/pubmed/11431224.

Kisiel, C., McClelland, G., & Torgersen, E. (2013). *Understanding the impact of dissociation in Illinois Child Welfare: Relationship to risk behaviours and trauma symptoms, and intensity of services*. Unpublished Manuscript.

Main, M., & Hesse, E. (1990). Parents' unresolved traumatic experiences are related to infant disorganized attachment status: Is frightened and/or frightening parental behaviour the linking mechanism? In M. T. Greenberg, D. Cicchetti, & E. M. Cummings (Eds), *Attachment in the preschool years: Theory, research and intervention*, pp. 161–182. Chicago, IL: University of Chicago Press.

Milot, T., Plamondon, A., Ethier, L. S., Lemelin, J. P., St. Laurent, D., & Rousseau, M. (2013). Validity of CBCL-Derived PTSD and dissociation scales: Further evidence in a sample of neglected children and adolescents. *Child Maltreatment, 18*(2), pp. 122–128. doi:10.1177/1077559513490246

Muris, P., Merckelbach, H., & Peeters, E. (2003). The links between the Adolescent Dissociative Experiences Scale (A-DES), fantasy proneness, and anxiety symptoms. *Journal of Nervous and Mental Disease, 191*, pp. 18–24.

Nijenhuis, E. R. S., & Den Boer, J. A. (2009). Psychobiology of traumatization and trauma-related structural dissociation of the personality. In P. F. Dell & J. A. O'Neil (Eds), *Dissociation and the dissociative disorders: DSM-V and beyond*, pp. 337–367. New York: Routledge.

Nilsson, D., & Svedin, C. G. (2006). Dissociation among Swedish adolescents and the connection to trauma: An evaluation of the Swedish version of Adolescent Dissociative Experiences Scale. *Journal of Nervous and Mental Disease, 194*, pp. 684–689.

Ogawa, J., Sroufe, A., Weinfield, N., Carlson, E., & Egeland, B. (1997). Development and the fragmented self: Longitudinal study of dissociative symptomatology in a nonclinical sample. *Development and Psychopathology, 9*, pp. 855–879.

Perry, B. D. (2001). The neurodevelopmental impact of violence in childhood. In D. Schetky & E. P. Benedek (Eds), *Textbook of child and adolescent forensic psychiatry*, pp. 221–238. Washington, DC: American Psychiatric Press.

Perry, B. D. (2006). Applying principles of neurodevelopment to clinical work with maltreated and traumatised children. In N. B. Webb (Ed.), *Working with traumatised youth in child welfare*, pp. 27–52. New York: Guilford Press.

Perry, B. D., Pollard, R., Blakely, T., Baker, W. L., & Vigilante, D. (1995). Childhood trauma, the neurobiology of adaptation and use-dependent development of the brain: How states become traits. *Infant Mental Health Journal, 16*(4), pp. 271–291.

Porges, S. (2011). *The polyvagal theory: Neurophysiological foundations of emotions, attachment, communication and self-regulation*. New York: W.W. Norton.

Putnam, F. W. (1997). *Dissociation in children and adolescents: A developmental perspective.* New York: The Guilford Press.

Reinders, A. A. T. S., Nijenhuis, E. R. S., Paans, A. M. J., Korf, J., Willemsen, A. T. M., & den Boer, J. A. (2003). One brain, two selves. *NeuroImage, 20,* 2119–2125. doi:10.1016/j.neuroimage.2003.08.021

Reinders, A. A. T. S., Willemsen, A. T. M., Vos, H. P. J., den Boer, J. A, & Nijenhuis, E. R. S. (2012). Fact or factitious? A psychobiological study of authentic and simulated dissociative identity states. *PloS One, 7*(6), e39279. doi:10.1371/journal.pone.0039279.

Rizzolatti, G., Fadiga, L., Gallese, V., & Fogassi, L. (1996). Premotor cortex and the recognition of motor actions. *Cognitive Brain Research, 3,* pp. 131–141.

Robertson, J., & Bowlby, J. (1952). Responses of young children to separation from their mothers II: Observations of the sequences of response of children aged 18 to 24 months during the course of separation. *Courrier du Centre International de l'Enfance, 2,* pp. 131–142.

Sar, V., Onder, C., Killicaslan, A., Zoroglu, S. S., & Alyanak, B. (2014). Dissociative identity disorder among adolescents: Prevalence in a university psychiatric outpatient unit. *Journal of Trauma & Dissociation, 15*(4), pp. 402–419.

Satir, V. (1965). The family as a treatment unit. *Confinia Psychiatrica, 8,* pp. 37–42.

Satir, V. (1983). *Conjoint family therapy* (3rd ed.). Palo Alto, CA: Science and Behaviour Books.

Satir, V. (n.d.). BrainyQuote.com. Retrieved from: http://www.brainyquote.com/quotes/quotes/v/virginiasa175186.html.

DSM-V and beyond, pp. 107–141. New York: Routledge.

Science Daily. (2015, August 17). *How traumatic memories hide in the brain, and how to retrieve them.* Retrieved from http://www.sciencedaily.com/releases/2015/08/150817132325.htm.

Silberg, J. (2013). *The child survivor: Healing developmental trauma and dissociation.* New York: Routledge Press.

Teicher, M. H., Samson, J. A, Polcari, A., & McGreenery, C. E. (2006). Sticks, stones, and hurtful words: Relative effects of various forms of childhood maltreatment. *The American Journal of Psychiatry, 163*(6), pp. 993–1000. Retrieved from http://www.ncbi.nlm.nih.gov/pubmed/16741199.

Tolmunen, T., Maaranen, P., Hintikka, J., Kylmä, J., Rissanen, M., Honkalampi, K., & Laukkanen, E. (2007). Dissociation in a general population of Finnish adolescents. *Journal of Nervous and Mental Disease, 195,* pp. 614–617.

van der Hart, O., Nijenhuis, E. & Steele, K. (2006). *The haunted self: Structural dissociation and the treatment of chronic traumatization.* New York: W.W. Norton.

van der Kolk, B. A., van der hart, O., & Marmar, C. R. (1996). Dissociation and information processing in posttramatic stress disorder. In B. A. van der Kolk, A. C. MacFarlane & L. Weisaeth (Eds), *Traumatic stress: The effects of overwhelming experience on mind, body, and society,* pp. 46–74. New York: Guilford Press.

Vásquez, D. A., de Arellano, M. A., Reid-Quiñones, K., Bridges, A. J., Rheingold, A. A., Stocker, R. P. J., & Danielson, C. K. (2012). Peritraumatic dissociation and peritraumatic emotional predictors of PTSD in Latino youth: Results from the Hispanic family study. *Journal of Trauma & Dissociation, 13*(5), pp. 509–525. doi: 10.1080/15299732.2012.678471.

Vermetten, E., Schmahl, C., Lindner, S., Loewenstein, R. J., & Bremner, J. D. (2006). Hippocampal and amygdalar volumes in Dissociative Identity Disorder. *American Journal of Psychiatry, 163*(4), pp. 630–636.
Waters, F. S. (1996). *Quadri-theoretical model for the treatment of children with dissociation.* Paper presented at the meeting of the International Society for the Study of Trauma and Dissociation, November, San Francisco, CA.
Waters, F. S. (2016). *Healing the fractured child: Diagnosis & treatment of youth with dissociation.* New York: Springer Publishing Company, LLC.
Waters, F. S., Marks, R., & Parker L. (2018). *Prenatal, preverbal & preschool trauma & subsequent development of dissociation.* Preconference workshop presented at 35th International Society for the Study of Trauma & Dissociation, Chicago, IL.
Watkins, J. G., & Watkins, H. H. (1997). *Ego-states: Theory and therapy.* New York: W. W. Norton.
Wieland, S. (Ed.). (2015). *Dissociation in traumatised children and adolescents: Theory and clinical interventions* (2nd Ed.), pp. 191–260. New York: Routledge.
Yoshizumi, T., Hamada, S., Kaida, A., Gotow, K., & Murase, S. (2010). Psychometric properties of the Adolescent Dissociative Experiences Scale (A-DES) in Japanese adolescents from a community sample. *Journal of Trauma & Dissociation, 11*(3), pp. 322–336. Retrieved from http://www.ncbi.nlm.nih.gov/pubmed/20603766.
Zoroglu, S. S., Sar, V., Tuzun, U., Tutkun, H., & Savas, H. A. (2002). Reliability and validity of the Turkish version of the Adolescent Dissociative Experiences Scale. *Psychiatry and Clinical Neurosciences, 56*, pp. 551–556.

Chapter 7

The power of care
The healing that comes from teaching non-offending parents how to regulate their child after physical and sexual abuse

Christine C. Forner

Introduction and case background

When I was first introduced to the client, he was 11 years old. John (pseudonym) suspected that his child was dealing with a dissociative disorder. He read a disparaging article about Dissociative Identity Disorder, which was rebutted in a letter to the editor co-authored by Dr David Spiegel (Brand, Loewenstein, & Spiegel, 2014). John felt that he had finally found information that helped him understand what might be occurring within his child. He was upset with the treatment his child was receiving through community mental health and the medical system and contacted Dr Spiegel, who referred both father and son to me.

John was quite distraught when we first spoke. At this time his son had been through a mental health nightmare. This boy was diagnosed with a host of ailments, such as Oppositional Defiance Disorder (ODD), childhood Obsessive Compulsive Disorders (OCD), childhood Bipolar Disorder (BD), Adjustment Disorder (AD), Conversion Disorder, Attention Deficit Hyperactivity Disorder (ADHD), and Generalize Anxiety Disorder (GAD).

The family separated about three years prior to my first meeting with the son, who was eight years old at the time. The reason for the separation was that the mother was very volatile, with a lot of screaming and yelling and John realized that this type of parenting was not healthy for his children. Before the separation, John was the primary caregiver for the children, David (pseudonym), his brother, and twin sister. Initially he lost custody of his children to the mother, who was the bread winner of the family. The separation was extremely hard on both father and children. While the family was under one roof, John could buffer the mother's volatility. After he left, however, he could no longer mitigate this. The mother's rage and temper increased post-separation. During the first year, when John was no longer there, the children reported that their mother would often play strange favourites, only reading to the twins and not to David who would become my client, for example. She would scream and yell, calling the children names. It was

DOI: 10.4324/9781003246541-8

David, who I treated, who received the brunt of the outbursts. John was no longer able to manage the hurtful aspects of the mothers parenting and the children started to show signs of the insecure home life.

David was very close to his father; when he was not under his father's protection mental illness ensued. It was only following the mother's forced separation of John and his children that his symptoms started.

During the initial part of the separation, David was described as happy, curious, and smart. When upset, he would become more stubborn and defiant than his siblings, but nothing that could not be managed with soothing. At this time, he was a "typical" child.

During the end of the first year of separation, David was diagnosed with ADHD and placed on 2 mg of Abilify and 36 mg of Concerta, to assist with ADHD and "anger" issues. The mother insisted that her son be put on medication.

By fall at the end of the first year of the separation, David began to hallucinate, resulting in the police being called to manage him. By the beginning of the second-year post-separation, David was starting to become more aggressive at home; the same time that John became very vocal about the use of Abilify; he noticed that his son's aggressive behaviour coincided with its use. He asked that the medication be stopped and the mother insisted on an increase of the Abilify dose to 5 mg, with which the paediatrician complied. Shortly after this medication increase David developed seizure-like activity. When the seizures started, he was also placed on 4 mg of Intuniv. Both drugs were stopped a year later.

At the start of the second year following the separation, the mother invited her father—a medical doctor—into the family home to help care for the children. The grandfather's violence towards David, and not his siblings, started within two weeks of his arrival; David was thrown downstairs and against furniture. Within four weeks, he started to choke David. In the following months, the child spoke to many health professionals and teachers about not being able to breathe and he clearly remembers thinking that he was going to die. He tried, unsuccessfully, to fight off the grandfather. Eventually David's grandfather stopped choking him and, as the child got up to walk away, he hit him hard on the back of the head several times. David's brother, sister, and mother witnessed these events.

At this time, David's aggressive behaviour at home increased. He began to simulate choking when he got upset. He started to talk about overtly sexual content, was swearing a lot more and being louder; he was escalating at a very fast rate.

During the day, and at school, he could keep himself "together" for the first year and a half following the separation. He still had friends, was doing okay, and liked school. His home life was filled with violence, such as his grandfather regularly restraining him by holding his head to the ground while telling him that he was too weak to fight him, too dumb to stop and that he would never win. Many of these incidents were corroborated by his siblings. David was always referred to as a very troubled child and the aggression towards him was characterized, by the grandfather and the mother, as being necessary to manage David's angry outbursts. The adults put all the blame into David for the chaos in the home.

By the end of the second year after the separation, David's father had a bit more contact with the children. He reported that David would rage a bit, but was still consolable. He felt that David was traumatized and extremely hyper vigilant, but there was no indication that the child had any dissociative identity confusion or identity alteration (Steinberg & Schnall, 2000). David heard no internal voices at this time and the vacant stare and odd eye twitching was not yet present.

By the beginning of the school year, two years after the separation (when David was ten years old) things started to change even more radically. There was another violent episode between David and his grandfather and the police were called; they took David into custody. David said that the police tasered him at the police station, to gain control over him. He also stated that he was tied to a chair and left in a locked room by himself for a long time. When his mother was brought into the room, David begged her to stay with him, but she left him there alone, scared and trapped. Eventually he was released and this is when the voices began.

The police were also called many times after this incident to control David. They were never informed of the choking, hitting, forced restraints, or name calling. The story for others—including me, several years after the commencement of the chaos—by David's mother was that David was severely mentally ill, out of control, a general menace and terrifying the family. David was constantly told that he was the problem, that everyone was afraid of him, that he was the reason for the family's stress, and that without him the family would be at peace. At this point, John had little say in what was happening to his son.

Now ten, two years after his parents separated and David had become, reportedly, out of control, David was put into a day treatment programme in a Children's Hospital, without John's permission. John was very concerned that his son was being removed from yet another school; school was David's only safe place. He told the treatment centre that he did not want his son removed from school, but David's mother removed him anyway. This is when serious hallucinations and serious memory problems began for David. He also started wandering off aimlessly in the middle of various activities and passing out. David's father told staff, at the treatment centre, who dismissed the symptoms.

An evaluation of David was conducted within the school environment, with his teachers noting that he might be the family scapegoat. The report also notes that no real remarkable behaviours were detected at school; in fact, the school reported no behavioural concerns, though they did highlight that he had been to a lot of schools before the age of nine. At this point, David was still able to self-regulate and calm down while at school. His teachers described him as insightful and capable, though a bit delayed in mathematics. David's teachers observed that his mother would scream and yell at the child. They wondered whether, because she had accessed many resources for her child, the mother was searching for pathology as, prior to the separation, there was no apparent need for the child to be diagnosed with any disorder. The reports also mention that the mother always sought immediate results and pulled the children out of school if there were problems; the teachers at the school wondered about the mother's mental health. David's mother stated, in an email to a teacher, that her child was suicidal, but never followed this up.

At almost 11, David was discharged from the day-treatment centre's outpatient programme after about six months. His father and school support workers all confirm that he was a lot worse when he came out of the treatment facility; he was no longer functioning at school, having seizures and passing out frequently. The violence at home was still escalating at this point. David was grabbed by the grandfather and repeatedly slammed against furniture—something corroborated by his brother, sister, and his brother's friend. Social services were called; the mother and grandfather both said that David was lying. Social workers did nothing.

A week after this, the grandfather locked David in the garage for a very long time. When he was let out, he was again restrained by grabbing his head and holding him down. David's brother called their father saying that he thought his grandfather was going to kill his brother and he was terrified.

A few days after this, David had a massive rage attack at school; the classroom had to be evacuated as David tore everything apart in the room. He has no memory of the event. David was tested for epilepsy, but there were no remarkable findings leaving seizure-like episodes unexplained.

By the beginning of the third-year post-separation David was out of control. The police and emergency medical services had to be called every three or four days. He was taken to the hospital many times, when his father would be contacted. John always attempted to inform the doctors about the violence at home and that it was this that was contributing to David's behaviour. The mother and grandfather always explained this by saying that John was abusive and attempting parental alienation. The doctors always believed the mother.

Finally, a different social worker was brought in during a hospital emergency visit. She stated that David was trying to send a message and suggested he might be better off with John. The social worker convinced the mother and grandfather that it was best for David to be with his father and so he went to live with him. Now living with him, John had enough time with his son to see the damage done; he barely recognized his son. He had no real idea what was wrong with his son, but he knew it was serious. He also saw his son's more subtle symptoms, such as an odd eye twitching he would do every morning or when he had a major mood switch. He also noticed that the twins seemed to still be okay; he did not see any of the same serious signs of disturbance in his other children.

John knew his son needed help, but felt very alone. The doctors and therapists that his son had seen were not helpful, with some being harmful and shaming and disbelieving David while vilifying John.

John had finally managed to get Abilify stopped, with medical supervision from a new family doctor, but David started to act delusional. If he had a bad day, he started talking in a different tone of voice, passing out and not remembering. His father asked him if he had friends in his head; David answered "yes". After yet another hospital stay—because of the passing out—John was told by the unit's therapist to ignore the voices and they will go away. Following this, John went "on a mission" to get his son appropriate assistance.

Other psychopharmaceuticals were tried through the new family doctor, who worked a lot with children with mental health concerns. John was the main contact and assisted by researching information; they had a good collaborative doctor/patient relationship. They put David on 150 mg Sertraline, which coincided with a lessening of the fainting. He was weaned off of Concerta and placed on 0.3 mg of Clonidine.

I started to see David and his father three times a week. I was also communicating with David's mother and invited her to the appointment, as well as inviting her to set up a separate appointment so that she could interview me to approve my treatment plan. This was the option she chose. I saw David and his father for two years, three times a week for six months and then a few times a month for a duration of our time together. Then it lessened to about once a month after the first year. Currently I see him only sporadically. During the same time, I met with the mother three times, twice on her own, and once with David and his father. She did not want to attend any other sessions, even though she was always invited to the sessions.

The first time I met David, his presentation to me was not that remarkable. He was engaged, asking questions, making jokes; I did not see any real signs of distress. During the initial visit I spoke mostly with John about what to expect and describe what modalities I use. I outlined Sensorimotor Psychotherapy (Ogden, Minton & Pain, 2006), Havening (Ruden 2005, 2011), Ego State therapy (Laidlaw & Malmo, 1990; Watkins & Watkins, 1997), and the International Society for the Study of Trauma and Dissociation Treatment Guidelines (Chu et al., 2011), as well as giving some general information about dissociation being the human way to cope with emotions and pain that are too big for us to handle. I explained that I would like to assist David and his father to do some diagnostic measures to see if this was dissociation or not. They were both happy to do the tests and measures. During the first session I was soft and gentle to the child and invited him to sit where ever he wanted. He played with a few hand squishy toys I have in the office and he left saying that he liked my office.

During the first session I also spoke with John about the need to learn the skill of regulation. I described the need for a parent to be a neuro-biological-affect regulator to their child (Schore, 1994, 2003a, 2003b). This is the main reason that I requested John's presence in sessions. It is much more effective to teach the parent how to manage a traumatized child rather than just solely working with the child. In this way, a child can get appropriate assistance all the time, instead of 1–3 hours a week I could provide. John was quite well read by the time he found me and invested in his child's health. He was researching dissociation and was familiar with the language, and much of the neurobiology of dissociation. What he did not know was how to talk to his child when other parts were out, how to calm his child down when a rage hit, or how to revive him when he was fainting. When I described that dissociation is an escape from the full sensorium of trauma, neglect, pain, chronic pain, emotional distress, and violence (Stone, 2006), he was tangibly relieved that he was finally speaking with someone who understood his child.

The next time I saw David he was spread-eagled on the floor of my waiting room; he looked like he was passed out. John looked visibly upset and said David was not feeling well; he looked concerned about my reaction. I gently told him that it's okay, that David is not going to be judged, and that this type of behaviour is not uncommon in the waiting room of a therapist who works with complex trauma and dissociation! I then suggested that we deal with David with curiosity and calmness, to see if we can learn what is happening. I suggested that the dad could wait in the office so that I could try to get David into my office, principally for privacy and safety.

John went into the office and I stayed with David. After a bit of encouragement I was able to get him off of the floor, saying things like, "it is safer for him in the chair" and "I share my waiting room with others and someone could walk in and not understand why he is lying in the middle of the floor". Once in the chair I asked him if he would like to come into the office so I could help keep him safe. He then mumbled in a very low voice, "there is nothing you can do to help me". I replied that I can think of at least ten different things we could try and if they don't work, I could think of ten more, and then ten more after that. I told him that I am an adult who is used to kids like him and I have millions of ideas and different ways I could help him. My intention was to let him know that I could handle him, that he was not a mystery to me. I wanted to convey that I am not at a loss and that my adult wisdom is able to provide care (Talia, Muzi, Lingiardi, & Taubner, 2018). I wanted him to know that he was not alone, that he was safe, and that someone could provide care with ease. I wanted to give him a totally different experience with regard to his trauma symptoms than those he had so far experienced. I knew that he had been failed by every mental health professional—except the social worker who suggested he live with his father.

When I told David that I could think of a lot of things to try he almost challenged me to prove it, so I did! We went into my office and he collapsed onto the floor; I joined him. I moved to his level and then said, if it were me, I might actually like to be in a fort, hidden. I was concerned with his primitive defences and thought of the Cascade Model of Defence (Bovine et al., 2014, cited in Ratner 1967; Schauer & Elbert, 2010; Lanius, Paulsen, & Corrigan, 2014). There are various stages related to our mammalian evolutionary response to predation. I was thinking that in times of death and dying fear, being hidden in a "cave" might feel better. He seemed to like this notion. We made a fort out of big pillows and a huge blanket in my office. He curled up in the fort. I also wanted him to be soothed, but having just met him, and not knowing the full story, I felt cautious with close proximity. I also wanted to try to do a gentle distraction, so I asked if he liked things that smell nice and I gave him some essential oils that I put into a Kleenex for him to smell. I wanted to introduce new associations and experiences that coincided with dignity and care; he could associate the fort being safe with these nice new smells. I also put some nice music on my phone and let him just listen. In giving him new sensory inputs, I could bring in new experience and assist in interrupting the possible, constant triggers that he was perhaps going through.

As I was doing this, I explained my actions to David's father. I described that when a human is scared, our usual way of being is overridden by our animal defences (Panksepp, 1998, 2002; Panksepp & Biven, 2012). When we are in our animal defences, our body's concern is not with enhancing life or being alive, its concern is with not dying. The difference between being alive and fighting death is enormous. I said it seems like your son is exhausted and needs gentle, kind, caring healing.

Every word I said I knew was being heard by David, so they were chosen to support him, to remove shame, and to verbalize the importance of being safe. I also repeated often that he was not expected to trust me, I had to earn this; it is my job as an adult to ensure he is safe. I also stated often that I trusted him, that I trusted his emotional reactions, the language of his upset, of his feelings, and of his actions. From a somatic psychological perspective, he was communicating something and my job was to hear, listen, and receive the communication.

I informed both David and his father that we were not going to focus on the hurts until he could feel the feeling of safe and calm inside as I further explained the importance of following the stages of treatment recommended in the ISSTD treatment guidelines (Chu et al., 2011). I wanted him to know that we were not diving straight into talking about the hurts until he knew that he could escape, settle, or calm the feelings inside (Ogden, 2009; 2012). I also explained to John that David needed to be able to be regulated with consistency before we process the trauma. I also discussed the first stage of treatment, according to the ISSTD guidelines (2011)—focus on symptom reduction and stabilization.

After he was settled, I checked with David in his fort by getting on the floor and asking for permission to enter his safe space. He said I could enter and, when I asked him how he was feeling, said he was feeling better. I reminded him that I had said that I could think of a lot of ways to help him feel better and he agreed that these things had made him feel better. I then asked how did he know that he felt better, as supported by the modality of Sensorimotor Psychotherapy (Ogden et al., 2006; Ogden, 2009; 2012). I asked him if he could feel the difference between not better and better. He said that he could feel his muscles and they were more relaxed; his head had less pressure and his voices were quieter. As we did this, I explained in a very simplistic way that the body is the purest form of communication in that it reacts to the environment. It is our minds and imaginations that adapt by inventing and creating as a way of interacting with our environment. Because of this ability to invent and create, sometimes our thoughts and beliefs can be misunderstood or be different to what an emotion is "saying". I talked about how dogs and cats don't question their behaviour, they just react, but we humans have minds and imaginations that help us change, question, create, and invent ways to live in our environment. So, as we begin this work, dealing with the sensations and emotions by learning how to regulate them is much more important than the words, narrative, and cognitions of what may or may not be an accurate account of the events that led to his dysregulation.

I said to David and his father that because humans are quite complex, doing some standardized measures that have been tested to see if they are measuring what they are intended to measure is very important before we begin. I conducted the Adolescent Dissociative Experience Scale (A-DES) (Smith & Carlson, 1996; Armstrong et al., 1997) and the Adolescent Multidimensional Inventory of Dissociation (A-MID) (Dell, 2006). He scored 32.5 on the A-DES, where the cut-off score indicating a dissociative disorder is 12 (Smith & Carlson, 1996; Armstrong et al., 1997; Farrington, et al., 2001). He also had an A-MID score of 21–40. Many cases of Posttraumatic Stress Disorder, Otherwise Specified Dissociative Disorder, and Dissociative Identity Disorder fall within this range (Dell, 2006). I wrote to both the mother and the father that David had a very high A-DES score and positive results from the A-MID. Within this letter I stated that David has childhood Dissociative Identity Disorder (DID).

Medication during stage one, two, and three

Once dissociation was determined to be an accurate diagnosis, I forwarded information to his family doctor and suggested that we should consider the possibility of prescribing Low-Dose Naltrexone (LDN) (Lanius et al., 2014,

2018) for the child. LDN is known for preventing some of the effect of the naturally occurring opioids and cannabinoids that are secreted during a dissociative episode as it is an opioid blocker (Lanius et al., 2014, 2018). With the guidance of the family physician, his father weaned him off of Sertraline. David also started to take LDN, starting at 2 mg once per day, working up to 3 mg twice a day. After three months of three times per week therapy, the doctor had him on 3 mg of LDN twice a day and Clonidine was reduced from 0.3 mg, to 0.2 mg to 0.1 mg. By the end of my first year with David, who was now in therapy once or twice a month, he was only on 0.5 mg of Clonidine at bed time and 3 mg of LDN twice a day. He is still currently on these doses of medications.

Ego State therapy and stage one work

After the positive diagnosis of DID, I recommended working with parts using Ego State therapy and Feminist Ego State therapy (Laidlaw & Malmo, 1990; Watkins & Watkins, 1997). When David was more lucid, we started to explore the inner world he had created to protect himself. There were four distinct parts, other than himself. One was very angry and rageful, one was quite pleasant and happy, one was good at taking him away to nothingness, and one was very shy. We gave the parts special rooms in an internal tree fort. The angry part was given the gift of a magic baseball bat that could smash things; when he was done smashing, the things would then magically repair themselves and could be destroyed again. To help this part we found, via YouTube, the sound of breaking glass; the angry part loved to use this when he was mad! Directed by David, I put the tree fort into a rain forest. I found rainforest sounds and instructed him to use these whenever he needed safety. We also used other sounds, all chosen by the part under discussion. Each part got their own special room in the tree fort with unique items inside such as an imaginary huge teddy bear with a heartbeat for the very shy part. I also put in places for each part to get food. They all slept in hammocks, all were able to swim or take showers to stay clean. I also set up a treadmill for the parts to walk on, trampolines to jump on, and video games for the inner parts to play with. Each item, as discussed with David and his father, was put in place to foster safety and care. I wanted the parts to be treated with dignity. The simple acts of eating, sleeping, being clean, having exercise, and having entertainment are basic ways we care for our young, ourselves, and each other.

The main intention of these interventions was to alter the end of the story he had had so far. Many of his experiences during times of difficulty ended with him being alone in his room. I wanted to introduce a different ending, where his inner parts have a fun, safe, new environment to go to. After a new room for a part was invented, I reinforced the experience of safety by bringing in somatic resources as well (Ogden et al., 2006; Ogden, 2009, 2012). For example, when the angry part got a room that was full of mirrors that he could destroy with the magic baseball bat, and we added the sound of smashing, with encouragement from me and his father I asked how he felt inside his tummy, lungs, muscles, and heart or gut. He was beginning to be able to feel himself calm down and recognize that when he was calmer, the parts went back inside.

Sensorimotor Psychotherapy with children and stage one work

Sensorimotor Psychotherapy is best explained as an intervention where bodily experiences become the main entry point of discussion and the focal point of the intervention. When emotions and sensations are the focus, meaning-making arises from the subsequent somatic reorganization of the trauma response (Ogden, Pain & Fisher, 2006). By working from the bottom up, rather than top down—or body to mind rather than mind to body—the person can direct their attention to the sensations and emotions rather than thoughts. As a result of paying attention to body reactions and desired actions, the more primitive, autonomic, and involuntary functions of the brain are understood differently and can be attended to (Ogden et al., 2006). By organizing a session in this way, it can be shown to the child and parent that through focusing on experience, the cognitive functions evolve from, and are dependent on, the integrity of limbic and reptilian structures (Fisher, Murray & Bundy, 1991). David responded well to a somatic approach as he was able to answer somatically based information occurring within his body. He was also able to have the lived experience of feeling better in the present moment.

In the first few months, there were many days when David would come in and be very aggressive; he liked to smash things. I have a Neurofeedback machine next to his favourite chair. In these moments, the child had to be care for in equal measure to his upset; I would have to hold him. I was very concerned about restraining/containing this child, because part of his original traumatic injury involved being held down. So when he flared into a rage and lunged towards my very expensive Neurofeedback machine, I would hold him in a big hug, face forward, and tell him that I don't want to hurt him. My only concern was his safety, and while I held him, I would say I don't want you to get hurt, or hurt my stuff. While we were doing this containment, as we all agreed this was a better name than restrain, I would ask typical Sensorimotor mindfully directed questions (Ogden et al., 2006; Ogden, 2009, 2012). I asked him to tell me what he noticed I was doing, or how was I acting that supports my words. I would ask him "what can [you?] tell, from observing my body, my muscle tension, or my eye contact, that could inform him if I am lying or telling the truth". How could he test my words? What would tell him if I was holding him to hurt him and what would tell him that I'm only interested in helping him? I would instruct him to be discerning in assessing my actions. As I was doing this, I was talking to John about my tone, my cadence, and asking him to take notes on how I was behaving and feeling, on the implicit forms of communication, such as emotions, intent, regulation of myself, and regulation of him. I asked and encouraged both David and his father to take what is typically implicit and make it explicit. I discussed the language of rage and asked them both to try out compassionate words, what anger might be asking for, and then explicitly provide that to the child.

During the time I saw David he only had two rages where I had to hold him for safety; each incident only lasted a few moments. He would often collapse after a short time and we would end up on the floor. My intention was to give him the explicit experience of safety during and after the rage attacks. I would talk to him about his internal experiences, such as what feelings he had inside and where he felt those feelings. We would search for sensations that might help him understand what his feelings or experiences are for him. I was not very concerned with the story of how this happened, but I was much more concerned with what was happening to him in the here and now. His father and I just focused on moment-to-moment experiences and directed mindfulness in order for the child to recognize feelings of anger and fear and experience resolution to his current fear and anger (Ogden and Fisher, 2015).

Each upset resulted in finding explicit words for the internal experiences he was having. For example, after he would collapse following a heightened emotional outburst, we would lie on the ground. He had a favourite pillow that I would put under his head and I would start to draw letters and numbers on his back to help him get back into his body. He was able to feel each number or letter, and this always calmed him down. As I was doing this, I would also describe what I was doing to John from a clinical perspective. I would explain that when we dissociate we lose contact with the body or we lose awareness of the feelings and when I draw letters on his back I am attempting to (a) settle him and (b) get him into his body so he can tangibly feel the feelings of going from upset to calm. I would also introduce the notion of the window of tolerance (Siegel, 1999; Ogden, et al., 2006). I gently encouraged John to do this every time the child went into a rage or terror episode at home.

We spent a lot of time on the floor, David lying on his stomach with his head on a huge pillow with me beside him on my own pillow. This is where a great deal of the work to help this boy learn how to be his own neurobiological-affect-regulator happened. As John watched, I reminded him of how we need to prove to his son's central nervous system and primitive brain structures that we were not a threat to him. We had to help him feel safe in order for his social engagement system to come back online (Porges, 1998, 2003, 2011).

Every time I introduced an intervention, like Polyvagal Theory, I would explain what I was doing and why to David's father. I explained that human higher functions—language, abstract thinking, and reasoning, for example—tend to go offline when our more primitive reactions—such as flight, fight, and freeze—kick in to save us. We have a system that helps us live and adapt and it is often inflexible. This child, he needed real-time soothing, and after the soothing was accomplished we could talk with him, ask questions about his inner experiences, and help him put those experiences into words, so that eventually he could feel and know what it is like to change states without switching.

During our time together from the beginning of the year until the summer months this boy started to heal. He was attending school for a few hours a day with the ability to leave if he was scared. The school psychologist became part of the team and used several of the Sensorimotor resources that David liked, such as hiding his face with his hoodie when he felt overwhelmed. This was explained as an attempt to hide from danger, and it helped David settle down in school. Another common resource was walking slowly and feeling the legs move, with directed mindfulness (Ogden, 2012). David reported that this helped him feel like he could get away when he felt trapped. These daily resources assisted him to learn how to settle himself down, and begin to recognize when he was triggered and what to do about triggers.

Modified Havening in stage one work

During the more difficult sessions where he collapsed a lot or was very dysregulated, I would use modified Havening. Havening is a method of attempting to reconsolidate memory by de-potentiating the amygdala with touch. It is based on the notion that touch and distraction can alter the encoded glutamate pathways that result from traumatic encoding (Harper, Rasolkhani-Kalhorn, & Drozd, 2009). It has been shown that EMDR has some efficacy based on amygdala de-potentiation (Ruden, 2005, 2011; Hong et al., 2011). Harper et al. (2009) theorized that EMDR's bilateral movements disrupted the activated glutamate receptors by a mechanism called de-potentiation (Ruden, 2011). Ruden explained that the principal mechanism for de-potentiation is the removal, by internalization, of activated glutamate receptors by the production of a low-frequency signal produced by eye movement. These receptors, now internalized within the neuron, cannot transmit a signal and the pathway is disrupted (ibid.).

Ruder continues that there are data to support that serotonergic modulation of GABA neurons is associated with an increase in low-frequency (delta) waves in the amygdala (ibid.). The delta waves produced during touching the face, arms, and palms, while using distraction, can be an effective way to alter the previously consolidated fear responses (ibid.). In this case using modified Havening—in which I only used touch (on the face, arms, and hands)—worked very well. As I was gently touching the face in a downward motion, arms from shoulder to elbow and palms from palm to finger, I explained to John why I was doing this and how it potentially affects encoded memories of terror. John used this intentional healing touch to calm his son whenever he was upset or sometimes experiencing nightmares. Near the end of our intensive sessions John and I used this method frequently. These sessions always resulted in David leaving calm and settled.

The turning tides

By the time summer came, David was swearing less, was switching less, had fewer nightmares, was able to spend more and more time at school, was catching up on school work, and was generally feeling like his old self. Exercise still triggered him, causing difficulties. He would switch into rage or faint, but these episodes became less frequent. At this time, I had only seen the mother once and the grandfather was asked to leave David alone with John insisting that there be no contact. The mother ignored this request once during the intensive six-month treatment. There was clear upset and very specific reaction from David upon having to be near the grandfather, at the insistence of the mother. After this, there was no further contact for the rest of the year. David was told by his father that he would care for him and protect him and this is what he was able to do. For me this was one of the most powerful interventions that was employed (Perry & Szaalavizs, 2010; Siegel & Bryson, 2011; Tronick & Beeghly, 2011). David had someone on his side, who brought in others who were also on his side. He had people fighting for him, helping him, keeping him calm and safe; he was being cared for in a predictable way. All of his feelings of fear, rage, shame, confusion, and overwhelm were being seen and specifically cared for.

The power of the parent in the therapeutic process

I would often tell John that PTSD and DD are the after-affects of a life-threatening event that has not been cared for. If the life-threatening event is ignored, denied, gaslighted, unseen, and unknown, there is a good chance that this event will result in disorders. The human body knows what to do with the internal residue of these life and death events, but this instinctual reaction and subsequent healing is heavily dependent on others. We need others to hold us, comfort us, reality test with us, and help us keep one foot in the present as we try to review and make sense and meaning of the traumatic event (Weinberg, Tronick, Cohn, & Olsen, 1999). Without care, the event will be too big or too much and dissociation will be needed to deal with the resulting reactions to the event. This child had no one and the result seems to be the development of a Dissociated Identity that became very disordered. He thrived once the care of his injuries was incorporated into his life.

Sensorimotor psychotherapy and stage two processing

At the request of David, I had only processed one event with David near the end of the six-month intensive treatment. He had become relatively stable and both John and I agreed that it was safe to move into the processing stage of treatment (Ogden et al., 2006; Chu et al., 2011). David told me that he wanted to talk about the abuse. We worked on the incident of being choked, as this is what he felt he wanted to work through. I used Sensorimotor Psychotherapy techniques of altering the current felt feelings of being choked and helped him follow his natural reaction to push the threat away, in very slow motion, so he could be curious as to how pushing was altering his current internal reaction. He was able to push me away, and discharge some of the intensity via somatic sequencing (Ogden et al., 2006). Following this the fainting stopped all together. David left the session saying he felt lighter and heavier at the same time; he liked this new feeling. He also noted the new feelings of being less scared, his parts being very quiet, and feeling like they were resting. I spent some time helping him solidify this by encouraging him to walk around while savouring this new feeling. He left with a very upright, prideful posture.

Agency and stage-three integration

The most contact that I had with David was three times a week for six months. John understood that if his son had room and space to heal, he would, and he did. By the fall, I only saw David about once a month, and this then tapered off. It was at the beginning of the new year that the final piece of the puzzle fell into place. David was forced to have contact with the grandfather during the Christmas break. This was another traumatic event, but which produced a very different reaction. At this time David was having fewer symptoms of trauma. He was being home schooled, to reduce stress, and was laughing again! When I saw him, our sessions involved colouring and talking, we would play patty cake (to help with body awareness and to counter dissociation), and his voices were a lot less intrusive. When the voices became loud, it was easier for him and his dad to communicate with the parts and understand their individual functions. For example, when the rage self was brewing, the child could ask him what his concern was and then—with the dad's help—David helped protect or address rage's concern. The more they did this, the less the voices took over.

When David was forced to have contact with the grandfather, he pulled his mother away from everyone else and stated that he was not supposed to. As the mother began to insist that David needed to have a relationship with his grandfather, David said, "that's it". He told his mother that the grandfather had raped him, something he had hitherto kept to himself, and called his father to come and get him.

What happened after this was one of the most amazing displays of self agency that I have ever seen from a child. He was not out of his window of tolerance at all when I saw him a few days later. He told me what he had said to his mother and father and then that he was anally raped by the grandfather, the first being the same day that he was held and tasered by the police.

We spent our next session processing the first rape, using the Sensorimotor techniques of finding his natural response and helping him push and move away from the danger. We also helped him find ways of protecting his bottom using a sweater to hold as a barrier between the threat and his body. He could sequence this event and he was able to feel the felt feeling of the assault. He cried and cried in this session as he was finally able to feel the grief and pain of the injury, and of not being cared for.

As we were working on this event he noticed, without any discussion from me, that he remembered the events differently. He was able to recall the beatings in first person (his words) and the rape was viewed in third person (his words). He had a perfectly clear picture of what he was wearing during the rape, as he could see himself in third person, but with the beating he could feel it, and it was less clear, he also had no idea what he was wearing. What was interesting to David, John, and me is that David could see, perhaps for the first time, how he dissociated the feelings and reality of these events. He stated that he always remembered the rapes, he just never felt like he should or could talk about it, but it was when his mother continued to not look out for him and protect him that he finally had the need and strength to tell. Social services and the police were called and he was able to tolerate rigorous interviewing while staying within his window of tolerance. The police officer mentioned that this child was one of the most articulate he had interviewed. There was a backlash from the grandfather and the mother, but David continued to stay within his window of tolerance. He still has moments of triggers and upset, and the voices are rarely there, but when they show up and when he is triggered, he knows what to do or he knows to ask his father. John can tell that his son is dissociating and knows how to address and care for each triggered reaction.

I have only seen him a few times since and he is still doing remarkably well. He has returned to school full time and there is no evidence of any learning difficulties; he achieved 95% in his grade 8 math. He can exercise now, and is a funny, bright curious child wise beyond his years. As of the writing of this chapter his A-DES score is 11.7 and his A-MID is 1–7, which are both non-clinical scores. He has told me on many occasions that he feels that he will be okay.

I feel that the largest influence on David's incredible recovery is his father's support. He listened, helped, and allowed me the freedom to teach him how to care for the trauma reactions that his son was communicating. Sensorimotor is an excellent intervention, Havening is very good in phase one for calming the body and deeper brain structures. Ego State therapy is brilliant in working with parts. The Polyvagal Theory is life changing in helping us understand why we react the way we react. But in the end, I think it comes down to taking care of the trauma reactions with kindness, wisdom, and dignity. There is a large difference between love and care. We can love a lot of things but doing the nitty-gritty constant care for others is a vital role in human health and without care of the pain and suffering, in equal measure to its occurrence within someone, the pain and suffering will likely not heal. This is a case where John did just that and dedicated himself, full-time, in the care of his child.

References

Armstrong, J., Putnam, F., Carlson, E., & Libero, D. (1997). Development and validation of a measure of adolescent dissociation: The Adolescent Dissociative Experience Scale. *Journal of Nervous and Mental Disease*, 185(8), 491–497. doi:10.1097/00005053-199708000-0000.

Bovine, M., Ratchford, E., & Mark, B. (2014). Peritraumatic dissociation and tonic immobility: Clinical findings. In U. Lanius, S. Paulsen, & F. Corrigan (Eds.), *Neurobiology and treatment of traumatic dissociation* (pp. 51–67). New York: Springer Publishing Company.

Brand, B. L., Loewenstein, R. J., & Spiegel, D. (2014). Dispelling myths about dissociative identity treatment: An empirically based approach. Psychiatry. *Interpersonal and Biological Processes*, 77(2), 169–189. doi:10.1521/psyc.2014.77.2.169.

Chu, J. A., Dell, P. F., Van der Hart, O., Cardeña, E., Barach, P. M., Somer, E., Loewenstein, R. J., Brand, B., Golston, J. C., Courtois, C. A., Bowman, E. S., Classen, C., Dorahy, M., ,Sar, V., Gelinas, D. J., Fine, C. G., Paulsen, S., Kluft, R. P., Dalenberg, C. J., Jacobson-Levy, M., Nijenhuis, E. R. S., Boon, S., Chefetz, R.A., Middleton, W., Ross, C. A., Howell, E., Goodwin, G., Coons, P. M., Frankel, A. S., Steele, K., Gold, S. N., Gast, U., Young, L. M., & Twombly, J. (2011). Guidelines for treating dissociative identity disorder in adults. *Journal of Trauma & Dissociation*, 12, 115–187.

Dell, P. (2006). The Multidimensional Inventory of Dissociation (MID): A comprehensive measure of pathological dissociation. *Journal of Trauma & Dissociation*, 7(2), 77–106. doi: 10.1300/J229v07n02_06.

Fisher, A., Murray, E., & Bundy, A. (1991). *Sensory Integration: Theory and Practice*. Philadelphia, PA: Davis.

Harper, L., Rasolkhani-Kalhorn, T., & Drozd, F. (2009). On the neural basis of EMDR therapy: Insights from qEEG studies. *Traumatology*, 15(2), 81–95. https://doi.org/10.1177/1534765609338498

Hong, I., Kim, J., Lee, J., Park, S., Song, B., et al. (2011). Reversible plasticity of fear memory- encoding amygdala synaptic circuits even after fear memory consolidation. *PLOS ONE*, 6(9), e24260. https://doi.org/10.1371/journal.pone.0024260.

Laidlaw, T. A., & Malmo, C. (1990). *The Jossey-Bass Social and Behavioral Science Series. Healing Voices: Feminist Approaches to Therapy with Women*. San Francisco, CA: Jossey-Bass.

Lanius, R., Boyd, J., McKinnon, M., Nicholson, A., Frewen, P., Vermetten, E., Jetly, R., & Spiegel, D. (2018). A review of the neurobiological basis of trauma-related dissociation and its relations to cannabinoid -and- opioid mediated stress response: A transdiagnostic, transrelational approach. *Current Psychiatry Reports*, 20, 118. https://doi.org/10.1007/s11920-0180983-y.

Lanius, U., Paulsen, S. L., & Corrigan, F. M. (2014). Dissociation: Cortical deafferentation and the loss of self. In Lanius, U., Paulsen, S.L., & Corrigan, F. M. (Eds), *Neurobiology and Treatment of Traumatic Dissociation, pp 5–28*. New York: Springer Publishing Company.

Ogden, P. (2009). Emotion, mindfulness and movement: Expanding the regulatory boundaries of the window of affect tolerance. In Fosha, D., Siegal, D., & Solomon, M. (Eds), *The Healing Power of Emotion: Affective Neuroscience Development and Clinical Practice*. New York: W.W. Norton.

Ogden, P. (2012). Embedded relational mindfulness: A sensorimotor psychotherapy perspective on the treatment of trauma. In Follette, V. M., Rozelle, D., Hopper, J. W., Rome, D. I., & Briere, J. (Eds), *Mindfulness-oriented interventions for trauma: Integrating contemplative practices, pp 227–242*. New York: The Guildford Press.

Ogden, P. & Fisher, J. (2015). *Sensorimotor Psychotherapy: Interventions for Trauma and Attachment*. New York: W.W. Norton & Company.

Ogden, P., Minton, K., & Pain, C. (2006). *Trauma and the Body: A Sensorimotor Approach to Psychotherapy. New York: W.W. Norton and Company*.

Ogden, P., Pain, C., Fisher, J. (2006) A sensorimotor approach to the treatment of trauma and dissociation. *Psychiatric Clinics of North America*, 29(1), 263–279, xi–xii. https://doi.org/10.1016/j.psc.2005.10.012.

Panksepp, J. (1998). *Affective Neuroscience: The Foundations of Human and Animal Emotions*. New York: Oxford University Press.

Panksepp, J. (2002). At the interface of the affective, behavioural and cognitive neuroscience: Decoding the emotional feelings of the brain. *Journal of Brain and Cognition*, 52(1), 4–14. https://doi.org/10.1016/S0278-2626(03)00003-4.

Panksepp, J., & Biven, L. (2012). *The Archaeology of the Mind: Neuroevolutionary Origins of Human Emotions*. New York: W.W. Norton & Company.

Perry, B. D., & Szalavizs, M. (2010). *Born for Love: Why Empathy Is Essential--and Endangered*. New York: Harper Collins.

Porges, S. W. (1998). Love: An emergent property of the mammalian autonomic nervous system. *Journal of Psychoneuroendocrinology*, 23(8), 837–861.

Porges, S. W. (2003). The Polyvagal theory: Phylogenetic contributions to social behaviour. *Journal of Physiology & Behaviour*, 79, 503–513.

Porges, S. W. (2011). *The Polyvagal Theory: Neurophysiological Foundations of Emotions, Attachment, Communication and Self-Regulation*. New York: W.W. Norton & Company.

Ratner, S. (1967). Comparative aspects of hypnosis. In Gordon, J. E. (Ed), *Handbook of Clinical and Experimental Hypnosis*, pp. 550–587. New York: Macmillan.

Ruden, R. A. (2005). A neurological basis for the observed peripheral sensory modulation of emotional responses. *Traumatology*, 11(3), 145–158. https://doi.org/10.1177%2F153476560501100301.

Ruden, R. (2011). *When the Past Is Always Present: Emotional Traumatization, Causes, and Cures*. New York: Routledge.

Schauer, M., & Elbert, T. (2010). Dissociation following traumatic stress: Etiology and treatment. *Zeitschrift fur Psycholgie/Journal of Psychology*, 218, 109–127.

Schore, A. (1994). *Affect Regulation and the Origin of the Self*. New Jersey: Lawrence Erlbaum Associates, Inc. Publishers.

Siegel, D. (1999). *The Developing Mind: How Relationships and the Brain Interact to Shape Who We Are*. New York: The Gilford Press.

Siegel, D., & Bryson, T.P. (2011). *The Whole-Brain Child: 12 Proven Strategies to Nurture Your Child's Developing Mind*. New York: Delacorte Press.

Smith, S. R., & Carlson, E. B. (1996). Reliability and validity of the Adolescent Dissociative Experiences Scale. *Dissociation: Progress in the Dissociative Disorders*, 9(2), 125–129.

Steinberg, M., & Schnall, M. (2000). *Stranger in the Mirror: Dissociation the Hidden Epidemic*. New York: Cliff Street Books.

Stone, J. (2006). Dissociation: What is it and why is it important? *Practical Neurobiology*, 6, 308313.

Talia, A., Muzi, L., Lingiardi, V., & Taubner, S. (2018). How to be a secure base: Therapists' attachment representations and their link to attunement in psychotherapy. *Attachment & Human Development*. https://doi.org/10.1080/14616734.2018.1534247.

Tronick, E., & Beeghly, M. (2011). Infants' meaning-making and the development of mental health problems. *American Psychologist*, 66(22), 107–119.

Watkins, J., & Watkins, H. (1997). *Ego States: Theory and Therapy*. New York: W.W. Norton and Company.

Weinberg, K. M., Tronick, E. Z., Cohn, J. F., & Olsen, K. L. (1999). Gender differences in emotional expressivity and self-regulation during early infancy. *Journal of Developmental Psychology*, 35(1), 175–188.

Chapter 8

Structuring treatment for dissociative children with the Sleeping Dogs method

Arianne Struik

Introduction

There are several excellent treatment models for dissociative children, with comprehensive descriptions of theory, psychoeducation and interventions such as Silberg (2013), Waters (2016) and Wieland (2015). However, working with these children can be challenging and it can be difficult to access their traumatic memories. They claim to have forgotten, are too afraid or become overwhelmed with anger when they would talk about their trauma. Caregivers and clinicians can start doubting whether these traumatic memories really need to be addressed or whether it is better to 'let sleeping dogs lie' and focus on the child's symptoms. However, focusing on symptoms often does not lead to an improvement without addressing the underlying traumatic memories, the so-called 'sleeping dogs'.

A wide range of issues can create barriers for chronically traumatized children to engage in trauma-focused therapy (Struik, Lindauer, & Ensink, 2017). Many of these children grow up in unstable families facing multiple social, and mental health problems, where child protection services have been involved. Some have been placed in out-of-home care and have had multiple placements in residential facilities or foster care. The chaotic circumstances, difficult behaviours and crises can make therapists lose track of where treatment is heading. Some dissociative children do not want or cannot attend therapy sessions. Children in out-of-home care can be reluctant to talk about their memories of traumatic events, because they fear that their disclosures will reduce contact with their parents or minimize chances to be reunified. The parent pressures or threatens the child not to talk. The lives of children in care can be complicated by decisions made by child protection workers and these decisions can either support or undermine treatment.

The Sleeping Dogs® method provides a framework to structure the treatment process and can be used in addition to these other treatment methods. This chapter provides a brief summary of the Sleeping Dogs method, which is described in the book *Treating Chronically Traumatized Children: The Sleeping Dogs Method* (Struik, 2019). In this chapter the terms abuser-parent

DOI: 10.4324/9781003246541-9

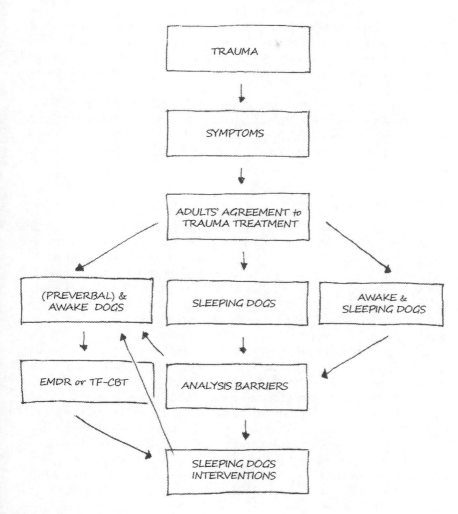

Figure 8.1 Flow Chart.
Source: Struik (2019).

is used for clarity purposes. Obviously, every parent is more than just an abuser-parent. The pronoun 'he' can also be read as 'she' (Figure 8.1).

The Sleeping Dogs method

The Sleeping Dogs method is developed for children who were severely and chronically traumatized in early childhood and for whom 'standard' trauma treatment is not possible, treatment is stuck or does not have the expected results. With the Sleeping Dogs tool, the child's circumstances are mapped out and the possible barriers to process traumatic memories are systematically analysed. Based on that analysis, interventions are planned to overcome those barriers, to support trauma processing, and to facilitate and improve integration and overcome the impact of developmental trauma. This tool (see Appendix 2) is based on both literature and clinical experience and it summarizes 19 different reasons that children and parents have described while working with them on their trauma. It is a work in progress and this second edition has integrated feedback of clinicians using it all over the world in the last ten years and can be downloaded for free on www.ariannestruik.com.

Key principles

The Sleeping Dogs method uses the principles of the Self-Determination Theory (Deci & Ryan, 2002), which describes autonomy, competence and a connectedness as the three basic needs determining human motivation. Most chronically traumatized children feel helpless, incompetent and disconnected from their families. They do not have these needs met at all. It is no wonder they present as unwilling or unmotivated to engage in trauma-focused therapy. The Sleeping Dogs interventions focus on increasing the child's feelings of competence, autonomy and connectedness.

As the child is not willing or able to participate in treatment at the start, collaboration with the child's current and past network is necessary. To motivate children, residential staff or caregivers or child protection workers can do interventions outside the therapy room. The Sleeping Dogs method uses active involvement and collaboration with child protection services. Child protection workers can make or review decisions that form barriers to the child. They can inform the child of the possible consequences of what they will tell the therapist about their memories. Many of the barriers concern the child's biological family, including the abuser, and they are included in treatment, provided this is safe. Biological parents are not judged nor criticized, but they are invited to assist their children to heal from the trauma they have (unintentionally) caused (Figure 8.2).

Motivation and psychoeducation

Sleeping Dogs method describes various metaphors and ways to provide the child with an explanation on different topics—such as the Window of Tolerance to explain stress reactions and motivate them to process traumatic memories, the Volcano to explain the relationship between trauma and current behaviour and motivate them to process traumatic memories, the Filing Cabinets (see Figure 8.3) to explain flashbacks and how these can

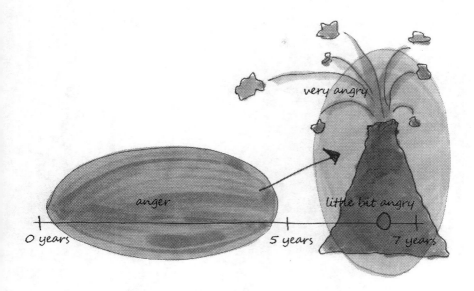

Figure 8.2 The Volcano.
Source: Struik (2019).

Figure 8.3 The Filing Cabinets.
Source: Struik (2019).

Figure 8.4 The Heater in Your Heart.
Source: Struik (2019).

be processed into normal memories, the Heater (see Figure 8.4), to explain how children need safe attachment to develop confidence. Psychoeducation for caregivers and (young) children not only helps them to understand themselves and their trauma reactions, but also helps them to understand how they could benefit from processing their traumatic memories. It increases their knowledge and competence and therefore motivation.

Children with a dissociative disorder often feel weird or they worry they are going crazy. Explaining structural dissociation with a Russian Matryoshka doll (a wooden doll filled with several smaller dolls, one inside the other) can be a great relief for them and it can help them to get more control over themselves.

Addressing the child's barriers

When motivation through psychoeducation is not enough and the child still cannot or will not talk about his traumatic memories, the child has so-called 'sleeping dogs'. Then the child's possible barriers are analysed. By mapping out the child's symptoms, the traumatic experiences and how these symptoms can be related, the clinician can get a better understanding of the child's inner world and the reasons behind the child's dissociation and behaviour. Then the clinician fills in a checklist of 19 questions to assess whether this item could form a barrier for the child to remember and process traumatic memories. Dissociative children can display severe symptoms, function very poorly in daily life on many areas and grow up in challenging circumstances but that does not mean all these items form barriers to discuss traumatic memories. The questions focus only on whether or not this item from the child's perspective potentially forms a barrier and do not reflect the child's daily life functioning. When a question is answered with yes, interventions are planned in the action plan to overcome these barriers. The following paragraphs describe the barriers and briefly some interventions to overcome them when identified.

Barrier 1: safety

(1a) Is not being or feeling safe because the abuse could happen again a barrier?

On-going abuse, being or feeling threatened, can form a barrier when the child is afraid that the abuse from the past will continue to happen in the future. Dissociative parts can feel like they are living in the past which makes them feel unsafe, while they actually are safe. The adults may know the child is safe, but the child has not been explicitly informed about the safety measures that are in place. Safety Planning approaches such as Signs of Safety (Turnell & Edwards, 1999) or Partnering for Safety (Parker, 2011) can be used to create more safety in families or to increase the child's safe feeling. The child can be currently unsafe because of problem behaviour or fighting in school, or bullying, but those only form a barrier when the child is constantly terrified and outside his window of tolerance.

(1b) Is not having an attachment figure or not being sure who is an attachment figure a barrier?

This can form a barrier, when child does not want to talk about his memories mainly because he does not have anyone who thinks of him and supports him. Why would he do it, for whom? For example, children in residential care with staff on a rotating roster without any contact with family can have this barrier, especially when they are dissociative. For those children an attachment figure needs to be found in order to wake up sleeping dogs. In the Sleeping Dogs method, an attachment figure is defined as someone who loves the child and who wants to stay in the child's life. The child does not have to live with the attachment figure or have intensive contact. The attachment figure can even be a father in prison, a grandmother who visits every two years or a mother with a borderline personality disorder who lives in a psychiatric hospital and has once every two months two hours supervised contact with her daughter. The primary focus here is the quantity 'is there an attachment figure?' The quality of the relationship does not have to be good and the child does not have to be attached to that person, as this is addressed in barrier 3.

(1c) Is not having regular contact with that attachment figure, or not being sure that contact is guaranteed to continue a barrier?

This forms a barrier when the child's main reason not to start talking about their painful memories is that he cannot rely on the attachment figure to continue to be there for him. The child needs to be certain that the attachment figure will stay in his life and cares about his well-being. Contact does not have to be regular or intensive, as long as the child has another temporary support person to talk to and the attachment figure has approved that. This can form a barrier for children in foster care or adopted children who may not know whether their foster or adopted parents want to have a life-long relationship with them, or are only daily caregivers until the placement breaks down or the child become 18. Dissociative children can have parts that think they can be abandoned anytime. Reassuring all parts of the child frequently that the attachment figure stays in his life, discussing future event such as becoming grandparents and helping the child move house when they grow up can provide the child with more internal safety. By collaborating with child protection services, decisions around contact with the biological parents, future arrangement or reunification can be reviewed and the child can be informed of these decisions.

(1d) Is being afraid that disclosures will have legal consequences and/or that contact arrangements will be changed, and/or that the child will be removed or not reunified a barrier?

This forms a barrier when the child is worried that talking about his memories will have consequences from people outside the family. The child can be afraid the police will be informed, and his parents or he himself will be convicted. Children can refuse to talk because they fear the legal guardian will reduce contact arrangements, not reunify the child or make contact supervised. Children can also fear the opposite—that the legal guardian will intensify contact, make contact unsupervised or reunify him with his parents because his problems are solved. Besides traumatic memories of incidents that were already disclosed or are known, the child may have secrets or think they have secrets, which would be new disclosures.

Reassurance needs to come from people outside the family. When child protection services are involved, they are very important partners in overcoming the safety barriers. With the child protection worker can be discussed what the possible consequences are of the child's disclosures. They can make if...then... scenarios. The child protection worker can be assisted in defining the possible actions. In many cases the plan is quite simple and the child's disclosures will not lead to any actions. The child protection worker can tell all parts of the child which information is already know, such as domestic violence, sexual abuse or neglect. The child protection worker can assure the child that the child disclosing further details about this would not lead to a change in contact because they have already intervened. Even if new disclosures may lead to contact being reduced or supervised or reunification being postponed or called off, it is important to inform the child about this and explain why that would be necessary. All those scenarios can be drawn on a flip-over with the child and caregiver.

(1e) Is not having permission from the biological parents to talk about the memories and being afraid to be punished a barrier?

This forms a barrier when the child is worried that talking about his memories will damage the relationship with one of his parents or both. The parent may have threatened him or the child is not sure if his parent approves of him talking. To overcome this barrier, the child needs reassurance from his parent. Parents can also fear consequences from outside the family, which can be the reason for them to tell the child not to talk. Reassurance from outside for the parents can also help to overcome this barrier.

When this forms a barrier, the parent needs to be involved in treatment to provide the child with this information, even when this parent has abused the child unless, of course, this would jeopardize the child's safety. Professionals or the other parent can question this by arguing that the parent does not have custody and therefore do not have to consent to treatment. However, the child is not interested in legal regulations. This is about emotional permission. The child does not want to be rejected by his parents or lose them. Involving the abuser-parent can actually lead to consent. An (alleged) abuser-parent who feels that his side of the story is also heard and is informed about treatment can be more willing to consent. Parents can be explained that the purpose of the child's therapy is to help the child overcome his trauma symptoms, not to investigate what happened in the past and to gather facts. When parents argue about facts, explain to them that the only thing that matters is the child's memories, not their version of reality. The parent is then asked to give their child permission to talk about all his memories in a subsequent session with the child. When direct contact is not possible, the parent can also do this via a video message, phone call, text message, a letter, etc.

When it is suspected that the child may struggle with a secret, parents or caregivers can explain to the child that there are good secrets, such as birthday presents, and bad secrets that make you sad and afraid. That it is important to talk about the bad secrets, despite what adults or other children may have said in the past, so your head gets clear. That 'drawing' what happened is not 'talking' about it. This conversation is prepared with the parent, caregiver or child protection worker before involving the child. When the parents have pressured the child into secrets in the past, this conversation can actually help the child to disclose the secret, despite the parent's pressure.

Some parents continue to refuse to give permission, even after investing in building a relationship with this parent. The child could overcome the barrier, by getting explicit permission from the other parent, or from foster parents for example. They will need to guarantee to take care of the child and to protect the child from the parent's possible rejection.

Barrier 2: daily life

Processing traumatic memories requires the child to be calm enough to focus on doing this. It can temporarily increase the child's symptoms. Problems in daily life can form a barrier when the child has too many problems to deal with and he refuses because he does not have the headspace to also dig up old memories. Or child either does not want to talk about his memories because he is afraid, he will get more difficult to handle and his (foster) parents, the residential staff or the school will be unable to handle that. The child's placement or school can be under pressure. These reasons are summarized into the following barriers.

(2a and 2b) Is having too many problems at home or at school, and/or the child being afraid to be removed from home or school a barrier?

(2c) Is the child or caregivers being afraid the child does not have enough distraction because the child does not have a daily routine a barrier?

(2d) Is the child or caregivers being afraid not being able to handle an increase in flashbacks and or sleeping problems a barrier?

(2e) Is the child or caregiver being afraid drugs and alcohol abuse will increase and/ or lead to serious problems a barrier?

When instability in daily life is analysed to be a barrier, interventions focus on making this instability manageable through for example caregiver support, psychoeducation, support for the child's school and interventions with the child. In order to prevent switching, the normal part of the personality needs to become stronger. That part of the child must learn to solve problems in daily life so the child does not need to switch. The child needs to learn interventions to control flashbacks, because when the child has flashbacks, these increase the anxiety and the phobia of the trauma and the other parts even more, and it strengthens the structural dissociation. A Safe Place or Safe Deposit Box can be created for the child, or several different ones for the different parts.

Children with a dissociative disorder experience their world different. It is essential to interact with these children, in therapy, at home and in school based on the reality. They are one child and one personality. Even though they do not know or feel that yet. When they say they did not do or say something, they are not lying but they have amnesia. The child has to be held responsible for all actions, including things he does not remember doing.

Barrier 3: attachment

The child needs to feel supported to process trauma. The child's attachment relationships can also form barriers to process traumatic memories as the child does not have enough support. These reasons are summarized into the following barriers.

(3a) Is the child being afraid to upset the attachment figure who would not keep a calm brain when the child would process the traumatic memories a barrier?

This forms a barrier when the child fears the attachment figure will become upset when he would talk about his memories. For example, when the attachment figure is traumatized, overwhelmed, has experienced the same trauma such as domestic violence, or has become upset in the past. By avoiding traumatic memories, the child cares for the attachment figure.

Rather than trying to change the child's or the caregiver's behaviour, which is often very difficult, a compensation plan can be made to provide the caregiver with extra support possibly from his network to compensate for what the caregiver is unable to do.

(3b) Is not having a support person with a calm brain in daily life who can compensate for the attachment figure with his permission a barrier?

This forms a barrier when the child's attachment figure does not have a calm brain and the child does not have anyone else to talk to, or the attachment figure does not allow the child to talk to this adult, or the child is not sure if he can. Children can worry that the caregiver of therapist cannot tolerate the horrific details of their memories. This does not form a barrier when the child's parent allows the child talk to the other parent, a grandfather or aunt, foster parents, residential staff or this can be a way to overcome that barrier.

(3c) Is being afraid that the child cannot stay in contact with the therapist during trauma processing a barrier?

This mostly form a barrier for children with a dissociative disorder as they experience severe problems in attachment. Improving the attachment relationships usually requires a lot of time. The child must learn that adult can help them. To achieve this, they will have to form a meaningful attachment relationship with someone and to overcome their fear of trusting people. Interventions may focus on increasing the child's support and the child's ability to connect and to regulate himself. Attachment is the third item because the child needs an attachment figure (1b) before being able to work on the quality of the relationship. It needs to be clear for the child who is going to stay in his life, before attaching to that person (1c). In order to be able to become vulnerable by working on improving the attachment relationship, the child needs to be safe (1a) and not have too many problems in daily life requiring attention (2).

Barrier 4: emotion regulation

(4) Is the child not being able to feel and tolerate bodily sensations (4a)/ feelings (4b) during trauma processing a barrier?

When bodily sensations or feelings are not tolerated and they need to be dissociated or blocked, this can form a barrier because trauma processing can overwhelm the child. This always forms a barrier for children with a dissociative disorder. The child needs to learn to deal with normal daily life feelings without dissociating and switching first. When the child is able to do that, he is ready to tolerate the old overwhelming feelings. Learning emotion regulation skills is an important part of the treatment of children with a dissociative disorder. However, working on emotion regulation, without providing the necessary safety and attachment relationship, can be dangerous. When these children start to feel how abandoned and sad and hurt they are, while still being alone, this may increase self-harm or suicidal ideation or even lead to suicide attempts. Therefore, this is the fourth item.

Barrier 5: cognitive shift

(5) Is the child fearing that the mother (5a)/father (5b)/other person (5c) blames him or her for the abuse or neglect and will reject him of her when the child would believe he or she was innocent, and the child does not want to risk this a barrier? This barrier is only relevant when the abuser is a parent or someone the child will maintain close contact with.

From a survival perspective it is imperative not to risk being rejected by 'the hand that feeds', otherwise you die. Children are therefore programmed to see their parents as 'absolutely good' and 'always knowing best' and idealize them. If their parents hurt them, they will first try to find out what they have done to cause this, which is logical from a survival perspective. It is better for the child to think that it is his own fault than that his parents are doing something wrong. Guilt and shame can help the child to continue to see his parents are good and idealize the parents.

In order to process traumatic memories and integrate them, the child needs to make a cognitive shift from strong negative cognitions (For example 'It's my fault' or 'I am bad') related to the traumatic memory ('I see dad beating up mum and I do nothing') to believe it he is innocent. To enable these children to make this cognitive shift, it is necessary that the child can openly say he was innocent or, even better, put the responsibility on the abuser (usually the parent), without the risk of losing 'the hand that feeds'. When the child's parent continues to holds him responsible, the child risks the parent getting angry. Making this shift seems dangerous and they rather not talk about their memories and feel guilty or bad, than talk about them and risk being rejected. Working on guilt and shame can be a lengthy process and children can get stuck.

Interventions on this barrier focus on working with the abuser-parent to acknowledge to the child that he did not have the responsibility for the trauma and that the parent will not reject the child when it would come to that conclusion. This can help to access the deeper dissociated negative ideas about themselves including the perpetrator parts. The abuser-parent can tell the child in a conversation, write a letter and make a recorded message to inform the child. When abuser-parents struggle to formulate their words or are unpredictable, they can make a trauma-healing story (Struik, 2017), which is a brief, simple language story with drawings describing the parent's views on the child's responsibility. With help, most parents can acknowledge that the child was not to blame for the past. They may continue to blame others instead of acknowledging their own responsibility, but for the child this is enough.

(5d) Is the child not having an alternative attachment figure acknowledging the child's innocence and the child not wanting to risk ending up alone a barrier?

If the parents continue to blame the child, the child needs to be able to rely on another attachment figure to take care of him. The child needs to have someone else to take care of him, so he can safely risk rejection by the abuser-parent. From the point of view of survival, there is then another 'hand that feeds' and that is safe. That is why interventions on the cognitive shift are done after removing barriers 1b, 1c and 3a, 3b, 3c first. Experience shows that with stuck case, this is very often one of the identified barriers. The child is thought to have trouble regulating feelings and emotion regulation skills are taught, without success. Everything seems stable but the child is still resistant to talk.

After analysing the main reasons, the child does not or cannot talk about his traumatic memories, the clinician drafts a customized treatment plan with a selection of interventions focused only on overcoming these barriers.

Trauma processing

The Motivation and Nutshell Checks

After having worked on the identified barriers, the child gradually starts to remember or becomes more willing and able to talk about his traumatic memories and process them. The 'sleeping' dogs become 'awake' dogs. To make sure that the child is really ready for trauma processing, the Motivation Check is done and the child is asked whether he wants to talk about his memories and if he can explain why this is beneficial to him. If the child passes this check successfully, the Nutshell Check is done and the child is asked to make an overview of his traumatic memories in clusters or on a timeline (explain in a nutshell). If the child can do that while staying within his window of tolerance, he is ready (Figure 8.5).

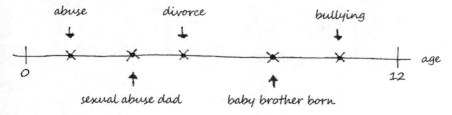

Figure 8.5 The Timeline.

128 Arianne Struik

Trauma-processing interventions

In addition to the Sleeping Dogs method, a directive therapy to process traumatic memories, such as EMDR therapy, is used. The Sleeping Dogs method provides interventions to support the child and family during this phase, as it can be quite challenging for children. For children who have suppressed their memories or dissociated, processing these memories could lead to a temporary worsening of symptoms (Figure 8.6).

Integration interventions

After the trauma processing has finished a new treatment, plan is made with a selection of interventions from the chapters on safety, daily life, attachment, emotion regulation and cognitive shift. The remaining problems in the child's life that were ignored in the stabilization phase can be addressed. It is important to continue treatment and increase the child's resilience to prevent future traumatization. The aim of the integration phase is to teach the child how to minimize the chances of being traumatized again and make him more resilient. In children with a dissociative disorder trauma

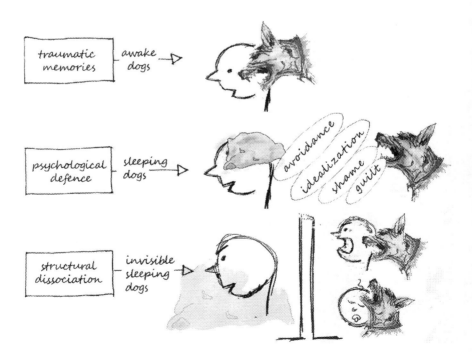

Figure 8.6 Psychological Defences.
Source: Adapted from Knipe (2018).

processing very often takes place in layers, especially when the structural dissociation is more elaborate. They go through several cycles of stabilization, trauma processing, and integration and back to stabilization.

Summary

To reduce dissociative symptoms, it is necessary to process and overcome adverse experiences. With chronically traumatized children, their life experiences or circumstances can make children avoid access to traumatic memories and they have 'sleeping dogs', some of which are even invisible through dissociative amnesia.

When treatment of dissociative children seems impossible, gets stuck, they refuse to engage with therapists; the Sleeping Dogs method can be used to find out the reasons for this and make a structured plan to address these barriers and engage and prepare the child for trauma-processing therapy. This method also provides extra support during trauma processing and a structured treatment plan for the integration phase.

Appendix I

Sleeping Dogs® Case Conceptualization Form

|—————|——————————————————————————|

Note the traumas and other important events for the child such as separation or going to foster placement on this timeline (conception–birth–now).

Child's Symptoms *Which trauma-related symptoms does the child display, that are expected to reduce after trauma processing?*

	Age: IQ if determined: Diagnosis if determined: Child Protection Order if applicable: Motivation for trauma treatment: Yes/Not sure/No

Traumas *Note the traumas from the timeline in keywords (for example DV/SA/Neglect) and circle whether these are awake (AD), sleeping (SD) or preverbal dogs (PD). Fill in the Barriers Form for the sleeping dogs.*

....	AD/SD/PD
....	AD/SD/PD
....	AD/SD/PD
....	AD/SD/PD
....	AD/SD/PD
....	AD/SD/PD

Network *Note here complicating factors with the biological mother and father, if applicable with others (foster parents/grandparents), such as parents' diagnoses, IQ, drug/alcohol use, imprisonment. Note here the contact arrangements in frequency, supervised or unsupervised. Describe the relationship briefly such as the child is overly loyal, close, normal attached or distant.*

Biological mother	Biological father
Contact arrangements with mother	Contact arrangements with father

Others/family
Contact arrangements

Questions/unclear?	How can I get this information?

Appendix 2

Sleeping Dogs® Barriers Form

Name child:					DOB:			Date:
Who is/are the child's main attachment figure(s)? ....
Who is/are support person(s)? ....
Which parent gives the child permission to talk about memories? ....

Sleeping dogs	Child's negative cognition	Shift to positive cognition

Fill in for which sleeping dogs the barriers are analysed, which dysfunctional cognition the child may have and which shift the child needs to make.

Instructions

The questions in the Barriers Form focus only on whether or not this item from the child's perspective potentially forms a barrier and does not reflect the child's daily life functioning. The goal of this form is to find out what could be the main reasons for the child not wanting or being able to talk about his/her traumatic memories. The questions are numbered 1a, 1b, 1c etc. The questions are answered from the child's perspective, what would he/she think or feel. Tick the box as yes or no. Focus only on the main barriers, so do not tick nearly all. Interventions are planned in the stabilization phase on the Barriers Action Plan. These interventions have priority.

Motivation and Nutshell Checks

(Y)(N)　The child has passed Motivation Check. If yes, discuss whether to fill in this form.

(Y)(N)　The child has passed Nutshell Check. If yes, discuss whether to fill in this form.

		Barrier 1 Safety
1a	(Y)(N)	Is not being or feeling safe because the abuse could happen again a barrier?
1b	(Y)(N)	Is not having an attachment figure or is not being sure who is an attachment figure a barrier?
1c	(Y)(N)	Is not having regular contact with that attachment figure, or not being sure that contact is guaranteed to continue, a barrier?
1d	(Y)(N)	Is being afraid that disclosures will have legal consequences and/or that contact arrangements will be changed, and/or that the child will be removed or not reunified a barrier?
1e	(Y)(N)	Is not having permission from the biological parents to talk about the memories and being afraid of being punished a barrier?

		Barrier 2 Daily Life
2a	(Y)(N)	Is having too many problems at home, and/or the child being afraid to be removed from home, a barrier?
2b	(Y)(N)	Is having too many problems at school, and/or the child being afraid of getting expelled from school, a barrier?
2c	(Y)(N)	Is the child or caregivers being afraid the child does not have enough distraction because the child does not have a daily routine a barrier?
2d	(Y)(N)	Is the child or caregivers being afraid of not being able to handle an increase in flashbacks and/or sleeping problems a barrier?
2e	(Y)(N)	Is the child or caregivers being afraid drugs and alcohol abuse will increase and/or lead to serious problems a barrier?

		Barrier 3 Attachment
3a	(Y)(N)	Is the child being afraid of upsetting the attachment figure who would not keep a calm brain when the child would process the traumatic memories a barrier?
Question 3b is only relevant when 3a forms a barrier		
3b	(Y)(N)	Is not having a support person with a calm brain in daily life who can compensate for the attachment figure with his permission a barrier?
3c	(Y)(N)	Is being afraid that the child cannot stay in contact with the therapist during trauma processing a barrier?

		Barrier 4 Emotion Regulation
4a	(Y)(N)	Is the child not being able to feel and tolerate bodily sensations during trauma processing a barrier?
4b	(Y)(N)	Is the child not being able to feel and regulate the feelings during trauma processing a barrier?

		Barrier 5 Cognitive Shift
5a	(Y)(N)	Is the child fearing that the mother blames him/her for the abuse or neglect and will reject him/her when the child would believe he/she was innocent, and the child does not want to risk this a barrier?
5b	(Y)(N)	Is the child fearing that his/her father blames him/her for the abuse or neglect and will reject him/her when the child would believe he/she was innocent, and the child does not want to risk this a barrier?
If applicable otherwise skip:		
5c	(Y)(N)	Is the child fearing that .... (other person) blames him/her for the abuse or neglect and will reject him/her when the child would believe he/she was innocent, and the child does not want to risk this a barrier?
Question 5d is only relevant when 5a and 5b both form barriers		
5d	(Y)(N)	Is the child not having an alternative attachment figure acknowledging the child's innocence and the child not wanting to risk ending up alone a barrier?

Appendix 3

Sleeping Dogs® Barriers Action Plan

Name child: Date:
DOB: Evaluation dates:
Current owner of the plan:

	Circle Barriers	Example interventions	Describe actions with barrier numbers	Who will do this?	With whom?	OK
1a	Safety	Safety Plan (SP) Inform child of SP				
1b	Attachment figure (AF)	Discuss with network who is AF Find new AF Inform child of AF				
1c	AF stays in child's life	Clarify with AF/child protection worker (CPW)/organization/police Establish or intensify contact with AF Inform child of contact				
1d	Consequence Disclosure	Clarify legal consequences Clarify consequences contact arrangements Inform AF and/or child				
1e	Emotional permission	Ask mother Ask father **Inform child**				

	Circle Barriers	Example interventions	Describe actions with barrier numbers	Who will do this?	With whom?	OK
2a	Home	Caregiver support and Compensation plan Within Window of Tolerance Prevent trigger plan **Safe Deposit Box** Safe Place Here and Now Relaxation School support and compensation plan Distraction plan Sleep plan Drug/alcohol plan				
2b	School					
2c	Daily routine					
2d	Flashback and sleep					
2e	Drugs Alcohol					
3a	Calm brain	Compensation plan AF Self-regulation AF AF informs child				
3b	Other calm brain	Assess other calm brain Discuss with AF AF gives child permission for other				
3c	Attachment system	Increase contact AF/ biological parents Life story work Attachment exercises/therapy				
4a	Bodily sensations	Sensory exercises/ therapy Relaxation				
4b	Feelings	Psychoeducation Management plan Self-harm/suicide plan Intensive work/ therapy				

5a	Mum not acknowledge	Discuss with mum/dad/other Find other to acknowledge Inform child in session/letter/video message or note Trauma Healing Story				
5b	Dad not acknowledge					
5c	Other not acknowledge					
5d	No other to acknowledge					
	Motivation	**Find princess** Filing Cabinets Window of Tolerance Volcano Heater Princess story Matryoshka **Motivation Check**				
	Nutshell	**Nutshell Check** Remote control				
	Trauma processing	Process awake dogs				

Instructions

Fill in the child's name, DOB, date and current owner of the plan. Circle the identified barriers. The numbers correspond to the barriers. Examples of interventions are listed. The **bold interventions** are frequently used. Describe concrete actions with the numbers of the barriers that are addressed by the action (e.g. 1b and 1c, 3a and 5b) or only one (e.g. 1e). Fill in who is going to do this action (e.g. foster care worker Sonja) and with whom this action is going to be done (child protection worker Tina, biological mother and child). Several interventions can be combined into one action. Note an evaluation date.

When evaluating this Action Plan, tick 'OK' for the completed actions. Describe new or altered actions. Note a new evaluation date. Continue until all barriers are removed. Then describe actions for Motivation, Nutshell and trauma processing. Note an evaluation date.

After trauma processing evaluate the child's symptoms. Set goals and describe actions for the integration phase. Note an evaluation date and evaluate until goals are reached.

Sleeping Dogs® Integration Action Plan

	Circle areas	Tick interventions	Describe actions with area numbers	Who will do this?	With whom?	OK
1	Safety	Safety Plan Find new AF Inform child of AF Execute consequences AF/CPW/organization/police Inform child Ask mother Ask father Inform child				
2	Daily Life	Carer support and home improvement plan School support and improvement plan Safe Place Relaxation Sleep plan Drug/alcohol plan Difficult circumstances				
3	Attachment	Improvement plan Therapy parent Assess other calm brain AF gives child permission for other Start contact with parent Increase contact parent/AF/siblings Reunification plan Life story/video Visit former houses Attachment exercises/therapy				
4	Emotion Regulation	Sensory therapy Relaxation Intensive work/therapy				
5	Cognitive Shift	Assess child's wish Family therapy Trauma Healing Story Forgiveness plan				

Chapter 9

Genesis of a dissociative child

Kayleigh's story – how 'I' became 'us'

Jo Russell

Kayleigh was a 15-year-old young woman who came to see me for weekly psychotherapy at an NHS CAMHS clinic following the distressing discovery of her double life. Kayleigh became one of the participants in my doctoral research (Russell, 2015) which used thematic analysis (Braun and Clarke, 2006) to investigate what additional types of therapeutic activity are needed when working with children that dissociate. My study was prompted by the uncomfortable reality that I regularly met dissociative children in my consulting room about whom psychoanalytic theory[1] seemed to have relatively little to say, and for whom a traditional analysing of the deepest lying anxiety by 'consistent interpretations, gradual solving of resistances and persistent tracing of the transference to earlier situations ...' (Klein, 1926, p. 137) appeared to only inflame distress and trigger further dissociation.

I feel privileged to have worked with Kayleigh; she applied a raw but keen intelligence to the ideas we exchanged with energy and commitment despite the pain of doing so. Kayleigh's naivety and thirst for understanding produced in me a powerful desire to do all I could to nurture her mind, whilst her alternative identity *Priti*'s fierce protective savvy impressed upon me the sadly very necessary adaptive capacities that a personified dissociative state, an 'alter', can bring to an oppressed child. Kayleigh generously gave her informed consent to my use of our work and the research findings in order to help others as, with some caveats, did *Priti*.[2] Her mother also gave consent.

Several elements make this a case that offers a rare perspective on how the generation of a discrete personified dissociative state may become established. First, Kayleigh herself was a 'good' patient; she was a regular and reliable attender of her weekly psychotherapy with me for over a year and was highly motivated by the desire to recover from her mental distress to become happier and more able to get on with her life. She had a strong conscious impulse to 'tell the truth, the whole truth and nothing but the truth' under the belief that if she could only garner thorough help to understand herself fully, she would be able to achieve the emotional stability she craved. This meant that I received a full and frank and consistent account

DOI: 10.4324/9781003246541-10

of her life story and its impact, albeit, of course, a subjective account and one subject to the vagaries of memory. Second, the manifestation of Kayleigh's dissociation was observable and stark: she had just one distinct alter in *Priti* (significantly pronounced 'Pretty') and as it transpired the history of *Priti*'s development was traceable for her. As the reader will see below, significant trauma is present and implicated in their life story: there is poverty, domestic violence, parental inadequacy and an unstable family situation, and there are several incidents of significant injury including sexual injury to Kayleigh's person. However, there is not the uninterrupted course of chronic pervasive abuse from multiple colluding adults that is so often tragically discovered behind the presentations of those living with multiple personalities. The expression of Kayleigh's dissociation in just two alternative personified states-of-being (Kayleigh and *Priti*) allows for relatively easy comprehension. In trying to map how her dissociation may or may not correlate with her experiences, we are spared having to try to navigate multiple contemporaneous assaults to body and mind. Lastly, Kayleigh was only in her mid-teens during our work together, her childhood and infancy were not so very many years distant and her mother was able to corroborate many of the factual elements within her account.

In this chapter, then, I employ Kayleigh's life narrative to trace how her dissociative expression may have been forged by relational trauma. This is important for our theoretical understanding of the dynamics of dissociative pathology but it is also central within any particular therapeutic endeavour with a child that has established dissociative states-of-being. Creating a shared subjective but coherent understanding of how 'I' became 'we' is vital in a relational therapy approach to trauma, notwithstanding whether additional techniques of psychoeducation, engendering self-soothing, active organising of confusions and so on are required alongside (Russell, 2015). We need to construct a dynamically true and meaningful narrative that incorporates all the parts of the self, which can then be expressed, explored and, maybe, transformed, in the service of more functional 'living together'.

The narrative which unfolds below is necessarily a heavily disguised and attenuated version of Kayleigh's life story. Interwoven are indications of where the external relational events may be impacting on her developing mind and personality. Using current theories regarding the aetiology of dissociative disorders, I highlight the significance of these within Kayleigh's internal landscape and offer a dynamic explanation of how, in her beleaguered life, 'I' necessarily became 'us'.

A dissociative internal landscape

Kayleigh's mother Jessica was just 16 when she became pregnant with her during her very first sexual relationship. Over her own teenage years, in a flurry of uncontained retaliatory remarks between her long separated parents for whom she was the only conduit, Kayleigh learned from her mother that her father, Ian, had persistently wanted her aborted and from her father that he had only 'got with' her mother 'because she was an easy lay'. During 'laddish' drinking sessions with a 13/14-year-old Kayleigh, her father further coloured her understanding of her conception with graphic descriptions of his and the teenage Jessica's perverse sexual activities, communicating powerfully to Kayleigh that although her mother might seem appropriately 'up tight' and strict in limiting Kayleigh's sexuality nowadays, underneath she was really 'just a dirty bitch'. Kayleigh was hence powerfully given to believe that the relational crucible for her conception was a union based on compulsive sexual excitement, of which she was an unplanned and largely unwanted by-product. Romance, affection, caring or thoughtfulness are absent from her understanding of how and why she was made.

So here then we encounter the first set of relational circumstances that will have contributed to Kayleigh's vulnerability to dissociation later on. Young people can be excellent parents if settled, supported and prepared; but as a naïve young woman finding herself unexpectedly pregnant with a volatile uncommitted partner, Jessica is likely to have been at the very least ambivalent and very likely highly stressed. As a foetus Kayleigh may well have experienced surges of intrauterine cortisol and adrenaline and as a neonate she will almost certainly have experienced an inconsistent 'facilitating environment' (Winnicott, 1965) in which the need to stay close to her caregivers required different behaviours from her at different points. Baby Kayleigh may well have quickly 'learnt' for instance that irritable crying and body squirming elicited warmth and soothing when Jessica's voice was low and heartbeat slow, but that frozen quiet and an averted gaze were best when voices got raised and the air became thick with stress hormones. Quite diverse *discrete behavioural states* (Putnam, 1988, 1997) experienced by the infant Kayleigh are likely to have become established as self-stabilising constellations of physiology and interaction: hyper-aroused active bodily communication when needing care in the orbit of a calm parent, hypo-aroused 'shut-down' body and mind when these parents became a danger.

This is precisely what Giovanni Liotti's plentiful research concludes (2004, 2006). Liotti explains this in terms of the infant's inborn motivational systems – on the one hand an attachment system which prompts behaviours aimed to make the child stay close to their caregiver, and on the other a defence system prompting behaviour aimed to make the child avoid (or possibly fight off) an environmental threat. Frightened or frightening or inconsistent caregivers simultaneously activate both systems at once, giving the infant or young child contradictory information about how to interact and diverse internal working models, 'IWMs' (Bowlby, 1973), that cannot be integrated into an organised representation of the self and the other. Disorganised attachment, which he (Liotti) asserts is fundamentally dissociative in nature, is the result.

Most importantly, in charting the rise of dissociative capacity from infancy, Putnam emphasises that the shifts between these states are *non-linear* and have the character of sudden *switches* rather than gradual reiterative flexible responses. This is adaptive in the short term:

> By binding these variables to discrete circumscribed dissociative states, the child protects him or herself against being overwhelmed by a flood of painful affects and memories during times when he is not being traumatised ... This enables the child to function successfully in other areas of his life.
>
> (Putnam, 1988, p. 26)

However, in a predominantly hostile landscape of anxiety, fear and trauma this response becomes habitual and problematic.

It seems unlikely that either Jessica or Ian would have been consistently thoughtful and attuned so as to finesse these physio-psychological states towards more functional integration and eventual self-regulation. In this important task they fell short of 'good enough'. In addition, unresponsive, frightened or frightening care-giving mitigates against secure attachment and is *in itself* experienced as stressful – relational trauma. For the neglected infant there is likely to be a repeated dissociation-building cycle in which an ordinary bodily need causes arousal and an attempt to engage the parent, a following ill-attuned response from the carer which then incurs additional trauma and consequent infant hyper-arousal, a state which when sustained in the context of inadequate parental response results in initial forays into hypo-aroused dissociative shut-down. Bruce Perry aptly describes this as a 'cascade of dysfunction' (Perry, 2009, p. 242) in which initial spontaneous neurological responses become rigid and automatic physiological and behavioural traits. An infant Kayleigh may have become familiar with dissociating right from the start.

Although he is not explicitly implicated in the sexual abuse she suffered later, Kayleigh's irregular encounters with him confirm that her father, Ian, consistently intruded on her with his own sexual preoccupations, and undermined her mother's attempts to instil appropriate sexual boundaries for their daughter. From the vantage point of her 16-year-old self, Kayleigh described Ian as 'like three different fathers'; in addition to his approach to her as 'one of the boys', which included talking about women as sexual objects and offering cannabis or alcohol, he could be flirtatious just up to but not beyond the point of 'playfully' smacking her bottom, and then, on occasion, be more appropriately protective of her as a young girl in his care. Given his own alcohol and mental health problems, and reports of himself as a victim of childhood sexual abuse, it is likely that Ian has always been unpredictable and quite possibly dissociative himself, hence Kayleigh's experience of distinct shifting parenting styles. What might the impact have been on the pre-verbal Kayleigh's developing mind?

One of the first organising tasks of the infant mind is to construct representations of the self and the care-giving others – IWMs – which comprise expectations about how both can be predicted to behave within the attachment system. These are the blueprint for all future relationships. They are initially held in the infant's implicit memory and do not require language or consciousness, though they will later, if all goes to plan, be consciously attributed to an attachment need and become part of the expressed narrative of the self. Daniel Stern understands this as the active construction of meaning from 'unformulated experience' in the interpersonal field (Stern, 2009). This is an impressive achievement for each infant-parent constellation, but if Ian offered wildly differing versions of 'Dad material' to the infant Kayleigh, then we can reasonably conclude that her capacity to formulate experience would have been further compromised. 'Dad-the-mate' may have prematurely treated Kayleigh as an equal, blind to her actual cognitive and social immaturity, 'Dad-who-needs-physical-satisfaction' may have cuddled his daughter too long, or tickled her too much without caring for Kayleigh's level of arousal and bodily cues that this was not pleasurable or comforting *for her*. Conversely sometimes Dad-as-father may have irregularly related to her with ordinary contingent responsiveness and welcome attunement.

In her infancy there is no sense that the little family had much time to enjoy each other and create the 'ordinary devoted parenting' required for making a good beginning (Winnicott, 1949, 1964, p. 17) before Kayleigh's father had left when she was under a year old. Certainly Kayleigh can remember very little from her time as a toddler, and has none of the reassuring nostalgia for a favourite toy, pet or game which conveys that a child has had sufficient enjoyed experience to form a benign focal memory. The net result is that Kayleigh cannot refer even symbolically to an idealised time when she felt safe and happy as the centre of her mother's world or the apple of her father's eye. Therapeutically this deficit, so familiar in the back-story of dissociative children, has implications, especially in the initial phase of treatment. Not only may engagement and alliance have to be achieved against the tide of internal distrust, but in addition the endeavour to build resources to help stabilise the young person when dysregulated (Silberg, 2013; Struik, 2014, pp. 37–39) will encounter a dearth of 'good internal objects' (Klein, 1932; Heinmann, 1949) around which to constellate these.

Surviving as a stranger in a strange land[3]: the need for an imaginary friend

Kayleigh's mother had a swift series of partners, and a second daughter, Natalie, was born when Kayleigh was three and a half by a father that Natalie never met. The little Kayleigh's shifting family landscape in which men came, were adored, misbehaved, abused and then left, was mirrored and further destabilised by a repeatedly shifting geographical landscape. Fleeing from one particularly violent man, just as Kayleigh had started in school, her mother briefly settled hundreds of miles north in Liverpool, where the other children's accents in the playground sounded like a different language to a four-year-old Kayleigh. Any developed hypervigilance to new sounds and meanings, and a capacity to quickly adapt her own manner and voice would have served her well if she were to survive and flourish.

However, Jessica was at once homesick, longed for her sisters' company, and spent the next eight years in sequential council house-swaps to 'get back home'. Kayleigh remembers getting on well at school and indeed being quick to make friends, but her mother's determined pilgrimage back to the capital meant that she was constantly uprooted and starting afresh. Kayleigh did not bemoan the many moves, other than the last at age 12 which had taken her from a group of slightly older boys (13/14) to whom she felt special. Given that she may have already become adept at keeping herself close to primary attachment figures by adapting to their shifting states of mind, Kayleigh is likely to have approached new social groups by 'fitting in', taking on the colours of the relational environment like a dissociative chameleon, rather than asserting her own 'true colours'. None of this makes for a firm sense of identity.

Jessica relates that she found Kayleigh no trouble at all throughout her young childhood (age 3–10), although she does recall that when partners 'got leery' or threatened to assault her, Kayleigh would become a little fireball of aggression, trying to get in the way and protect her. Kayleigh even became known in the extended family, with some misplaced affection, as 'Mummy's Little Rottweiler'. For an otherwise quiet compliant little girl, this reactive fluorescence of protective fury seems to have merited its own moniker, and we can imagine that the concomitant 'non-linear' switching between submissive and aggressive states of mind also honed dissociative skills that brought Kayleigh closer to the creation of a 'non-linear' personified dissociative state in *Priti*.

Kayleigh is unable to pinpoint the time when *Priti* first came into being;[4] nevertheless, by age eight, *Priti* was present as a helpful imaginary friend that kept Kayleigh company when lonely or bored. Kayleigh had to adapt to an attachment environment in which she was faced with a contradiction of needing quick access to sufficient passivity to be uncomplaining about yet another move, sufficient optimism, confidence and social skill to fit in and make friends in yet another new peer group, and simultaneously quick access to sufficient aggression to defend her only permanent carer. In conclusion, whilst Kayleigh's early life circumstances conspired to significantly compromise her opportunity to internalise reliably attuned and caring parental figures from which secure base she could meet and negotiate what was to come, her latency years compounded non-linear shifts and a somewhat fluid identity.

Precipitating trauma – a first incidence of sexual abuse, (imaginary friend) *Priti* becomes more than 'just pretend'

When she was just six years old, Kayleigh's mother fell into another new relationship which there seemed good reason to hope would be different. Anthony came with no baggage in terms of previous children or 'difficult' ex-wives, and was a hard worker, lifting the family clear of precarious finances. Kayleigh remembers she and Natalie had their own rooms for the first time, there were new clothes and a telly each. After several months Jessica agreed to marry him, and Anthony set about formally adopting Natalie. Kayleigh describes feeling that they had become 'normal'. In reality, this new normal still included regular loud arguments between the adults which threatened to become physical, and a certain amount of rough handling and forceful chastisement of the children, but for Kayleigh none of this was out of the ordinary, it was pretty much all she and Natalie had ever known and anyway *'Mum was happier than she had been in a long time'*.

However, whether planned or spontaneous, Anthony sexually abused Kayleigh at a family party when she was aged just eight, and Kayleigh told her mother who, to her credit, immediately phoned the police. Anthony was arrested, her clothes were taken away and examined, as was she, and he was charged. This event led to a huge change in family fortunes. To the trauma of the abuse, which Kayleigh remembers as mentally confusing rather than painful or repulsing, were added the seriousness of police interviewing, the paradox of being the chief witness in the judging and punishing of a previously loved family member, the immediate breakdown of the relationship in which her mother had finally been happy, her sister's loss of a newly adoptive father, a house move, a school move and an inevitable slide back into poverty. Kayleigh recalls that, having had the courage to speak up, she felt exhausted, overwhelmed by guilt and that she retreated to quiet compliance; yet there was still so much she needed strength and sociability to manage. Kayleigh is clear that it was around this time that *Priti*, having previously been just an important imaginary friend, became a person in her own right, arriving to help Kayleigh who often no longer felt strong or confident or capable. She would *come out* (or at this early stage perhaps she *was allowed to take over* is a better description) with cleverness and attitude when Kayleigh felt inadequate and small.[5] In due course Anthony was convicted and Kayleigh's mother told her that he had gone to prison.

A compounding trauma – perceived discovery of maternal betrayal, *Priti* is invited to take over

During the subsequent years, Kayleigh remembers little of note and imagines things rumbled on much the same as before, although Jessica met Harry during this period, a hard-working unassuming man who remains the somewhat 'silent partner' in their family to this day. However, around her 11th birthday, her father, Ian, visited and let slip that Anthony had not in fact gone to prison, and Kayleigh aggressively confronted her mother to be told that this was true. Her mother had lied because she thought this was best for Kayleigh, feeling that justice ought to have been seen to be done in her little girl's world. For Kayleigh it was as though a time bomb had gone off, shattering their relationship for ever; all her rage about her mother's mistakes and inadequacies flew down the lightening rod of this well-meaning deceit and appeared to her as entirely unforgivable. In her view her mother had betrayed her far worse than Anthony had ever done.

Kayleigh was on the cusp of puberty, and the revelation that Anthony was not in fact punished seemed to trigger a determination to actively involve herself in any sexual liaison on offer. Kayleigh increasingly felt compelled to engage with men in a bold flirtatious way, often consciously sending *Priti* into the fray when as Kayleigh she felt too shy or lacking in allure. Indeed, Kayleigh declared that it was one of *Priti*'s defined jobs to 'get us a boyfriend'. If we return to the theory that dissociation is the corollary of disorganised attachment in which the child develops a series of self-states aimed to maintain close contact with diverse parental states, then we can understand this as a part of Kayleigh's divided childhood identity. This discrete self-state was forged by the infant's need to engage a parent with highly responsive entertaining confidence, originally developed to secure an intimate attachment relationship and now seeking this out in the shape of a romantic/sexual partner. When self-confidence and extrovert sociability were required by the attachment challenge, *Priti* was the attractive young woman for the job.

To start with Kayleigh kept what she knew of *Priti*'s activity to herself, rightly deducing that her family would not understand or approve, and evidently, at this stage, having sufficient control or cooperation between the two to execute such a self-state management strategy successfully. If Kayleigh had not suffered the second trauma, we might have predicted that a working co-consciousness would have remained and that no amnesia between the two would have developed. We could therefore reasonably have hoped that ordinary developmental processes, including the readjustments to identity that every adolescent must negotiate and resolve, would have helped Kayleigh continue to grow up with a less divided self.

A second precipitating trauma – violent sexual assault at age 14

Unsurprisingly Kayleigh and *Priti*'s pursuit of sexual encounters drew her into the local gang in which the largely dominant young men had very little respect for the largely objectified young women. At 14, Kayleigh was so pleased to be selected as a *bona fide* girlfriend for one of the key players that any intelligent appraisal of 17-year-old David was entirely overrun by delight that she could now finally *belong* to a man and so belong to a group. Whilst being accepted within a group of peers is an important developmental step for all adolescents, this is imbued with a sense of survival for the dissociative child who is all too used to morphing into the required 'norms' of the other in order to stay safe in the orbit of a perplexing/abusive carer. If the 'assets' of the body (as Kayleigh's father referred to her developing breasts and womanly shape) are what keeps a child wanted and 'safe' by achieving proximity to the primary carer, then an identity and sense of self-worth that coalesces around those 'assets' is likely.

A tragic series of events unfolded between them. When David raped Kayleigh for the first time, she remembers protesting but very little detail since she was so very 'out of it'. Her experience is in line with Schore's assertion that despite observed hypo-aroused behaviour, the dissociative response is indicative of extreme emotional arousal and a profound detachment from an unbearable situation, and includes a dissipation of consciousness (Schore, 2009, p. 113). In the event, Kayleigh went home but told no-one since she knew her mother and grandmother would be appalled and would be likely to prohibit her movements. She tried to avoid David over the next few days, but he professed contrition, holding alcohol and cannabis rather than himself responsible, and so Kayleigh, a great champion of giving men second chances (as the hopeful daughters of feckless fathers may have to be), felt impelled to try to 'maintain the situation of tenderness' (Ferenczi, 1949, p. 228) with this abusive man and agreed to see him again.

We can imagine that she was also psychologically at sea, having exiled her actual mother for lying to her, and having no reliable internal mother or father figure to advise or protect her. Of course, the capacity to make a good judgement would have already been compromised by her dissociative landscape: if cognitive development and social development happen in somewhat segregated silos then not *all* learning is available. Instead she had *Priti*, confident and sassy, created and then installed to help her feel stronger and less alone, to manage what Kayleigh herself could not. Just two months later, once more under the influence, David again pressed her for intercourse, she resisted and he became violent, holding her up against a wall by her throat and raping her both vaginally and anally.

It is perhaps telling of the fundamental lack of trust she felt in relation to her mother, that she kept her distress to herself and only some days later, when still bleeding from the attack, she turned to her father, who she judged would be more accepting, telling him what had happened and asking if the bleeding was only to be expected. This enquiry sounds immensely naïve, but is congruent with Kayleigh's fragile sense of self: she had insufficient anchoring self-worth or orientating relational common sense to appreciate that she was the injured party in every sense of those words. *Priti* might hold these capacities, self-confidence and protest, but Kayleigh did not. It seems that, to Kayleigh's mind, the event itself, despite being a terrifying ordeal, had not registered as an act for which David was culpable rather than herself, let alone as a crime of which she was the victim for which society might rightly pursue prosecution. The dissociative child is to some extent a pawn in other's games, forged by other's needs and desires, where these are fluctuating and contradictory and unpredictable. The agency of the child themself, the grammar of needs and wishes (after Alvarez, 2012, pp. 78–89), and, we might add, the grammar of *rights*, is very underdeveloped.

She felt herself to blame not only because she had returned to a relationship which she 'should' have walked away from, but also because internally she was forced back around the circuit of her former experience of sexual abuse from her stepfather at age eight for which she had also felt responsible. The response she received is further testament to the confused sexual mores of Ian and those in his orbit; whilst interested and believing, he put his partner Cheryl on the phone who in the spirit of 'all us girls together' sought to reassure Kayleigh by telling her that she (Cheryl) had 'a lot of tricks up her sleeve' which she could pass on, so that next time this sort of thing happened Kayleigh could make sure it was less painful.

So Kayleigh did not, as a first response on disclosing violent rape, receive comfort, righteous outrage or important medical attention, including the sensitive gathering of forensic evidence. Instead she had her suspicion that this was a fairly normal sexual event confirmed, and was given the idea that growing up was going to be about learning to manage sexual trauma with less fuss. This feels perilously close to her earliest experiences of having to manage relational trauma (inconsistent, frightened or frightening parents) with little fuss – *the person you love will also be the person who hurts you*. It may also have chimed with the lived consequences of having 'made a fuss' when Anthony sexually assaulted her as an eight-year-old – *if you tell that the person you love is hurting you then other people you love will be hurt*.

This time around, Ian told her mother Jessica, who was appalled by his response, frustrated with Kayleigh and immediately referred the matter to the police. However given the delay in reporting, the presence of alcohol and drugs, and the circumstantial reality that Kayleigh had initially gone willingly with David, it was never going to be an easy case to prosecute and Kayleigh's perception that she was treated like a time waster feels sadly credible, further confirming, perhaps, that it is wrong, or at least unproductive, to 'make a fuss'. In her psychotherapy Kayleigh repeatedly recalled the moment when a police woman shouted in her face because she could not remember important details about the evening in question; this event stood out for her as significantly shocking, confirming yet again that she could not have confidence in her felt experience, that she was inadequate, wrong, bad.

This was just one of many points at which Kayleigh's position has echoes of Fairbairn's identification of the 'moral defence' by the victims of abuse: Fairbairn theorised the internalisation of bad objects and subsequent identification with these as a way of preserving the sense of good objects and a good world. Going beyond Anna Freud's view of identification with the aggressor as a normal stage of superego development (Freud, 1936), Fairbairn conceptualises the abused young child's need for and use of a 'moral defence' (Fairbairn, 1943, p. 65) in which conceiving of himself as conditionally bad is preferable to understanding himself to be in an unconditionally bad world – 'better to be a sinner in a world ruled by God than to live in a world ruled by the Devil' (ibid., p. 67). Such a defence is especially necessary for children whose real-world parents are neglectful and abusive, preserving some hope of security and redemption but at the cost of guilt, impoverished self-esteem and relentless internal persecutions. From here it is easy to see how an abusive internal voice or personified state would become the segregated expression of the internalised abuser in children who have already had recourse to dissociative manoeuvres. I have heard this so many times from dissociative children, a self-recrimination that they 'should have known' or 'should have told' and *Priti* would regularly castigate Kayleigh in just such a way.

Returning to her sad story – if we understand the neuroscience correctly, Kayleigh's inability to remember details of this second violent rape is hardly surprising; indeed, it is almost diagnostic of a dissociative response to trauma. Kayleigh remained consistently frightened of police women, the police uniform and police in general, and her poor experience of being contained by a good authority figure was compounded. As with her enduring fury at her mother's 'betrayal' in lying about Anthony's sentence, the most coherent memory, in which strong emotion and narrative are comprehensively matched, is that of being maltreated by a female 'who should have known better' (the policewoman).

Dissociative escalation – *Priti* takes over uninvited

Possibly if Kayleigh had been offered an opportunity to talk and think about what had happened *at that time*, and if she could have allowed herself to engage with such an offer, then she could have begun to process both sets of abuse and to heal. There could have been validation of her distress and protest thus allowing core aspects of Kayleigh (unwitting 'victim') and *Priti* (outraged protest) to come together. But Kayleigh was already adept at dissociating in order to manage situations she felt overwhelmed by; if defensive strategies are etched into our neurology by the well-travelled physical pathways between neurones, then a dissociative neural highway was already firmly constructed within her. From Kayleigh's perspective, it was at this juncture that *Priti* got cross with her for being 'so weak' and took matters into her own hands, no longer coming on board to take over at Kayleigh's request when she (Kayleigh) felt faced with scary social situations, but instead taking over uninvited and actively creating an alternative romantic life, first via social media and then in real time and space. In addition, Kayleigh now experienced confusing amnesia for much of what *Priti* got up to, would find several hours of the day unaccounted for, or would 'come to' with people she did not know, dressed in unfamiliar clothes, and have to make a sharp exit covering her confusion. All of this she kept to herself for fear of being seen as mad.

Matters came to head when *Priti*'s determination to spend time with her boyfriend Josh, 15, broke through to interrupt Kayleigh's hitherto protected life at school. The liaison with Josh, a studious young man on the other side of London, was one of which Kayleigh had no conscious direct knowledge, only a dim awareness that *Priti* was 'trying to sort out a boyfriend for us'. Prior to this Kayleigh was recognised by staff and peers alike as an earnest, creative, diligent young woman, both sensitive and likeable, transparent in declaring her anxieties and in appealing for extra help both academically and socially. Later her teachers would concur that it was puzzling how such an able girl could be simultaneously so naïve, and surprising that she remained a bit of a loner socially when she had such a good rapport in class, but they had previously put this down to her late arrival into year ten following her unplanned move, rather than more serious emotional difficulties.

Priti managed to secure several permissions to go to 'appointments' and finally a whole morning off school for a fictitious medical investigation. In terms of how different *Priti* and Kayleigh were, it is worth noting that the contained presence of mind needed to fabricate and sustain this sort of deceit is quite beyond Kayleigh, who wears her heart on her sleeve and is liable to say rather too much truth, all in a rush, rather than to lie. *Priti* could contain her emotions, was bold in manipulating others and could tolerate not being liked or trusted by people in authority; indeed, Kayleigh rather envied her easy liberty of 'not caring'. It was during this longer outing, meeting up once more with Josh at a park café some 20 miles from home, that Kayleigh/*Priti*'s double life got dramatically found out. Jessica could not reach Kayleigh on her mobile phone and so in a state of some anxiety called the school, which broke confidentiality to let her know about the 'medical' appointments. A phone call to their GP, and a scan of the most recent Facebook contacts on the family computer revealed where she was actually intending to be, but could not confirm the identity of the young man she was meeting. No one could determine whether 'Josh' was actually 15 or a dangerous predatory adult. An emergency police hunt ensued culminating in the couple being confronted in the middle of their date. Understandably Josh was utterly shocked to find himself not only in such serious trouble but also to have been 'lied to' so thoroughly by the young woman he thought was his girlfriend, and immediately declared he wanted nothing more to do with her. *Priti*'s exposure and humiliation was compounded by huge distress at the loss of the precious relationship to which all the effort had been directed and she became physically distraught. Attempts to abscond led to her being forcibly restrained and returned home.

Her mother and stepfather were at once furious with and fearful for her, caught between their frustration that she had determinedly caused so much dramatic upset, and fearful that she was seriously mentally ill. Her mother, in particular, was deeply affected by witnessing the state she was in when brought home by the police that day:

> It wasn't her, it wasn't Kayleigh, she was completely someone else. I can't say whether it was Priti or not, I'm not sure what I think about all that, but it definitely wasn't my daughter, I could hardly recognise her!'
> (Introductory meeting with mother, Jessica)

On 'coming to' later that evening, Kayleigh herself was mortified and became somewhat frightened of *Priti* who had previously always been much more of a help than a hindrance, albeit somewhat domineering and critical. Over the next few days, she was continually tearful, remorseful and despairing, begging to be allowed to apologise to Josh face to face, '*to try to explain*', and feeling that she would be better off dead.

Within a week Kayleigh was urgently seen for psychiatric assessment and then referred to myself so that we could make a decision together on whether psychotherapy seemed likely to be of some help.

Final thoughts

Multidisciplinary colleagues in the UK NHS community CAMHS team, where I met Kayleigh and where I continue to be referred dissociative children, still question multiplicity with concern as to the *true* validity of alternative personified self-states. Experienced professionals may feel thrown off balance in both formulation and treatment planning by a preoccupation with *discovering the truth*. I am often asked if I *really believe* that these children and young people 'can't help it' or if I am not secretly suspicious that they are rather just very troubled, emotionally unstable young people dramatically 'putting it on'? Sometimes there are implications that I am overly gullible or even narcissistically caught up in the supposed 'glamour' of such florid presentations. This chapter is in part a response to those who struggle to find dissociative multiplicity in children credible. I hope that Kayleigh and *Priti*'s story shows how very possible, indeed likely, if not inevitable, this is, when we apply our current understanding of how developing brains respond to adverse childhood experiences in the realms of relational trauma and abuse.

In terms of our therapeutic technique with dissociative children, what *we believe* as a child's therapist about the varying versions of events given by diverse self-states, or the admittedly convenient amnesia or the degree of consciousness of one state for the actions of another, is not necessarily relevant to healing. Forensic investigation of the 'reality' of alters is usually immaterial to our approach in therapy.[6] What is more important is our belief that all communications are meaningful and our understanding that multiplicity is the best adaptation the child's developing brain could fashion in such a compromised and abusive relational environment. Our distressed and impaired dissociative children and young people have been forged in relational adversity and their multiple versions of being are the result.

So I emphasise to these sceptical colleagues that to fully understand and help a dissociative child, our attitude needs to be one of welcoming *all*, of accepting the truthfulness of all self-states and all accounts of past and present experience, even where these are contradictory or mutually exclusive because they necessarily 'express and/or enact crucial dynamics and subjectively experienced historical material' (Kluft, 2009, p. 609). This approach is Kluft's alliteratively named 'invitational inclusionism' (Kluft, 2000, 2009, p. 608) and shares, at its heart, Shakespeare's conviction that 'though this be madness yet there is method in't' (1603, 2(2): line 195). The particularities of the self-states are not random but purposive, and tracing these back to their original usefulness at creation is the journey we need to embark on with the child. Only then, as we take time to understand how 'I' became 'us' for *this* particular child, can we begin to fathom out how that 'us' might now grow together into a more functional integrated 'I'. From this viewpoint, a psychodynamic relational approach is uniquely well suited to working with children who have developed multiple self-states as a response to trauma.

Acknowledgements

I would like to thank Valerie Sinason for her incisive supervision of my work with Kayleigh and her consistent enthusiasm for the research, and Miranda Passey for her helpful reading and editing of first drafts of this chapter. My greatest thanks to Kayleigh, *Priti*, and Jessica for their permission to share our work together in the hope of helping others.

Notes

1 Certainly *British* psychoanalytic theory as taught on our NHS child psychotherapy trainings.
2 For a discussion of seeking consent from alters in this case, see Russell (2015, pp. 57–58).
3 'I have been a stranger in a strange land'. Exodus 2:22.
4 Many dissociative children answer this question about the beginning of a first alter with, often initially benign with a puzzle '*I think they were always there*' – it appears that genesis may often predate memory.
5 See Silberg (1998, p. 66) for a similar description of development of DID by her 12-year-old patient Lizzie.
6 It is of course not immaterial to a court, but that's another paper!

References

Alderman, T. & Marshall, K. (1998). *Amongst Ourselves: Self-help Guide to Living with Dissociative Disorder.* Oakland, CA: New Harbinger Publications.
Alvarez, A. (2012). 'Moral Imperatives and Rectifications in Work with Tormented and Despairing Children', in A. Alvarez, *The Thinking Heart: Three Levels of Psychoanalytic Therapy with Disturbed Children*, pp. 78–89. Hove, East Sussex and New York: Routledge.
Bion, W. R. (1962). 'A Theory of Thinking', in W. R. Bion, *Second Thoughts*, pp. 110–119. 1967. London: Karnac.
Bowlby, J. (1973). *Attachment and Loss, Vol. 2: Separation: Anxiety and Anger.* London: Hogarth Press.
Braun, V. & Clarke, V. (2006). 'Using Thematic Analysis in Psychology', *Qualitative Research in Psychology*, 3, pp. 153–171.
Fairbairn, W. R. D. (1943). 'The Repression and the Return of Bad Objects (with special reference to the 'War Neuroses')', in W. R. D. Fairbairn, *Psychoanalytic Studies of the Personality.* (Reprinted 1952) London: Tavistock Publications Limited.
Ferenczi, S. (1932/1949). 'Confusion of Tongues between the Adults and the Child', (Published 1949) *International Journal of Psycho-Analysis*, 30, pp. 225–230.
Freud, A. (1936). *The Ego and the Mechanisms of Defence. Reprinted in The Writings of Anna Freud Vol. 2.* New York: International University Press, 1974.
Heinmann, P. (1949). 'Some Notes on the Psycho-analytic Concept of Introjected Objects', *International Journal of Psycho-Analysis*, 22, pp. 8–17.
Klein, M. (1926). 'The Psychological Principles of Early Analysis', in M. Klein, *Love, Guilt and Reparation and Other Worts 1921–1945*, pp. 128–138 (1975). London: The Hogarth Press.
Klein, M. (1932). *The Psychoanalysis of Children.* London: The Hogarth Press.
Kluft, R. P. (2000). 'The Psychoanalytic Psychotherapy of DID in the Context of Trauma Therapy', *Psychoanalytic Inquiry*, 20(2), pp. 259–286.
Kluft, R. P. (2009). 'A Clinician's Understanding of Dissociation: Fragments of an Acquaintance', in Dell, P. F. and O'Neill, J. A. (Eds), *Dissociation and the Dissociative Disorders: DSM-V and Beyond*, pp. 599–623. New York: Routledge.
Liotti, G. (2004). 'Trauma, Dissociation, and Disorganised Attachment: Three Strands of a Single Braid', *Psychotherapy: Theory, Research, Practice, Training*, 41, pp. 472–486.

Liotti, G. (2006). 'A Model of Dissociation Based on Attachment Theory and Research', *Journal of Trauma and Dissociation*, 7(4), pp. 55–73.
Perry, B. (2009), 'Examining Child Maltreatment Through a Neurodevelopmental Lens: Clinical Applications of the Neurosequential Model of Therapeutics', *Journal of Loss and Trauma*, 14, pp. 240–255.
Putnam, F. W. (1988). 'The Switch Process in Multiple Personality Disorder and other State-change Disorders', *Dissociation*, 1(1), pp. 24–32.
Putnam, F. W. (1997). *Dissociation in Children and Adolescents: A Developmental Approach*. New York: Guildford Press.
Russell, J. (2015) Dissociative identities in childhood: An exploration of the relationship between adopting these identities and painful states of mind in three young people. Are there implications for psychoanalytic technique?. Source: http://hdl.handle.net/10552/4581.
Schore, A. N. (2009). 'Attachment Trauma and the Developing Right Brain: Origins of Pathological Dissociation', in Dell, P. F. and O'Neill, J. A. (Eds), *Dissociation and the Dissociative Disorders: DSM-V and Beyond*, pp. 107–141. New York: Routledge.
Shakespeare, W. (1603). *Hamlet*. Reprinted 2006, Edited by Taylor, N. and Thompson, A. London: Arden Shakespeare.
Silberg, J. L. (1998). 'Interviewing Strategies for Assessing Dissociative Disorders,' in Silberg J. (Ed), *The Dissociative Child: Diagnosis, Treatment and Management* (2nd Edition), pp. 47–68. Lutherville, MD: Sidran.
Silberg, J. L. (2013). *The Child Survivor: Healing Developmental Trauma and Dissociation*. New York and London: Routledge.
Stern, D. (2009). 'Dissociation and Unformulated Experience: A Psychoanalytic Model of Mind,' in Dell, P. F. and O'Neill, J. A. (Eds), *Dissociation and the Dissociative Disorders: DSM-V and Beyond*, pp. 653–663. New York: Routledge.
Struik, A. (2014). *Treating Chronically Traumatised Children: Don't let sleeping dogs lie!* Hove, East Sussex and New York: Routledge.
Winnicott, D. W. (1949). *'The Ordinary Devoted Mother and Her Baby' from 'Nine Broadcast Talks*. Republished in The Child and the Family 1957. London: Tavistock Publications.
Winnicott, D. W. (1964). *The Child, the Family and the Outside World*. London: Pelicam Books.
Winnicott, D. W. (1965). *The Maturational Processes and the Facilitating Environment: Studies in the Theory of Emotional Development*. London: Karnac.

Chapter 10

The Inside-Outside Technique

Exploring dissociation and fostering self-reflection

Sandra Baita

Two decades ago, I was working with a highly dissociative little girl whom I have written about elsewhere (Baita, 2015a). Her presentation was baffling to me, considering my complete lack of knowledge and experience in the field of dissociation and related disorders. Besides, I lived and practised in a country where there was not much information about trauma-related dissociation; I keep saying to myself that I have treated this girl in a most intuitive way. However, I like to think that I keep learning from her and from my work with her. The Inside-Outside Technique (Baita, 2007, 2015b) was born within her treatment, and I usually say that it was born as an unexpected way to fight despair. This chapter will show the evolution of some of the things I've learned from Dalma's treatment.

I will introduce the readers into Dalma's life before speaking further about the technique.

I first started seeing her when she was four years old. She was in foster care, living with two older siblings and a younger sister. All of them had been sexually abused by her biological father – who was in turn the stepdad of her older sister – and both parents were charged with sexual abuse: The father for his active participation, the mother for her neglect to protect the children. At the time in which Dalma and her siblings were put in foster care, the father had run away, and the Family Court had forbidden any kind of contact with the mother. The contact between mom and her children resumed after one year into treatment and it was full of surprises: Mom had married another man and was pregnant with his child.

The Family Court had then allowed mom visits only within a therapeutic setting which she first attended on a regular weekly basis, until she gave birth to the new child. After that she attended family sessions intermittently, and when she did, she used to carry the baby with her. The older sister refused to be part of these sessions; the older brother and the younger sister were completely detached from their mother, passively rejecting her or overtly avoiding her. Dalma, however, was lovely, obedient and polite towards her mom. And so she spent the entire sessions sitting very close to her mom, willing to share her scarce attention with the new "intruder" rather than being entirely left away. The price for this devoted attitude towards mom was a complete shift into a wildly sexualized dysregulated self- state right after mom left the setting and Dalma had to start her individual therapeutic session. I remember having spent session after session just trying to calm her down, reassuring and reminding her of the safety she could experience with me in my office. But I didn't have a single clue about how to effectively link these two dissociated self-states. I guess most of her calming down was intended to calm myself down as well.

One day, Dalma came to my office very upset. She said she didn't like her siblings calling her crazy.

- So tell me, why do they call you like this? – I asked Dalma.
- They say sometimes I act like a normal girl and sometimes I act like a baby girl and sometimes I act as a crazy girl. But that's not true!
- Well… I have seen you acting in two very different ways. Let me tell you what do I see… Every time your mom comes to visit you and your siblings, I see a very polite and lovely Dalma, who speaks perfectly well to mom; but after she leaves, and we come here to my office, I see a very different part of Dalma, jumping and moaning and screaming… I can barely understand what this part says, it really looks like a baby part talking… – Dalma was attentive to my words, so I decided to move forward – I wonder whether this is the kind of changes your siblings might see… only that they don't know how to call this nor they can understand what is going on with you… would you like to look into it and see whether we can get an answer to this mystery?

What I did was to reflect on her behaviour in a very respectful, non-judgemental way and try to engage her curiosity. Having her on board I proceeded by drawing a circle on a white piece of paper and asked her: Tell me, how do you think you look like when your siblings call you crazy? And after she completed the task, I turned the sheet, draw a second circle and asked her: And now let's see… what do you think there is inside of you when you act in the way your siblings call crazy?

This second drawing would allow Dalma to see, understand and explain her internal, dissociated experience as being part of herself for the very first time in her therapeutic process.

Why would that be so important?

What do I think? How do I feel? Who am I?

During her first grade Dalma was assigned a very simple task: She had to draw herself and complete the sentence I am….

While she was able to complete the first part of the task – the drawing – she was unable to fulfil the second part. It wasn't that she didn't know how to write. It was that she didn't know what to write. How could she answer a question about who she was when her experience about herself was so varied and shifted from a calm girl to a younger sexualized one, to a younger needy one, to a mean one, as if each of them was felt and perceived by her as a different separated girl?

Let's start with a simple question: How do we know who we are? How are we able to speak about our feelings, our inner world, our thoughts?

Putnam (1997) states:

> (...) parents and other caretakers are instrumental in helping children integrate information and behavior across behavioural states and social contexts. The caretakers remind the children of what they have learned in other states and contexts and help the children to adapt and apply this previously learned information to new situations.
>
> (p. 163)

How do parents and caretakers complete this task? By mirroring the child's behaviour, providing interpretation and feedback about it and reflecting back to the child the link between the observed behaviour and the possible explanations for it. In doing so, parents help the child provide meaning to experience and learn about their own feelings, thoughts, behaviours and internal processes.

Within the same line of reasoning, Siegel (2003) describes five key ingredients of the interactive experiences that promote secure attachment: Contingent communication, which involves the perception of the child's signals ("I see you are crying"), the meaning making of these signals in terms of what they imply for the child ("You probably are afraid of thunders"), and a timely and effective response ("Come with Mummy, I'll hug you and the fear will fade"); reflective dialogue, which involves the parent's discussion of contents of the mind such as thoughts, feelings, sensations, perceptions, memories, etc.; emotional communication, which includes the sharing and amplification of positive emotions and the sharing and soothing of negative ones, including the reflection upon what have caused these emotions, in order to enhance the child's self-understanding; self-regulation which makes for repair of the logical and expected disruptions that happen within every human communication, and which involves acknowledgement of the disruption that drives disconnection and moving towards reconnection; and coherent narrative as means to make sense of our own lives and others.

A parent who is able to make a good distinction between his or her own life and history and the child's is in better shape to feed the interactive experiences with the child with these ingredients, promoting secure attachment. The foundations for growing up with a strong sense of self and an increasing capacity for self-regulation have been laid.

This would be a child able to fulfil both tasks given to Dalma, a child able to shift between different emotional states without losing a sense of continuity, who would increasingly perceive herself as one, rather than several girls.

Self-reflection, complex trauma and dissociation

According to the *Merriam-Webster Online Dictionary* self-reflection is the examination of own thoughts and feelings. Synonyms are self-examination and self-observation, and related words are self-awareness, self-exploration, self-knowledge, self-concept, self-image and self- perception. Many of these processes are relevant in the therapeutic work with any kind of client of all ages, but we are going to explore the challenges involved in the specific work with dissociative children.

Self-reflection, a specific element of metacognition (Lysaker et al., 2011), was found to be helpful to perceive social cues, generate social emotions such as guilt and contribute to emotion regulation, self-awareness and self-insight (Philippi & Koenigs, 2014). Putnam (1997) states that "metacognitive capacities emerge over the course of development and are strongly influenced by the input of significant others" (p. 297); however, "metacognitive, self-reflective and integrative capacities are often disrupted in traumatized individuals" (p. 297). The exposure to interpersonal chronic violence that leads the path towards complex trauma and dissociation faces the child with an impossible situation, an attachment paradox: In order to keep closeness with the attachment figure, the child must "accept" whatever comes with the interaction, being this sexual abuse, emotional abuse, physical abuse, neglect or a combination of many of these traumatic events. So the meaning of experiences will be distorted (like in sexual abuse where the offender explains his or her behaviour in terms of tenderness, affection or playfulness), and the sense of self will be shaped by this same distortion: When the sexual offender tells the child I did this because you like it, the child might assimilate this statement as I like this, then I am disgusting; when a parent abuses a child saying You deserve this, the child might assimilate this statement as My Dad beats me because I deserve it, so I am mean. These are just a couple of examples, because the reality shows that these children, later adolescents, later adults, will assimilate several contradictory messages about themselves within a shifting interaction with an attachment figure as long as the abuse will last.

In describing how abusive families behave, Putnam (1997) states that they

> ...often maintain significant discrepancies between public and private behaviour, so that the child alternates between two dramatically different social contexts. Abusive parents may even actually prohibit the child

from generalizing across these two domains, thus creating multiple realities that require differing responses to the 'same' situation.

(p. 172)

This situation worsens if we consider that abusive parents show these dramatic discrepancies within their own private behaviour, as is the case of a sexually abusive father who acts in very different ways while abusing the child by night and taking lovely care of her by day. This was the exact experience of Dalma.

Within this scenario, how could a human being answer the question who am I?

And what about exploring own thoughts and feelings, when they are extremely confusing and painful, and too negative and intense?

Self-reflection, self-exploration and avoidance

In her Affect Avoidance Theory to explain childhood dissociation, Silberg (2013) states that the traumatic interactions with abusive or neglectful parents elicit intense negative emotions that the child will try to avoid. These are not one time experiences, but rather they are repeated over and over again, and so is the affect avoidance pattern. According to Silberg:

> The mind becomes organized around the principle of dissociation from affect, which generalizes to not remembering experiences related to the affect, or to not feeling pain related to the affect.
>
> (Silberg, p. 21)

The construct of avoidance has a significant place in theorizing dissociation. Van der Hart and colleagues (2006) and Steele and colleagues (2017) state that maintenance of structural dissociation of personality in adult clients, even when the individual is no longer exposed to the same traumatic events that gave birth to it in the first place, is possible due to the phobic avoidance of trauma-related content, experiences, memories and even the existence of dissociated self-states.

Self-exploration is a pillar of any therapeutic work. Every single question the therapist poses to the client implies for her the action of going inside and find the answer: How did you feel? What were your thoughts? What happened? However, we have learned that dissociation creates barriers to the knowledge a client can find inside, and avoidance is a powerful and helpful tool to elude the intense pain this knowledge might bring. Are we therapists at a crossroad? If our clients avoid self-exploration, how can they reach self-reflection?

Exploration entails curiosity, interest, seeking, expectation and openness to novelty (Ogden, Minton & Pain, 2006). It is only within a safe interaction with a secure attachment figure that we dare to explore the world around us and within ourselves. But chronically traumatized children have learned that the world can be a very dangerous place, relationships are barely safe and they can only expect more danger. They must remain hypervigilant, there is no place for curiosity. When they look inside themselves, they might find reflections of this same dangerous world: Negative cognitions about themselves; negative and intense feelings; awful, splintered and confusing memories; and sometimes a pervasive feeling of not me (this didn't happen to me, I am not this child). So, there is very limited interest in going inside.

Chronically traumatized children come to see us expecting the same kind of danger and rejection, and with scarce motivation to dig inside the reasons for the behaviours that brought them into therapy. How do we help them engage with us and the therapy itself?

One way could be by role-modelling curiosity for them in a very respectful way. The Inside-Outside Technique is only one way to do so, and it has been so rewarding to me in my work with dissociative children that I would like to share with the reader what I have learned.

The Inside-Outside Technique: Let's get started

Imagine you are in your office and this is one of the first meetings you have with the child. You are both getting to know each other. And then you pick up a white piece of paper and draw a big circle on each side of it. While you are doing this, you start saying to the child: Did you know there are some things everyone can see of your head? What things do you think they are? If the child remains silent you can move forward and ask: Do you think everybody can see your mouth, your eyes, your hair? Once you are sure the child is on board, keep going: Good! But did you know there are other things that are stored inside your head that nobody can see nor listen but you? What kind of things do you think they are? Most children will reply "The brain" or "The skull". In that case, you go on with a statement like this: Yes, you are right. I can't see your brain or your skull right now... however there are some ways in which both your brain or your skull could be seen... if you fall and badly hit your head there is the chance that your doctor might take a picture of your brain or even of your skull [I actually have an x-ray of my own skull and an MRI of my own brain to show them; and when I do so I ask the child]: Tell me... do you see any thoughts or any memories in these pictures? And that's because there are some things stored in my head that I am the only one who knows. That's exactly what happens with your head as well. There are thoughts, affects, memories and so many other things stored inside that only you know.

The Inside-Outside Technique 161

Thus far your job as a therapist has been to engage the child's curiosity into some sort of exploration, one that you are role-modelling by putting yourself as an example. Now, let's go a little bit further: Some of the things that happen to us can be easily seen by others: If you have tears someone might think you are crying because you're sad. But what causes your sadness might remain unknown for the person who is with you. The only one who really knows what's going on, what's inside your head, what makes you feel sad and cry, it's you. And you are the only one who has the power to solve the mystery, because you are the only one who really knows why you are sad, and you are the only one who can decide to answer this question or not. To be a child entails to be powerless. To be a traumatized child entails to be atop of powerlessness. Through this statement you as a therapist give to the child a sense of mastery: The child is the only one who knows something you don't and has the power – and the right – to share with you something of her inner experience that is unique. Now, we are probably ready to move to the drawings: I have this piece of paper with two big circles on each side. I would like you to draw on one side what everybody can see of what is outside your head, is that ok for you? Good. Encourage the child to make this drawing as she or he wants, no matter whether the eyes are closed or wide open, whether she or he draws a mouth or not; we don't intervene in what the child wants to draw of her outside. Once this first drawing is done, keep going by saying: And now, would you like to draw in the other side of the paper all the things that only you know that are inside your head, and might be worrying or bothering you? This could help me understand and help you better. If the child refuses to draw "all the things", tell her: Fair enough… you can also draw the things you want to share with me right now… is that ok for you? If the child keeps refusing to show the things that are bothering her inside her head, you can say: I see there is something inside of you that doesn't want you to show me what's inside your head. Sometimes we have inside our heads a helper that doesn't want us to feel bad by remembering awful things; sometimes we have a reminder, like a warning system, telling us it's better not to talk until we feel safer, or it's better not to talk because that would upset someone we care about. Is anything like this inside your head? How would you draw it? I think it's very important to know it so I can remember what things I can or cannot ask you. Sometimes children refuse to draw, but they do accept writing: That is perfectly allowed.

Only when the drawing of the inside and outside is completed, the therapist can ask the child about any details of both drawings that stand out: Why are your eyes closed? I see you didn't draw your mouth, I wonder why?

These first drawings are usually the doorway to a first glance into the internal world of the child. From now on the therapist can use the drawings as tools to explore and discuss with the child her internal states at any given time: What's inside your head when mom tells you have lied to her? And

162 Sandra Baita

how do you look in your outside when she tells this to you? What's inside your head when you remember all these things? Can you show me how does your face look like when these things happen inside of your head? What do you think others can see when you have these feelings inside of you/when you have this voice inside of you/when you remember the things Dad did to you? These are just a few examples of the questions the therapist might ask to the child.

But, why do we ask for the outside, not just the inside?

Some children will show some differences between the self as displayed in the outside and the self as experienced in the inside (Blaustein & Kinniburgh, 2010) like the girl in Figures 10.1–10.3. In her drawing of the inside (Figure 10.1), L. portrays her confusion and desire for her dad to leave her classroom, where he has arrived unexpectedly after breaking a court order of not approaching his daughter. Dad didn't exactly approach L., he just stayed at the door chatting with her teacher, who was unaware of the Court order, and then left.

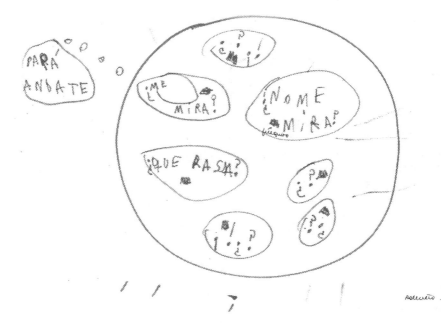

Figure 10.1 L.'s drawing of the inside

The Inside-Outside Technique 163

But when L. made the drawing of her outside (Figure 10.2), she portrayed a smiling face that didn't seem to match the inner confusion and disorientation.

When the therapist finds this kind of inconsistencies, this is a good chance to explore further by reflecting upon the mismatch between the internal experience and the external demeanour:

> What is this picture of your outside head saying? How do you look like here?
> Happy.
> And when you see what was inside your head, how does it look like? Does it look like you felt happy inside of you?
> No… it looks like I wasn't happy at all…
> How would you like to express with your outside head what was going on inside your head at that moment?
> (Figure 10.3 L. is screaming "Dad get out!")

In order to successfully achieve self-regulation, Blaustein and Kinniburgh (2010) state the child will need to have some awareness of her internal states

Figure 10.2 L.'s drawing of the outside

Figure 10.3 L.'s drawing of L. screaming "Dad get out!"

(going inside), some ability to communicate her experience to others (going outside) and an understanding of what influences internal experience, and how all its aspects are interconnected.

In order for traumatized children to go inside and explore their inner experience they will need the guidance and support from a safe, consistent adult; to be able to properly communicate this experience, they will require some psychoeducation and to gain understanding they will need a reflective action from the adult world.

- It looks like you were very confused when you heard your Dad's voice at your classroom door, and you knew he was not allowed to stay there, but since your teacher was chatting with him you weren't sure whether you could express how you really felt inside... sometimes our brain acts in a very wise way, protecting us from things that can be upsetting... together we can keep exploring all the feelings you have inside of you and how would you like to be able to express them, to show them and talk about them...
- I was afraid Dad could see me...

In her art work using masks with children who have suffered injuries, Sanders Martin (2008) states that "Helping children and adolescents learn that some internal emotions may be expressed in external behaviours can aid in increasing self-awareness and self- regulation of behavior" (p. 126). She provides a mask to the child and encourages her to paint the outside and represent the internal content of her experience inside the mask, allowing the child "to separate what is expressed to others and what is internal" (p. 126).

By using these kind of techniques – both the masks and the drawing – with dissociative children, we are helping them to acknowledge these internal experiences as belonging to them, and not to someone else, the very first baby steps to erode avoidance.

The Inside-Outside Technique and dissociative parts: Acknowledging and connecting them

An important part of the treatment of dissociative children is the assessment of dissociative parts. Other authors have described different ways to achieve this goal (Putnam, 1997; Silberg, 2013; Waters, 2013, 2016). The Inside-Outside Technique can be used to complement the assessment. In the experience of this author, some children have first disclosed the existence of dissociative parts using this technique. A five-year-old child drew a sad face in the Inside drawing, and when asked about what she had drawn she said: It's a little voice I have inside of me, it is sad, it is calling me, I don't know why… A seven-year-old girl came to a therapy session concerned about the fact that she had found herself saying things she didn't want to. When asked about what was inside her head when she said those things she didn't want to, she drew a little girl inside a circle surrounded by "garbage": It's like a little me, like a five-year-old, she wants me to throw all my stuff, she says this is garbage and she doesn't want it. She is very angry at me and I am angry at her. Another five-year-old girl drew a little girl with an angry face sitting on top of the girl's brain: The little girl is furious about her nanny [who had sexually and physically abused her]. The nanny is inside her brain and she doesn't want to be there with her. She wants to get out of there and sometimes when she is afraid she makes me wet my pants.

In the three cases these drawings provided an opportunity to explore more information about the depicted part and other potential dissociative parts.

When the child displays more than one part, we can use the technique to assess the relationship between all of them. I like to use the metaphor of a house to introduce the issue of internal communication:

Imagine that the inside of your head is like a house. Houses have doors that separate what is inside of them from the rest of the neighbourhood. And if you want you can open the door to let things come in or out. Inside this house there are also walls that separate the different rooms. You can go from one room to another by walking through a corridor or by opening a door. In this house there are also private places and common places, and there are closets where you can keep or hide things. Now that we have known all these parts of you, let's draw another big circle and see what place in this house inside of you would each of them stay in. Now let's see: Do they know each other? Do they like each other? How do each of them feel about each of the other parts? In what part of the house would you put each part? How would they communicate/relate to each other?

The visual aid of the drawing is very helpful to work with children who have amnesia for things that they have said to us before: The last time I saw you, you told me about a part that was very afraid, the one that you draw here... but now you say you don't remember anything about a scared part... we could try to find out where this part has gone, we could try to ask the other parts in the drawing to help us find the scared one... and to figure out what made you not remember it today... are you ok with that?

The Inside-Outside Technique: Limitations

I was asked several times how this technique could help to assess and address somatoform dissociative symptoms. I think this is the main limitation of the Inside-Outside Technique. What I have found more useful is to learn about the child's own experience of her body; most traumatized and dissociative children lack a language for body sensations, and a very important part of the first sessions will be to teach the child a language to speak about the body. But in order to do so, the child will need to experience the body, which is the first step towards body awareness (Baita, 2014).

Another important limitation is related to the lack of external safety. If the child is not safe the efficacy of the best treatment conducted by the wisest therapist will be restricted and dissociation will keep helping the child to feel protected or to protect parts holding confusing feelings and disturbing memories. For these children to express what is inside of them could be really dangerous. I was taught about that by a seven-year-old girl who was in custody with her abusive father and not allowed to see her mom. Her outside drawing showed a smiley girl, while in the inside she painted all in black. When I asked her what was under all this black colour inside her head she said: Inside it is all dark so I won't remember things Dad told me not to recall.

References

Baita, S. (2007). What's Inside My Head? How to Explore and Explain Trauma and Dissociation with Children. ISSTD International Conference. Philadelphia, USA.

Baita, S. (2014). Where Do You Feel it in Your Body? Creating a Language to Help Traumatized Children be Aware of Their Bodies. Lecture at the conference on Complex Trauma bij kinderen: de focus op behandeling. Utrecht, The Netherlands.

Baita, S. (2015a). Dalma (4 to 7 years old) – "I've Got All my Sisters with Me": Treatment of Dissociative Identity Disorder in a Sexually Abused Young Child.

In Wieland, S. (Ed), *Dissociation in Traumatized Children and Adolescents. Theory and Clinical Interventions*. Second Edition, pp. 41–88. New York: Routledge.

Baita, S. (2015b). The Inside-Outside Technique: Exploring Dissociation with Children. ISSTD International Conference, Orlando, USA.

Blaustein, M. & Kinniburgh, K. (2010). *Treating Traumatic Stress in Children and Adolescents: How to Foster Resilience through Attachment, Self-Regulation, and Competency*. New York: The Guilford Press.

Lysaker, P. H., Buck, K. D., Carcione, A., Procacci, M., Salvatore, G., Nicolò, G. & Dimaggio. G. (2011). Addressing Metacognitive Capacity for Self reflection in the Psychotherapy for Schizophrenia: A Conceptual Model of the Key Tasks and Processes. *Psychology and Psychotherapy: Theory, Research and Practice*, 84, pp. 58–69. doi: 10.1348/147608310X520436.

Merriam- Webster Online Dictionary. Self Reflection. Source: https://merriam-webster.com/thesaurus/self-reflection Retrieved on 12/16/2017.

Ogden, P, Minton, K. & Pain, C. (2006). *Trauma and the Body: A Sensorimotor Approach to Psychotherapy*. New York: W.W. Norton.

Philippi, C.L. & Koenigs, P. (2014). The Neuropsychology of Self-reflection in Psychiatric Illness. *Journal of Psychiatric Research*, 54–63. doi: 10.1016/j.jpsychires.2014.03.004.

Putnam, F.W. (1997). *Dissociation in Children and Adolescents: A Developmental Perspective*. New York: The Guilford Press.

Sanders Martin, E. (2008). Medical Art and Play. Therapy with Accident Survivors. In Malchiodi, C.A. (Ed), *Creative Interventions with Traumatized Children*, pp. 112–131. New York: The Guilford Press.

Siegel, D.J. (2003). An Interpersonal Neurobiology of Psychotherapy: The Developing Mind and the Resolution of Trauma. In Solomon, M.F. & Siegel, D. J. (Eds), *Healing Trauma. Attachment, Mind, Body and Brain*, pp. 1–56. New York: W.W. Norton.

Silberg, J. (2013). *The Child Survivor. Healing Developmental Trauma and Dissociation*. New York: Routledge.

Steele, K., Boon, S. & van der Hart, O. (2017). *Treating Trauma-related Dissociation: A Practical, Integrative Approach*. New York: Norton.

van der Hart, O., Nijenhuis, E.R.S. & Steele, K. (2006). *The Haunted Self: Structural Dissociation and the Treatment of Chronic Traumatization*. New York: Norton.

Waters, F.S. (2013). Assessing and Diagnosing Dissociation in Children: Beginning the Recovery. In Gomez, A. M. (Ed), *EMDR Therapy and Adjunct Approaches with Children. Complex Trauma, Attachment and Dissociation*, pp. 129–149. New York: Springer.

Waters, F.S. (2016). *Healing the Fractured Child. Diagnosis and Treatment of Youth with Dissociation*. New York: Springer.

Chapter 11

Severe and unusual self-harm in DID
Motive, means and opportunity

Adah Sachs

Introduction

My first experience of dissociative adolescents was rather specific: they were all psychiatric inpatients. Their behaviour (particularly their eating disorders and self-harm) had been so dangerous and disturbing that their GPs, paediatricians or mental health practitioners had to refer them to a specialist unit.

This was nearly 25 years ago. Most of my colleagues, and certainly I, knew little or nothing about dissociative disorders: it was one of those curiosities, a debatable disorder, which was deemed 'extremely rare' in the DSM-III (1980). No one that I knew expected to actually meet a person like Sibyl (Schreiber, 1974) or Eve (Thigpen & Cleckley, 1957) in real life, and I was certainly not ready to meet one in an adolescent unit. In hindsight, I have met several.

DID diagnosis in children

Identifying dissociative disorders in children and adolescents is more difficult than in adults. This is due to several reasons:

A   Behaviours which in adults would be deemed abnormal are not uncommon in young people. Absorption, 'moodiness', contrariness, secrecy, some delinquency and high-risk behaviour are frequently seen in adolescents; and conversations or arguments with an imaginary friend (or friends) are not uncommon in children.
B   Criterion A of DID, – the existence of two or more distinct personality states, – is not always present in children: 'children usually do not present with identity changes' (APA (2013), p. 294).
C   Young people, especially adolescents, are often uncomfortable talking about their feelings and can be evasive in their responses, making assessment interviews or the use of structured diagnostic tools less effective.

DOI: 10.4324/9781003246541-12

D   Most young people live with their families (natural, adoptive or fostering) or in care, and depend on the adults who care for them (their *attachment figures*). This dependency is greater the younger the child is (up to total dependency in babies). Children are thus bound by their dependency; and where a carer demands silence from the child, the child is unlikely to divulge information about their home-life to anyone, including to well-meaning professionals.

Dissociative children thus often 'slip through the net' and are not recognised. For some, the dissociation provides a refuge, which keeps the worst of their distress out of sight. These children can draw less attention (e.g. from teachers, neighbours, social workers or GPs) than the ordinary 'naughty child'. We probably know the least about this quiet group. Sometimes, they only get noticed many years later, if they are referred to adult mental health services due to further deterioration in their symptoms.[1] Many of these children, however, may never come to our attention at all: these invisible dissociative children become invisible dissociative adults, and spend their whole lives suffering and unhelped.

The clinical experience

The dissociative children I have met as inpatients, however, were not the invisible kind. They were the most difficult cases we had – the most risky, confusing, difficult to reach and often impossible to understand. Despite their dramatic presentation, however, they, too, often remained unhelped. Most of these young patients were hospitalised because of severe, persistent and dangerous self-harm (including very severe eating disorders), and following several pervious treatment programmes in other units.

The failure to help them was not due to lack of trying. All our patients received a wide range of intensive psychological interventions, including psychotherapy, art therapy, Systemic family work, EMDR and group therapy, as well as a high level of nursing support and psychiatric care. Indeed, most of the patients made a good recovery. Looking back at the ones who did not improve, I suspect that many of them suffered undiagnosed dissociative disorders, which accounted for their lack of progress.

It was quite apparent that while all our young patients were very unwell, some of them were even more so. They never got better. Some of them are now dead. Some of them, in their 20s, have become 'career patients', spending years in and out of hospitals, collecting an ever longer lists of diagnosis. I remember each of them distinctly, as they had a particular air about them: they were desperately and frantically waving for help while sinking in quicksand. We saw the frantic waving, but we didn't know how to stop them from sinking.

During the course of our patients' lengthy stay and intensive therapy, we often heard very difficult stories. Many, who initially seemed to be 'good kids from good homes', turned out to have grown up with domestic violence, parental mental illness, war trauma, bullying, unreported rapes and other highly traumatic life events. In fact, I can hardly think of an example of a patient in the hospital who did *not* have some form of traumatic history.

But amongst all these youngsters with difficult symptoms and difficult histories, there was that smaller group whose presentation was particularly severe, and particularly difficult to help.

Those of them who were anorexic were brought to the hospital literally at death's door. Their suicide attempts were always serious, and sometimes successful.[2] Their self-harm was the most severe, and the most unusual: a girl caused herself deep burns, holding cigarettes to the inside of her elbow for a long time. A boy cut the muscle of his arm all the way to the bone, till the muscle flopped open. A girl removed the skin off her face using sand paper. A boy poured acid on his leg and sat there for a long time, watching the skin disintegrate. A girl peeled off her toe-nails, one by one, and another one chewed and swallowed broken glass and metal staples. They seemed to be deterred by absolutely nothing.

These children were also very puzzling. Many of them had several diagnoses, all 'atypical' and none of them conclusive; and their stories, inasmuch as they were able to tell them, were not only distressing but also strange: a girl disclosed that she was raped by an eight-year-old boy. A boy talked about gatherings of 'some people' in a field around a small lake, and then insisted that he had never mentioned any lakes and had no idea who told me such rubbish. A 15-year-old girl kept wetting her bed and, in the therapy room, walked on all fours and acted like she was a dog sniffing for food in the corners. A boy who was an only child said that he had murdered his brother.

I highlight the strangeness of these children's presentation because it is suggestive of a dissociative process; however, none of these young people was deemed psychotic. These were occasional, isolated events. Most of the time they all struggled with eating disorders, and were otherwise able to think and relate coherently. James was one of these people.[3]

James

James was admitted to a psychiatric hospital at the age of 13, following his third serious overdose. It was hard to say what exactly was wrong with him: he did not appear to be depressed, was not psychotic, and most of the time was warm, eloquent and insightful. He had an eating disorder, on which he reflected intelligently; he also had several broken fingers and a broken arm in a big plaster cast. The broken bones were the result of him hitting furniture, handrails, trees and other hard objects, for no apparent reason.

The first time I saw him doing it was startling: he was walking along a corridor, and without changing his pace leaned slightly back and hit a sideboard with a ferocious bang, continuing to walk as though nothing had happened. When asked what was this about or why he had done this, he looked quite puzzled and said 'I don't know' with an expression of a real surprise on his face.

His puzzlement extended beyond his self-harm. Unlike many of our young patients, who often expressed vehement resentment about being 'stuck in hospital', James was just very confused by it. Whenever anyone asked him how he was feeling, he would say that he was perfectly fine, and wondered why he was asked, and why was he in a hospital at all. His puzzlement was so genuine, natural and convincing, that it was almost possible to forget for a moment how ill he was.

To protect him from breaking more bones, James was accompanied by two nurses at all times. He also had psychotherapy, group therapy and some medication. But weeks passed, and other than managing to break his other arm there was no change in his condition. It was obvious that we were missing something, but we had no idea what that was.

His family history was rather unclear. He was an only child, and lived with his mother and step-father. His father died when James was very young, but the circumstances of his death had not been explained. His mother had an extensive record of alcohol-related issues, self-harm and a few suicide attempts. There had been a suggestion of her being abused by both her first and second husbands, and perhaps by her parents, but she was vague about the details. There were also concerns regarding physical violence and sexual abuse of James by various male relatives, which James had once disclosed but then denied he had ever made such disclosure or that any such things had ever happened. James's school had reported frequent absences, and some 'concerning bruising'. Social services have been involved since he was in nursery, as the family appeared 'at risk', but did not have more information.

Such family history where so much is implied and suggested yet so little actually known, the air of confusion, of things untold and of vague suggestions of violence, and of course James's bone-breaking violence towards his own body are obviously very worrying. James himself, however, had always maintained that 'nothing bad had ever happened to him', a claim that not many of us could make. And the calm, friendly and open way in which he said it, without a trace of anxiety, fear or upset – was simply incongruent with the clinical picture of a child at risk, with bruised face and several broken bones.

These puzzles were never answered. Shortly after his admission James's family moved out of the area and he was transferred to another hospital. I was later informed that he was transferred again, and was not doing well.

Olivia

I'd like to give another example of a very odd and very extreme act committed by a young patient. The following is based on her own accounts in therapy as well as on her records.

Olivia, aged 18, held a kitchen knife at her victim's open mouth. The victim was sweating and shaking, but didn't scream. Olivia tilted her victim's head back, and started to push the knife into her throat. The victim coughed and moaned a little, but didn't move; she might have been too frightened. Olivia kept pushing, slowly and carefully. She wondered if she could make the knife disappear completely. The victim turned very pale and started groaning. Olivia didn't like the sound, and told her to shut up. She could hear the noise of the cutting of the knife, and then everything went completely silent as the knife disappeared. Olivia wondered for a moment if her victim was dead, but then she was mostly aware of feeling elated, so she didn't care. She sat motionless on her bed in the darkening room and waited. She felt deeply contented, her mind at peace. Some time later, she thought someone had come into the room, and then she heard the siren of a car approaching the house and stopping. In a daze, she remembers being taken out of her room, put into a car and then brought into hospital. The pain was unbearable, and she passed out into the comforting arms of the general anaesthetic. She was operated on successfully, and the knife was removed from her stomach. The victim was Olivia; and this was the fourth time she had done it.

An extreme story like Olivia's leaves us dazzled, shocked, sick and horrified. Olivia, however, did not seem to feel any of these reactions. She told me her story very gradually, over many months. And she always told it in a rather detached way, as though it had little to do with her personally, as though she was not the person who had been so brutally cut. Had I not known from her medical records that she had indeed swallowed four kitchen knives, I might have doubted that this was actually true.

I've told Olivia's story as if it was acted by two people because this was her experience. She told her story calmly, as if this awful thing did not happen *to her*; as though it was not even awful. She was quite distant. She described 'wondering if she could make the knife disappear completely', as if with academic interest. She was completely unaffected by the terror of being cut inside, because she was only engaged with the person doing the cutting, and unaware of the experience of the girl who was being cut, even though this was her own body. While this act lasted, she was completely dissociated from that girl – from her body, her fear or her pain. She remembered everything in minute detail, *but only from the perspective of the perpetrator*: this is because at that time, she *was* the perpetrator. The part of her who was a girl being terrified and tortured, or any part of her who might have stopped her actions, was just not present. Furthermore, all her memories of the pain following the previous times she had swallowed a knife were also dissociated, and thus they, too, did not serve to stop her. The feeling of pain had hit her as a real shock only hours later, in hospital, when she had 'switched' into another part of her dissociative self, a part who could feel pain.

Notably, she always struggled to explain why or how she could do it. She said she hated her body, because she was abused as a child. She said she felt dead inside, so she wanted to feel something, and pain was a feeling. She said she wanted to punish herself for complying with the abuse in her childhood. She also noted, with some confusion, that when she swallowed a knife she didn't actually feel any pain, and she also didn't feel punished. Her explanations were ones that were frequently given by other patients during group therapy, and she was familiar with the wording; but they did not actually fit with her experience.

Moreover, the complete sense of horror that we all feel when hearing about such severe self-harm means that for most of us, even if her explanations made sense, and no matter how much we may 'understand why', it would still be impossible to even imagine doing such violence to anyone, let alone to our own bodies.

Olivia's acts point to a very severe DID, where the amnesic barriers between parts are so solid that her body could sit still while her intestines were cut with a knife by her own hands. And it seems that both her *motive* for self-harm and her *ability* to do so were qualitatively different from those of her peers.

Discussion: severe and unusual self-harm as an indicator of DID in non-psychotic[4] young people

As I've mentioned at the start, my sample of dissociative young people was of a specific group: children whose symptoms were severe enough to warrant long hospitalisation. However, none of these patients had a diagnosis of DID or of other dissociative disorders. This was due to the general lack of awareness regarding these disorders (which has somewhat improved over the years), as well as to the difficulty that clinicians still face in making the diagnosis at a young age.

As correct diagnosis is crucial for appropriate treatment, it is important to identify further indicators which could help clarify a diagnosis of DID in young people. I would like to suggest that *severe and unusual self-harm* can be an indicator for DID.

Characterising severe and unusual self-harm

Most self-harm in adolescents ('group 1') consists of relatively superficial self-cutting, eating disorders or both. Conversely, self-harm in people with DID[5] ('group 2') is often characterised by tolerance of very high levels of pain – causing permanent, serious or potentially lethal damage to the body; and making seemingly bizarre choices regarding the form of self-harm.[6]

I suggest that while both categories of self-harmers express distress that they are unable to process, they are qualitatively different from each other.

Motive, means and opportunity

To understand the qualitative difference between the two categories of self-harm, I'd like to first highlight their common ground: either one of them, done to *another* person, would be deemed a serious crime. As both types are done to the body of a child, they are both criminal acts against children.

Defined as crimes, they could be compared to each other regarding the motive, means and opportunity which enabled them to happen (see Table 11.1).

Motive will answer the question 'why': why would a young person want to do damage to their own body?

Means will answer the question 'how': how could he or she manage to actually do it?

Opportunity is about the 'when': when does the perpetrator have a chance to be in close proximity to the victim, without being observed or interrupted?

Motive

Most self-harmers (Group 1) describe feeling an overwhelming *urge* to self-harm, and feeling better (for a short while) afterwards. Where they are able to reflect on their motives, three themes seem to come up in their narratives most frequently: the first is to do with needing to 'drown', 'shut down' or 'distract from' an unbearable mental pain, which just can't be stopped in any other way. The second is a feeling of numbness or 'deadness' inside, which the physical pain (or the sight of one's own blood) can break through, bringing a feeling of 'aliveness'. The third is a wish to punish oneself, for things that are felt deeply shaming or hateful (e.g. for having been abused).

With all the distress that is being conveyed in these acts and feeling, I want to highlight an unexpected, positive element that should not be missed. In fact, bringing it up in therapy has invariably been liberating to my young self-harmers: each of these 'reasons' for self-harm contains in it an element of *ownership* over one's own body and mind. In each of these situations, the young person takes, without asking or sharing with anyone, a remedial action: to stop the pain, to break through the 'deadness' or to punish badness also means that a part of the child sees him- or herself as powerful and 'good'. Most importantly, each of these young people is making a claim on their body, as though saying 'I can hurt this body because it is mine'.

For some of them, these acts are their first steps into establishing a separate identity. Their motive, for all its obvious pathological overtones, is actually also a developmental milestone.

Group 2 consists of the young people whose self-harm can be defined as severe and unusual. I suggest that their motive is *attachment*.

Attachment is our earliest survival mechanisms. It is the instinctive reach towards the protection of another, and it can be seen in new-borns almost as early as their first breath. It is shared – in different forms – by all living creatures, from insects[7] to humans. This special connection lasts at least until the creature reaches physical independence – in other words, for as long as protection is essential. In some species, this connection lasts a whole life time: the *attachment figure* changes over time, but the *attachment relationship* continues to exist between the individual and another individual (e.g. a partner) or between an individual and a group (or flock, pride, pack, family). In all cases, the severance of contact between an individual and his/her/its attachment figure is a drastic injury, which could potentially lead to death. All creatures know this instinctively; and all creatures guard this contact with all their might. Long before the formulation of *attachment theory*, Suttie and Suttie (1932) observed: 'the helpless infant will do *everything within its powers* (italics added) to preserve itself, i.e. to maintain its close association with the mother'. But what can a 'helpless infant' actually do?

The human baby has minimal physical abilities with which to hold on to an adult. A human baby can't walk, chase, grab, fly or even see properly. But human babies have the ability to sense moods and feelings, and they quickly learn which of their behaviours not only bring their attachment figure physically near, but also make her or him attentive and engaged. Being able to call for this attention and engagement at a time of distress or danger is a matter of survival for an infant; so the behaviour that engages their attachment figure soon becomes deeply imbedded in the baby's mind to mean safe, protected, loved, happy. This imbedded link between the deeply contented state of a baby in the arms of their attachment figure and a particular behaviour becomes one's life-long attachment mode.

Most parents instinctively (Liotti, 2017) engage with a very wide range of their babies' behaviour: laughs, cries, feeding, discoveries, illness, anger, play, distress and a hundred others all elicit parental attention. Subsequently, most babies develop a wide range of emotional states and behaviours and are eager to continue to widen their range of experience, knowing that their attachment figure will follow. This is the basis for secure attachment, which implies, in turn, that the child can safely be who he or she really is and develop a healthy sense of identity or Self.

Some parents, however, are limited by their own emotional handicaps and can only engage with a narrow range of the baby's feelings and behaviour.[8] The narrower the parental range, the less secure the attachment.

As the parental engagement is essential for the infant's survival, the infant does 'everything within its powers': that is, adjusts his or her behaviour to fit the parent's narrow range of responsiveness. Such a baby is not free to develop his or her own identity, because their responses and behaviour must stay within the range of tolerance of the attachment figure – even if that behaviour is in itself distressing, frightening or painful.

While the self-harmers in the first group must also have had a relatively narrow range of responses from their attachment figures, which accounts for their very negative view of themselves, their emotional pain and the drastic acts that they have to take in order to liberate themselves and 'make a claim' over their body in such a harsh way. Fortunately, however, that range was wide enough to allow them to retain sufficient Self or identity to be able to rebel.

The attachment figures of Group 2, by contrast, were only able to be fully engaged in moments of extreme intensity of negative emotions, such as rage, fear, sadism, pain, violence, sexual aggression, despair or suicidality. At other times they are distracted, unresponsive, self-absorbed, irritable or just distant. The child of such a parent, by necessity, spends much of his or her life in the shadow of such emotions. In particular, when the child is scared or distressed, their attachment needs will force them to fit into the only behaviour which strikes a chord and creates a deep connectedness with the attachment figure. In the case of an attachment figure who is only moved by extreme negative emotions, the child will have to invoke these emotions in the parent. This means that when the child is in distress, he or she will have no choice but to become a victim or a perpetrator of serious crime, in pain or in rage, suicidal or the silent recipient of abuse. Each of these roles is an *infanticidal attachment behaviour*[9] of a child who is desperately trying to engage an attachment figure in a moment of high distress. And each of these roles can be fulfilled by severe and bizarre self-harm.

These behaviours may endure even when the attachment figure is not watching or is not even alive (Sachs, 2017). This is because in the child's mind (for all the years to come, into the child's adulthood) there is that deeply imbedded connection between the specific attachment behaviour (i.e. severe and bizarre self-harm) and a feeling of peace, contentment and safety that came because the attachment figure became fully engaged. Olivia even called this 'feeling elated'.

Means

The two categories of self-harmers also diverge regarding the *means* for carrying out their self-harm.

For Group 1, the means (i.e. what makes them able to commit the act of self-harm) is moments of heightened *motive:* when the bad feelings (shame, self-hate, pain, 'deadness') become very intense, the urge to feel better is like a powerful wave that carries them into the act.

Conversely, Group 2 has usually no idea why they do it, or even that they are actually doing it. This is because the means for committing severe and bizarre self-harm is profound dissociation. James felt only confused when

Table 11.1 Self-harm: motive, means and opportunity

	Most self-harm	Severe and unusual self-harm
Motive	Pressing urge to remedy pain, numbness or badness	Pressing need to engage an infanticidal attachment figure
	Claiming ownership of one's body and Self	
Means	Intensity of distress	Profound dissociation
Opportunity	Readily available, as the perpetrator and the victim are the same person (or share one body)	

asked why had he just hit a table, and seemed quite unaware of the pain of all his broken bones. And in Olivia, the Self who committed the act was completely separate from the pain of the Self who was being hurt, as well as from the fear, horror or common sense which might had been felt by other selves (and might have stopped the act).

The extreme levels of pain of such self-harm, the brutal sadism, the total disregard for the body's future and the very close brush with death which characterise these kinds of self-harm can only be endured through the means of profound dissociation, such as in severe DID.[10]

Opportunity

For committing any kind of self-harm the *opportunity* is readily available, because the victim and the perpetrator are one and the same person (or at least share one body). The perpetrator is thus always physically close to the victim, and both are often unobserved. The two categories of self-harm are identical in this respect.

Conclusions

The difficulties in diagnosing DID in children mean that many children with the disorder are not identified, and subsequently are not treated appropriately. Some of them may have to wait many years before they receive a correct diagnosis and treatment. Others never receive it at all. Not being treated has grave consequences for a child's mental and physical health, and sometimes life. It is thus important to find additional indicators for the disorder in children.

In this chapter, I have highlighted severe and bizarre self-harm as a potential indicator for DID. This suggestion is based on (a) clinical observations, which show frequent connection between this type of self-harm and DID; (b) the fact that such self-harm requires deep dissociation in order for a person to be able to actually perform it; and (c) comparing *most self-harm* behaviour with the *severe and bizarre* type, based on the *means, motive* and *opportunity* for each of the crimes. While the *opportunity* is the same for both types, they are qualitatively different with regard to their *means* and *motives*. The ability to distinguish clearly between the two groups can thus allow us to use the severe and bizarre presentation of self-harm as an indicator of profound dissociation and likely DID.

Postscript: Olivia and James

Olivia died, aged 20.

James is now 35. He's had a lot of psychiatric input over the years, but his DID has never been diagnosed or treated. He suffers serious, chronic health problems, some of which are related to his self-harm and some to his childhood abuse. He also suffers from the chaos of a life managed by many alters, some of which are intent on harming the others; the persistent mental anguish of some of his alters; and frequent suicidal despair. Remarkably, he has not lost hope. He is still searching for – in his words – 'the **right** kind of help'. I'd like to hope that our moments of attunement may have been a factor in his continual search over the following decades.

Notes

1. The DSM 5 points out (p. 294) several conditions, including leaving home and having children, which may cause 'psychological decompensation' and bring about the full-blown presentation of DID and the appearance of distinct personalities. As these conditions are normally linked to growing up, their absence contributes to the difficulties in diagnosing children.
2. The DSM 5 quotes a figure of 70% for suicide attempts amongst people with DID.
3. All identifying details have been changed.
4. DID is a trauma-based rather than a psychotic disorder (APA, 2013).
5. Another difference is that people with DID often continue to self-harm into their adulthood, which isn't common in other self-harmers. Identifying severe self-harm in adults can thus also support the diagnosis in adults. However, as this chapter is concerned with the more pressing need for indicators of DID in children, I will not elaborate on this point.
6. Severe and bizarre self-harm may occur in psychosis too, as does dissociation. The clinician needs to consider whether the overall symptom picture is better explained by psychosis (primarily Schizophrenia) or by DID.
7. In some species, where the new-borns are not raised by the mother the attachment is to a flock, shoal or siblings. In species where the mother normally raises the young but is absent, they will treat a substitute (even from a different species) as a surrogate mother.
8. For further discussion of disorganised attachment and its sub-divisions, see Kahr (2007), Sachs (2007, 2011, 2013a, 2013b, 2013c, 2017).
9. See Kahr (2007), Sachs (2007, 2011, 2013a, 2013b, 2013c, 2017).
10. See also endnote 6.

References

American Psychiatric Association. (1980). *Diagnostic and Statistical Manual of Mental Disorders*, Third Edition. Arlington, VA: American Psychiatric Association.
American Psychiatric Association. (2013). *Diagnostic and Statistical Manual of Mental Disorders*, Fifth Edition. Arlington, VA: American Psychiatric Association.
Kahr, B. (2007). The Infanticidal attachment, pp. 305–309 in *Attachment: New Directions in Psychotherapy and Relational Psychoanalysis,* 1(3).
Liotti, G. (2017). Conflicts between motivational systems related to attachment trauma: Key to understanding the intra-family relationship between abused children and their abusers, pp. 304–318. *Journal of Trauma and Dissociation, (18)*3.
Sachs, A. (2007). Infanticidal attachment: Symbolic and concrete, pp. 297–304. *Attachment: New Directions in Psychotherapy and Relational Psychoanalysis,* 3.
Sachs, A. (2011). As thick as thieves, or the ritual abuse family: An attachment perspective on a forensic relationship, pp. 75–82 in V. Sinason (Ed.), *Attachment, Trauma and Multiplicity, second edition*. Hove: Brunner-Routledge.
Sachs, A. (2013a). Intergenerational transmission of massive trauma: The Holocaust. In J. Yellin & O. Bedouk-Epstein (Eds.), *Terror Within and Without: Attachment and Disintegration: Clinical Work on the Edge*. London: Karnac.
Sachs, A. (2013b). Boundary modification in the treatment of people with Dissociative Disorder, pp. 159–169. *Journal of Trauma and Dissociation, (14)*2.
Sachs, A. (2013c). Still being hurt: The vicious cycle of dissociative disorders, attachment and ongoing abuse, pp. 90–100. *Attachment: New Directions in Psychotherapy and Relational Psychoanalysis, (7)*1.
Sachs, A. (2017). Through the lens of attachment relationship: Stable DID, active DID and other trauma-based mental disorders, pp. 319–339. *Journal of Trauma and Dissociation, (18)*3.
Schreiber, F. R. (1974). *Sybil*. New York: Warner Books.
Suttie, I., & Suttie, J. (1932). The mother: Agent or object?, pp. 199–233. *British Journal of Medical Psychology,* 12.
Thigpen, C. H., & Cleckley, H. M. (1957). *The Three Faces of Eve*. New York: McGraw-Hill.

Chapter 12

I didn't know where you were

In the play space of treatment with a young dissociative boy

Eva Teirstein Young

Playing

> It is in playing and only in playing that the individual child or adult is able to be creative and to use the whole personality, and it is only in being creative that the individual discovers the self....
>
> (Winnicott, 1971, p. 54)

Children express themselves through action. Engaged in play children experience freedom of expression without judgment. Through play they explore conflicting feelings, and gain a sense of control in their lives (Landreth, 2001). Play is a child's "most natural of all activities" (Gil, 2010). Through play, children express thoughts, feeling states and sensations that can't be put into words. Babies and toddlers play peek-a-boo with their caregivers, then hide and seek with their playmates. Whether playing house, restaurant or fairy land children explore different ways of being while trying on different roles.

But not all children are able to play successfully. Early in her career, Arietta Slade (1994) was surprised at the chaotic play of her young patients. She found that the therapist working with disorganized children must be able to simply play. Therapists can be "organizing, enhancing and engaged play partners" (p. 81) when they suspend interpretation and engage in the play itself. Meaning is discovered as it develops in the play space.

> Psychotherapy is done in the overlap of the two play areas, that of the patient and that of the therapist. If the therapist cannot play, then he is not suitable for the work. If the patient cannot play, then something needs to be done to enable the patient to be able to play, after which psychotherapy can begin.
>
> (Winnicott, 1971 p. 54)

Winnicott cautions clinicians about inhibiting play with interpretations "the patient's creativity can be only too easily stolen by a therapist who knows too much" (p. 57). The play space itself holds the potential for growth, meaning and hope.

Attachment and play

Human beings instinctively seek help and comfort from familiar members of their social group (Bowlby 1969, 1979, 1982). A child falls, and looks for mommy. A frightened child grasps onto a parent's hand. Children with secure attachments develop trust that their adults will be reliable when they are in need of care.

Healthy attachments lead to the child feeling recognized and known in a meaningful way. When the environment is consistent, children are able to experience and express a range of affects while maintaining a sense of continuity in the world of self and others. A sense of cohesiveness develops through intimate interactions with a caregiver that are gratifying, disappointing, dramatically sad and gleefully exciting.

The infant's ability to survive depends on the mother's ability to respond to its needs (Winnicott, 1965). The secure, omnipotent infant cries and squeals, creating the reliable mother who understands his expressions and the play space begins to develop between them.

Securely attached children sense that they are a whole person in relation to other whole persons in relation to the larger world. They will develop skills for regulation, words for communication and a flexible repertoire of language and imagery that informs their play.

Trauma disrupts attachment bonds and impedes a child's natural use of play. The play of the simultaneously approaching and retreating disorganized/disoriented child (Main & Solomon, 1986) tends to lack structure and is difficult to follow. These children need their mother yet they are fearful of her at the same time. The child with a disorganized attachment style will create situations that seem to trap everyone around him in impossible predicaments.

A disorganized pattern of attachment combined with early childhood chronic trauma is a precursor to dissociation (Liotti, 2009). When a child is told that unbearable pain must be kept secret from the people that he or she instinctively goes to for help, the child becomes bewildered and disoriented. The traumatized, disorganized child is not able to make coherent sense of himself. His experiences remain unthinkable. We see a child who has difficulty remembering events and day to day thoughts and feelings, we see a child who doesn't feel real, we see a child who lacks the ability to speak coherently, we see a child who repeats grim, unchangeable scenarios in play (Terr, 1990) or who exhibits quick shifts in affect. We see a child who finds himself in one solution-less predicament after another. These are some of the signs and symptoms of dissociation.

The dissociative continuum

Children dissociate easily. Dissociation can be an adaptive, creative response and is helpful to a child who cannot escape a terrifying situation. It can also become a pattern of responding long after it is necessary causing serious problems at home, school and in relationships (Silberg, 2013, Waters 2016, Yehuda, 2016).

> Dissociation...is a basic process that allows individual self-states to function optimally (not simply defensively) when full immersion in a single reality, a single strong affect, and a suspension of one's self-reflective capacity is exactly what is called for or wished for...In other words, dissociation is primarily a means through which a human being maintains personal continuity, coherence and integrity of the sense of self.
>
> (Bromberg, 1998 p. 273)

Dissociation is a normal aspect of mind and brain functioning. When trauma is experienced repeatedly, normal processes of dissociation become pathological and the mind becomes structured by dissociation (Itzkowitz, 2015).

Problematic dissociation is considered mild, moderate or severe. Dissociative children and adolescents present symptoms that interfere with daily living and cohesive development, including trance states, autobiographical forgetfulness, fluctuations in attention and knowledge, inconsistent memory and changes in mood and behavior. Dissociative Identity Disorder is the most extreme form of dissociation. A diagnosis of DID includes the presence of self-states, sometimes called parts or ways of being. These distinct ways of being the child hold separate feelings, behaviors and memories. Also prevalent in DID are depersonalization, de-realization and severe difficulties with regulation (International Society for the Study of Dissociation, 2004).

Self-states or ways of being

Children with healthy attachments will move from one affect state to another, cranky, alert, sleepy, hungry, while sustaining a continuous sense of themselves in relation to others. This is a hallmark of healthy development. Traumatized children are unable to develop this internal flexibility. They develop fear-based states related to state-dependent memories. These discrete behavioral states (Putnam, 1997) create a system of dis-regulation and separateness. Furthermore, in severe dissociation, children may not be aware of the different self-states inside making it impossible to think about emotionally charged experiences in a coherent way (Silberg, 2013).

Dissociative parts control both awareness and behavior, disrupting identity while keeping feelings and somatic sensations from ongoing awareness. One self-state will not be aware of the experience of another. If one self-state experiences abuse, another self-state can function without knowledge of the experience or the resulting emotions.

Shifting self-states can be confusing and enraging for a parent who does not know what is happening inside the child. The child and the caregiver are often unaware of the protective motivations of an aggressive, defiant part. Often a volatile self-state still believes traumatic events are ongoing. This part of the child is in a constant state of alert to danger from others. Psycho-education about dissociation is critical in developing the understanding, cooperation and respect needed for successful healing across all self-states.

Young children have not developed the capacity to manage intense fear and pain. They cannot remove themselves from threatening situations by themselves and they cannot comprehend why nobody is coming to the rescue. Just as the most important task for the infant is to develop a secure attachment, the traumatized child's need to preserve attachment bonds becomes paramount (Silberg, 2013).

Traumatized children are vigilant for the slightest signs of danger. Even a subtle change of expression on a parent's face can seem threatening. Anger threatens the attachment bond. The child's fear heightens his alert system, which triggers the presence of a controlling perpetrator/protector self-state, pulling the child and the caregiver into the spiraling pattern of approach and retreat that renders them all helpless (Potgieter-Marks, 2012).

Treatment

The play space of therapy offers a child and parent the opportunity to be valued across all self-states within the context of a consistent relationship. The earlier the dissociative defenses are recognized the more the child is able to reach across dissociative barriers developing a more cohesive, age-appropriate sense of self and others (Silberg, 2013).

In a treatment room that supports free expression and hope, parent and child can create meaningful connections to past relational experiences that have contributed to the child's emotional and social difficulties (Waters, 2016). When a therapist is curious and interested in what is being created, the child can develop alternate coping strategies, learning to regulate emotions while also identifying resources in the world (Gil, 2010).

The therapist becomes attuned to the cues of dissociation. Eyes blink, a brief turn of the head, disruption in the play, a faint "accidental" image in a drawing, a growl in the midst of a conversation. The sensitive therapist will invite all the ways of being into the play space, while also allowing the child to set the pace (Waters, 2016).

The capacity to use language develops along with attachment bonds (Yehuda, 2016). Traumatized children who have experienced attachment ruptures typically have difficulty using words effectively. Art making can provide the bridge for communication while also reflecting affect, creating links to history and inviting projections of wishes (Spring, 2001). Communicating through pictures bolsters the abused child's capacity to assert control (Cohen & Cox, 1995). When traumatized children struggle to find the words, they often tell me, "I can draw it better".

In the sessions described below, a severely dissociated young boy and his parents discover the dynamics underlying the child's internal dissociative system. The therapist responded with attunement, respect and acceptance as together, they reached into the play space where the potential for attachment, repair and making meaning was waiting.

Andrew

Andrew came to his first weekly psychotherapy session soon after his fifth birthday. His family moved to the United States after learning that he had been victimized by an organized child pornography ring that reportedly targeted families in their tightly knit neighborhood. Andrew, a bright, intellectually gifted boy, reported that he had been taken from school repeatedly beginning at three or four years old. He described physical, emotional and sadistic abuse. Aside from threats against talking about the abuse, he was told that his Mommy and Daddy were not his real parents and that the abuse, which also targeted Andrew's sense of cultural norms, had been condoned.

Andrew's symptoms included violent outbursts, lashing out suddenly at peers and siblings, nightmares and difficulty with bowel and bladder control. He seemed to ignore people when they spoke, he often appeared to be in a daze and he began to disregard cultural rituals that he had always taken part in with his family. Andrew insisted he had magical strengths that kept him from feeling pain. Frightened and concerned, the family re-located to pursue psychotherapeutic treatment with someone specializing in pathological dissociation.

Accompanied by his mother, Andrew entered my office for his first session. He was curious and engaged. His small body explored the office and art materials. He read a child's book with precocious inflection. Then he noticed large toy animals on the shelf and suddenly began to violently throw plastic elephants and dinosaurs against each other. He stopped, asked for more animals and carefully organized them into a line (Figure 12.1). We sat in stillness together observing the line of creatures. I turned to Andrew. He looked into my eyes, tilted his head to the side and put his thumb in his mouth, staring as if in a trance. I looked back into his eyes and gently said,

Figure 12.1 Animals organized into a line

"hello". He added a few more animals to the line, climbed onto his mother's lap and continued to suck his thumb while silently twirling his hair with his other hand. After a short rest he returned to his play. Alliances with parts can begin to form in the first session. In this first session Andrew showed me his curious, competent self, a way of being that is powerful and angry, and a passive infant self-state who can utilize his responsive mother for soothing.

Thumby and Water

Andrew told me about Thumby and Water. He seemed to be describing Stephen Porges' Polyvagal Theory (2011) as he explained that Water alerts Andrew to danger. Water lives in Andrew's feet and tells him when something is scary. When danger is sensed, Water travels from his feet up a wire (Figure 12.2). When Water reaches Andrew's neck he can decide which self-state will help him to regulate. He can choose Thumby, who sucks his thumb and twirls his hair, or another way of being Andrew that has more power. Andrew explained that sometimes he gets a "Topsey-Tangle" in his head. Thumby helps him to bury the Topsey-Tangle in his hair. He said, "it makes me take more time to remember what I thought". I had met Thumby in our first session (Figure 12.3).

I'm not a bad guy

When Andrew was six, his mother had a baby. His father accompanied him to the play space. At this time Andrew's family was trying to manage a particular self-state named Flared-Up-Anger (Figure 12.4). Andrew told us that Flared-Up-Anger is "always mad, even when there is nothing to be angry at. His whole body is red, red, red, even his hands". He explained

Figure 12.2 Water part for if something is scary

that Flared-Up-Anger does bad things – like earlier that week when he poured milk on the floor, threatened his mother with a knife and almost hurt the baby. Andrew told me that he felt "embarrassed" and this made the part inside angrier. It took over his whole body. There was no time to think. And it is contagious! Mommy gets Flared-Up-Anger too. Then Andrew becomes very confused and thinks Mommy is a bad guy, "look at you. You're a bad guy. Look at your face! You're a fake Mommy! You're going to kill me!" Then nobody knows what to do. Everyone becomes stuck in the Topsey-Tangle. Typical of a child with disorganized attachment, Andrew was unable to mobilize when he felt threatened by his mother's reaction to his behavior and he also needed her for regulation and soothing at the same time. Flared-Up-Anger came in with a fury to protect Andrew from perceived dangers and from intense feelings inside, especially shame.

> The oscillation occurs because the rageful self-state can only be maintained briefly before fear of abandonment or annihilation triggers the idealizing self-state, which in turn, can only be maintained for a short while before fear of vulnerability triggers the rageful state.
>
> (Howell, 2014. p. 57)

Figure 12.3 Thumby

Figure 12.4 Flared-Up-Anger

Figure 12.5 Flared-Up-Anger feelings outside of body

He drew pictures about the part. Disavowing the somatic sensations that contribute to a whole unified self, Andrew did not include his red, angry body in his drawings. Flared-Up-Anger does to others before they can do to Andrew. There is no time for Andrew to think about what he needs. Fear, shame and rage take over. These are the feelings that activate the way of being him that is expressed through Flared-Up-Anger. These feelings are simply too big to fit into Andrew's little body (Figure 12.5).

He wrote the name of the self-state on the dry erase board in what he called "Flared-Up-Anger letters" and included his growl (Figure 12.6).

Then he drew a picture of Flared-Up-Anger, with no body (Figure 12.7).

I invited Andrew to show us what it is like to be Flared-Up-Anger. He clenched his fists, grit his teeth and growled. He yelled really loud, "I'm a good guy. I'm not a bad guy! A good boy, not a bad guy!" His father joined him in the play. The two of them grit their teeth and clenched their fists and roared as if their entire bodies were filled with Flared-Up-Anger.

Playing and pretending to be this self-state is much different than switching to the Flared-Up-Anger way of being. Andrew was beginning to work on repairing the dissociative split between his mind and his body. Before leaving the session, he added a body to his drawing (Figure 12.8).

I didn't know where you were 189

Figure 12.6 (Drawing re-created)

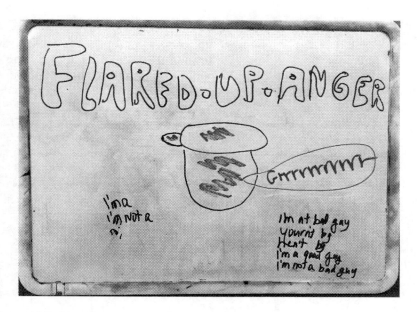

Figure 12.7 (Drawing re-created)

Figure 12.8 (Drawing re-created)

Mommy and Andrew

Meanwhile, emotional eruptions were increasing at home. While Andrew and his father were discovering affects and self-states in sessions, Andrew was also re-experiencing feelings of vulnerability and terror from a time when he desperately needed his mother and he did not know where she could be. I asked his mother to return to the play space.

Andrew walked into the office while his mother was parking the car. I noticed what appeared to be a wet tear on his cheek. He sat down on the floor and started to draw a picture of a map. Drawing maps had become a way for him to organize and orient. Andrew's mother joined us and sat next to her son. When she reached out, he defiantly pushed her hand away. She told me that she had left him in the car for a moment to pay the parking meter and when she returned Andrew was sobbing and kicking his feet, refusing to open the door.

Andrew looked up from his drawing, "I didn't know where you went, I didn't know where you were". He had brought us to the core of the conflict. Andrew returned to drawing, his agitation escalating. He tried to erase a mistake with his finger; instead, he made holes in the paper. "Now you've wasted time telling Eva what happened. I want the time back!"

He stomped to the far end of the room and sat on the floor, his back to us. The holes in his red map were beginning to resemble eyes (Figure 12.9).

I didn't know where you were 191

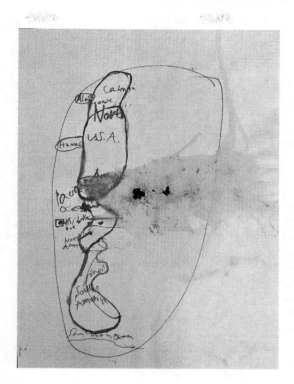

Figure 12.9 Andrew's Map

His mother sat near Andrew on the floor. Soon we had formed a small circle. I noticed that I felt like I could not move. This awareness alerted me to what might be happening. "Andrew, we're stuck! It's just like we were talking about with Daddy. You got stuck and now we are all stuck in the Topsey-Tangle!" He turned and looked at me with recognition. I wondered if we could tell Mommy what we knew about Flared-Up-Anger and what happens when Andrew is stuck.

Together we explained that when Water alerts him that there is something scary, Flared-up-Anger suddenly takes over his entire body. Andrew added, "that's when I do the things I do". We told Mommy that Andrew becomes ashamed of what he has done and Flared-Up-Anger becomes even more agitated because that's a hard feeling to manage. Then Mommy gets angry and Andrew feels scared and vulnerable. Then Flared-Up-Anger says things to mommy like, "You are a bad guy. You are going to kill me". That scares Andrew, his mommy and his entire family. Everyone gets stuck in the Topsey-Tangle and the whole thing starts all over again.

Andrew's mother smiled with relief, "That is what happens all of the time". Something was beginning to make sense. Once the self-state's role in avoiding affect was addressed there was a calm, related feeling in the room. I asked Andrew, "What do you need from Mommy right now?" He thought before asking.

ANDREW: Where are you when I go to school?
MOMMY: I go to work
ANDREW: But where *are* you?

Mommy looked perplexed.

EVA: Mommy, Andrew needs the details.

Mommy proceeded to tell him all about her week beginning with bringing her children to school on Monday. She told him where she works, what she does and who she works with. She did the same thing for every day of the week. As Andrew took in every word, his foot, which had been curled underneath him, slowly emerged, stretching across the space between him and his mother until it rested against her ankle. Mom smiled and continued to give details about her week. They laughed when she told him that she tells the man at the grocery store to wait to deliver the groceries until she gets home from picking Andrew up at school. Like a child who has enjoyed the most gratifying play with a grown-up, he asked her to tell him again. Which she did and they laughed together again.

Andrew and his mother had moved from being stuck in a place of doing, undoing and not knowing toward a place that was thinkable and knowable. As he reached his little foot toward his mother and joined her in the grocery store man chorus, he was connected to himself and to his mother at the same time. They were beginning to play, stepping into the transitional space that held the potential for deep connection and love, while also allowing for separation and autonomy (Winnicott, 1971).

Andrew returned to his drawing. Mommy told us that she needed to put money in the parking meter. He nodded as she left and then looked toward me. It was time for the therapist to simply play.

"Andrew, do you want to watch Mommy from the window?" He ran to the couch by the window overlooking a courtyard that exits to the street outside my ground floor office. Standing on the couch we waited for Mommy to emerge from the vestibule door.

I playfully anticipated, "Where is Mommy? keep watching...she's coming soon". Suddenly she appeared. "There she is!" we announced. Andrew waved and knocked on the window. Mommy waved back, running toward the sidewalk where she disappeared behind the courtyard wall. "Where'd she go"? Andrew and I looked at each other with dramatized concern. For a moment she reappeared in between an opening in the wall, "There she is. Hi Mommy!" She vanished again, finally returning to the courtyard and waved before disappearing into the vestibule.

Excited and grinning from ear to ear, Andrew leapt off the couch, flung open the office door and ran down the hall just as she was coming through the door. He jumped into her arms with glee, "MOMMY!" They embraced. Mommy carried him down the hallway until he slid down to the floor and together they walked back into the office. With a loud sigh of relief, they sank into the couch together, reunited in the play space. Andrew began to breathe long, calm breaths. From my chair across from them I began to match Andrew's long inhales and exhales. I knew that this calm sense of security could change at any moment.

> Play is immensely exciting. It is exciting not primarily because the instincts are involved, be it understood! The thing about playing is always the precariousness of the interplay of personal psychic reality and the experience of control of actual objects. This is the precariousness of magic itself, magic that arises in intimacy, in a relationship that is found to be reliable.
>
> (Winnicott, 1971, p. 47)

A growl emerged from his breath. The session was ending. The realities of the world outside were beginning to impinge on the play space. Flared-Up-Anger was on alert. I acknowledged the presence of self-states, "Now it's time for all the ways of being Andrew who go to school to come forward. All the ways who are not helpful at school need to please step back so Andrew can continue to have a successful day. You are welcome to return next week". It had become routine for us to end sessions this way, orienting the parts inside, reminding all his ways of being that they are welcome to return to the play space.

Andrew cuddled against his Mommy. "I wish we could sit like this all the way home in the car". Mommy suggested that they could sit closer to each other if he moved to the middle seat from his seat in the back. This was too much for his delicately regulated, obsessive system to bear and he began to cry, "that's not my seat! I can't sit there!" Feeling protective of the bond that had just been strengthened, I announced, "How about a string? Andrew, you hold one end from your seat in back and Mommy you hold the other while you're driving. You will be connected by the string". While much repair had been done in this session, Andrew's confidence in his ability to feel held in his mother's mind was still fragile (Fonagy et al., 2002). Andrew responded, "I want a wire". Realizing the significance of the wire that provides the path for the part called Water and in awe of the symbolic umbilical cord, I brought him a package of different colored strands of long soft, pliable wire. I tied the pieces together until it was about 12 feet long. Mommy took one end, Andrew took the other and together they left my office, practically skipping down the hallway.

When they returned the following week they had a funny story to tell. Mommy, pre-occupied with holding her end of the wire, forgot to put on her seatbelt. A policeman stopped the car and gave her a ticket. Andrew proudly told me that he first thought that the cop was a bad guy. But then, he thought again! He remembered that the bad guys were far, far away and a long time ago. He was safe *now*. It is important to emphasize the *then* and the *now* whenever the opportunity arises (Silberg, 2013).

In this session meaning making began with the words, "I didn't know where you were". Andrew then moved away from his mother, this time being the one to initiate the separation which would lead to a series of separations and reunions during the session. Turning his back on Mommy and therapist, reaching his foot to rest on Mommy's foot, watching Mommy disappear and re-appear like a game of peek-a-boo, opening the office door and jumping into his mother's arms, walking beside her to the couch and finally maintaining a connection with a wire that left enough distance for both mother and child to exist together and apart at the same time.

When Andrew saw the policeman approach the car, he initially responded to familiar internal cues alerting him to danger. However, he did not have to go into a trance and bury the Topsey-tangle in his hair. He had just, in a sense, gone back to a time when babies explore object constancy, Mommies are reliable, and separations and reunions are repeatedly practiced (Mahler, 1975). During this session, the Topsey-Tangle that had previously made it impossible for Andrew to think began to unravel.

Continuity

Months later, accompanied by his father, Andrew continued to explore attachment themes, this time in the sand tray. He built a tower of plastic lions (Figure 12.10). In size order, with the largest lion standing as a base, he placed one lion on top of the other, squeezing the legs of a smaller lion over the back of the one before. He struggled to create a secure base with the first two figures. His father watched from across the room. I sat next to Andrew as he squeezed and pushed, attempting to fit one lion onto the other's back. With a halting, pressured tone Andrew stammered, "this one…" he pushed some more. "this one is attached …" then some more struggle, "this one is attached to…"

He asked me to help. My grown-up hands joined the two lions for him at the base and he continued to play, pushing more lions on to the one before while at the same time pushing out words until they started to flow like

Figure 12.10 Tower of lions

a song. "His...his daddy...um...so, his daddy is attached to his daddy, his daddy is attached...he's attached to his daddy, his grandfather is attached to his daddy, his great grandfather is attached to his ancestor who is 120 years old". Andrew chuckled with joy as he gestured to the smallest lion that he had connected to his Daddy's tail. "oh...look at him!" he cried with endearment. "Look at him, attached to his Daddy" I responded.

I was struck with his emotional and physical exertion, initially pressured in struggle before releasing into playful rhythm. His tower of lions communicated a sense of continuity and history, culminating with Andrew's expression of joy and compassion for his little self.

He turned to his father, smiled at him and turned back to the sand. Andrew was discovering a meaningful, lively self in relation to others in his family.

I wondered aloud, "Andrew, we've been talking a lot about the bad guys. Who are the good guys?"

ANDREW: You...and Mommy and Daddy, my sisters and brother and Aunt Jenny, my friends and my teachers...

EVA: There are so many good guys *now*. What does it feel like to know you are with the good guys?
ANDREW: Like you are a person. Like you are a person that is really, really, really alive. That *I* am an alive person!

We often talk about "the session with Mommy". When it comes up Andrew recalls his feelings about the broken map and laughs about the grocery store man. We also remember how Mommy began to understand about the Flared-Up-Anger way of being Andrew. He is now communicating more with this part inside. He told me, "There was a time when I listened to it, before I started to talk about it". He recently wrote a letter to Flared-Up-Anger, acknowledging its attempts to be helpful. He also invited this way of being him to think about more constructive ways to be protective. He offered some very practical suggestions. Perhaps, without fear of retribution, and with compassion for himself, Andrew has invited Flared-Up-Anger to play.

References

Bowlby, J. (1969). *Attachment and Loss*. New York: Basic Books.
Bowlby, J. (1979). *The Making & Breaking of Affectional Bonds*. London: Tavistock Publications.
Bowlby, J. (1982). *Attachment*. New York: Basic Books.
Bromberg, P. (1998). *Standing in the Spaces: Essays on Clinical Process Trauma and Dissociation*. Analytic Press.
Cohen, B. M., & Cox, C. T. (1995). *Telling Without Talking: Art as a Window into the World of Multiple Personality*. New York: W.W. Norton.
Fonagy, P., Gergely, G., Jurist, E., & Target, M. (2002). *Affect Regulation, Mentalization and the Development of the Self*. New York: Other Books.
Gil, E. (2010). *Working with Children to Heal Interpersonal Trauma: The Power of Play*. New York: Guilford Press.
Howell, E. F. (2014). Ferenczi's concept of identification with the aggressor: Understanding dissociative structure with interacting victim and abuser states, pp. 48–59. *The American Journal of Psychoanalysis*, 74.
International Society for the Study of Dissociation. (2004). Guidelines for the evaluation and treatment of dissociative symptoms in children and adolescents, pp. 119–150. *Journal of Trauma and Dissociation*, 5(3).
Itzkowitz, S. (2015, May). *Engaging the Extremely Dissociated Patient: Anger, Aggression, and Self-harm*. Presented at the EDCAS Program of William Alanson White Institute. New York.
Landreth, G. L. (2001). *Innovations in Play Therapy: Issues, Process and Special Populations*. Philadelphia, PA: Brunner-Routledge.
Liotti, G. (2009). Attachment and dissociation, pp. 53–65. In Dell, P. F. & O'Neil, J. A (Eds), *Dissociation and the Dissociative Disorders: DSM-V and Beyond*. New York: Routledge.
Mahler, M. S. (1975). *The Psychological Birth of the Human Infant: Symbiosis and Individuation*. London: Hutchinson of London.

Main, M., & Solomon, J. (1986). Discovery of an insecure-disorganized/disoriented attachment pattern: Procedures, findings and implications for the classification of behavior, pp. 95–124. In Brazelton, T. B. & Yogman, M. (Eds), *Affective Development in Infancy*. Norwood, NJ: Ablex.

Porges, S. W. (2011). *The Polyvagal Theory: Neurophysiological Foundations of Emotions, Attachment, Communication, and Self-Regulation*. New York: W.W. Norton.

Potgieter-Marks, R. (2012). When the sleeping tiger roars: Perpetrator introjects in children, pp. 87–110. In Vogt, R. (Ed), *Perpetrator Introjects: Psychotherapeutic Diagnostics and Treatment Models*. Kroning: Asanger.

Putnam, F. W. (1997). *Dissociation in Children and Adolescents: A Developmental Perspective*. New York: Guilford Press.

Silberg, J. L. (2013). *The Child Survivor: Healing Developmental Trauma and Dissociation*. New York: Routledge.

Slade, A. (1994). Making meaning and making believe: Their role in the clinical process, pp. 81–107. In Slade, A. & Wolf, D. P. (Eds), *Children at Play: Clinical and Developmental Approaches to Meaning and Representation*. New York: Oxford University Press.

Spring, D. (2001). *Image and Mirage: Art Therapy with Dissociative Clients*. Springfield, IL: Thomas.

Terr, L. (1990). *Too Scared to Cry: Psychic Trauma in Childhood*. New York: Harper & Row.

Waters, F. S. (2016). *Healing the Fractured Child: Diagnosis and Treatment of Youth with Dissociation*. New York: Springer Publishing Company.

Winnicott, D. W. (1965). Ego integration in child development, pp. 56–63. In *The Maturational Processes and the Facilitating Environment: Studies in the Theory of Emotional Development*. Connecticut: International Universities Press.

Winnicott, D. W. (1971). *Playing and Reality*. London: Tavistock Publications.

Yehuda, N. (2016). *Communicating Trauma: Clinical Presentations and Interventions with Traumatized Children*. New York: Routledge.

Chapter 13

A journey of discovery

Joy Hasler

Nadine stood in front of me holding the card I had given her. 'Can he read?' she asked me. I told her that I thought he probably couldn't. She replied 'because he is asking me to read it to him'. This was a lightbulb moment for me when I realised that I could communicate with one of her alter parts.

In 1996 I was working with Nadine, age 12, and her mother Chris as part of my music therapy practice with adoptive families. Nadine talked about having two people in her head, or sitting on her shoulders, telling her what to do. One (male) would tell her to hurt people and the other (female) would tell her to do kind things for people. I realised that I needed to find out about this phenomenon so I set out on a journey that has engaged me ever since.

My experience of childhood trauma was as a foster carer, an adopter and a music teacher in a special school for children with emotional and behavioural difficulties. I had an understanding of the therapeutic power of rhythm and music-making so I decided to retrain as a music therapist specifically to work with traumatised children in adoptive and foster families. From very early on in my work as a music therapist, I discovered the benefit of working with parents and children together, using rhythms and musical improvisations to help build positive attachment patterns which could lead to developing trust, and healing the negative effects of the children's early trauma. I set up a company called Catchpoint to offer a range of creative therapies for adoptive and foster families who have a child affected by complex trauma. Some parents asked me what good banging drums and painting pictures could do to help their child, but when they saw the impact of the shared creative activities on their child, they accepted the therapy process and worked with us.

My starting point for discovering about dissociation was to talk to other therapists, friends, and read books and articles on 'dissociation'. This opened the door to a whole community of people working and researching in this field. It led to a journey of discovery, and I learned a lot from the families I was working with. I also discovered that there were other psychologists, psychiatrists and therapists of many different disciplines exploring 'dissociation' in the context of working with children with complex trauma

DOI: 10.4324/9781003246541-14

and attachment difficulties. Over the next few years, I met so many people sharing their findings, reassessing their approaches and trying to change the attitude of 'the public' about dissociation. I picked up an excitement in the topic (Perry and Szalavitz 2006; Silberg 1998; Sinason 2010; Weiland 2011; Van der Kolk 2015 and many more).

In my searching I was advised that I could try to befriend angry parts, so I decided to write a short message in a card to the angry part of Nadine, and to thank him for helping to keep Nadine safe when there was no one else looking after her. This led to him asking her to read it to him. When I wrote it, I had no idea that befriending could actually mean communicating directly with this part. I still thought the parts were like imaginary friends – inside her head, and to discover that I could communicate directly was a moment of enlightenment. From then on, I read books and articles on dissociation with a different perspective. Sadly I still hear of professionals telling children suffering from complex trauma that these parts are 'just your imaginary friends' and telling the child that 'we will get rid of them'.

At Catchpoint we have worked with many families and most of the children fit between the scores of 17–27 in the Putnam Child Dissociative Checklist where a score of 12 'should be considered a cut-off above which a dissociative disorder should be suspected' (Putnam, Helmers and Trickett 1993 Volume 17, pp. 731–741). Just looking at the range of questions in the checklist helps parents make sense of the pattern of their children's behaviours, and this is an important part of trauma work.

My personal journey of discovery became quite an adventure, taking me to places around the world as well as many conferences across the UK put on by organisations like ChildTrauma Academy, European Society for Trauma and Dissociation ESTD, Positive Outcomes for Dissociative Survivors PODS, Trauma and Abuse Group TAG and First Person Plural. In all this journey I met enthusiasm, dedication and determination. I undertook a one-year psychotherapy course with International Society for the Study of Trauma and Dissociation (ISSTD) in London led by Remy Aquarone from the Pottergate Centre in Norwich.

In the mid-1990s I set up a group of therapists also working with adoptive families, under the auspices of Adoption UK. We became the 'Rainbow of Adoption Therapies'. The idea was that we could be therapists from a wide range of therapeutic disciplines but that we were working with the common issues shared by many adoptive families – caring for children with attachment difficulties, complex trauma and dissociation. This later became a group called 'Attachment in Action' which organised training and forums about working with the effects of trauma. These therapists have gone on to found some of the current national Adoption Support Agencies, offering therapy, support and information to adoptive and foster families, and from this group have come several publications including a book that I co-edited: *Creative Therapies for Complex Trauma* (Hendry and Hasler 2017).

Dissociation is a spectrum spanning from daydreaming, which we all do, to DID – Dissociative Identity Disorder – with plurality of personality. But it is only a 'disorder' if it is not understood and leads the person into major difficulties which then become disorders. It is not schizophrenia, it is not a serious mental health disorder, it is not a personality disorder, but it is a naturally occurring response of the brain to overwhelming trauma which, if experienced as chronic and complex trauma by a young child or infant, becomes an embedded pattern of protection for that child. Dissociation is a means of surviving the effects of severe early trauma or developmental trauma. As such it should be embraced by the therapist and worked with to encourage integration and understanding for the child and the parents or carers. The difficulties arise when the child's brain instigates protective behaviours for everyday stresses and challenges, preventing trust developing in caring relationships, spoiling potential learning environments and blocking self-regulation. Sadly the symptoms are still often misdiagnosed as a variety of disorders, and then inappropriate support maybe offered.

I learned a lot from the children themselves, such as how freeing it is to emerge from their protective bubbles and engage with the world without continuous fear. This is a continuous journey because there is always ongoing research giving new insights into trauma and dissociation, and different ways to work with dissociative clients, adults, children, youth and families.

Through working with families, I learned that 'normal' parenting strategies of rewards and sanctions or consequences are usually not effective with traumatised children. The child lacks trust in their parents that the promise will be honoured, so to be in control they may need to sabotage the reward offered which is then a puzzle to many parents. Getting a reward or having a nice time also contradicts the negative self-belief of the child. This is the experience of so many families. Many dissociative children cannot associate a consequence that they get as a result of something one part of them did when they are in another part. Then when they say they didn't do it, they are accused of lying. This also makes learning from 'cause and effect' difficult, which is a recognised symptom of early trauma. So most consequences do not have the desired result of teaching the child to behave in a different way. It is important for everyone around the child – parents, teaching staff, club leaders, extended family – to have a common understanding of developmental trauma and the effect on the developing brain so that they can support each other. It is important to appreciate that their experience of the child is not necessarily the whole child, and so by interacting they can put the pieces of the child's jigsaw together. This integration of the people around the child is the start of the process of integration for the child.

So from the start at Catchpoint we worked with children and parents together and built up an informal support network around the family so that parents are understood by their supporters when they don't use conventional parenting strategies. There are many so-called supporters who think they know how they would parent these children, who make comments like: 'all children do that', 'you just need to be firmer', 'have you tried star charts' and more. The dissociative child can have a charm part reserved for these visitors, but the parents see the immature, hurt, angry and controlling parts. Understanding the effects of trauma, including attachment difficulties and dissociation, requires thinking outside the box of behaviourist parenting. This requires a back-to-front way of thinking. Here are just two examples of this. We ask parents to:

1. Refrain from offering rewards to encourage a child to complete a task. Instead offer spontaneous praise in terms of how you feel to help the child realise that he can be responsible for someone else feeling good. This is less likely to trigger a rejection.
    - 'I really enjoyed this afternoon with you'.
    - 'I like that lovely picture you have drawn'.
2. Help a child to feel safe, and avoid shaming the child before any discussion about negative behaviours or any consequences, and never ask 'Why?' (they usually don't know why). Shame is toxic and if triggered it will move the child into fight/flight/freeze mode.

This is backed by Dr Bruce Perry who advises, in his publications and presentations, that the sequence of managing difficult behaviours should be: Regulate > Relate > Reason (Perry 2009, p. 252). This is working lower brain up, instead of top brain down. Top down is the direction of brain activity when an adult tries to explain to a disruptive child what she has done wrong and then deliver a punishment. Instead Bruce Perry recommends:

- help the child feel safe – Regulate
- listen and relate with empathy – Relate
- when the child is relaxed, talk and listen about the whatever had been difficult – Reason

At this point we also advocate using PACE – Playfulness, Acceptance, Curiosity and Empathy (Golding and Hughes 2012, pp. 19–20). This works well with dissociative children as it reduces stress and helps to regulate the child and the parent. If parents and teachers can be helped to understand this sequence then alternative strategies make sense. It is hard for some parents/teachers to move away from the belief that a child must learn from consequences, and should not 'get away with' negative behaviour. But when parents/teachers can understand the underlying messages of the child's behaviours, they can adjust to thinking in a different way and exploring what patterns there are in the child's behaviours, which would then give them insight into which triggers raise anxiety.

Building an informal network of people around the family, which at Catchpoint we refer to as a 'Circle of Support', can make a huge difference to the welfare of a family caring for a traumatised child. I realised that this was essential for many families.

> The more isolated physically and socially a family becomes, the more vulnerable a child becomes. ... The primary therapeutic implication is the need to increase the number and quality of relational interactions and opportunities for the high-risk child. ... The therapeutic approach must address the process of helping to create a 'therapeutic web'. ... This simple but powerful fact appears to underlie the efficacy of intervention models with high-risk children.
> (Perry 2006 p. 46)

My journey of discovery was much enhanced by the young people I was working with. They showed me what it was like to live with dissociation day to day, and how it affects their decision making, their perception of the world around them and all their relationships. Here are some of my learning points from the children themselves.

Sally: In a therapy session we were playing a musical game of follow-the-leader. At the end of each turn, the leader chose the next leader. Sally (age nine) was chosen to be the leader which she enjoyed. I invited her to choose the next leader and she got completely stuck. After several minutes of discussion about how we make choices, she was still stuck. I asked her what was happening for her. She said that the different people inside her each wanted to choose someone different and if she chose someone, then the parts that wanted someone else would be angry.

I learned how difficult it can be for a dissociative child to make choices in so many everyday situations, and how easily this can be misunderstood, at home and at school.

Carrie: I was having a silent written conversation with Carrie (age ten). The written dialogue became quite in-depth, with Carrie telling me about her parts, and which ones caused her trouble and which ones were helpful. Then she wrote: 'Please don't read this out loud because my people can't read and they don't know what I am telling you. They'd be very angry'.

I learned that there are different ways of communicating with different parts and have encouraged parents to have written chats with their children.

Georgie and Kim are two sisters placed for adoption together with their younger brother. The girls had been abused and were dissociative. Their younger brother was not. The girls told us that there was something wrong with him because there is only one of him.

This taught me that parts could connect with each other across from one person to another.

Izzy had several parts who she could talk to. She would ring me up and ask me to speak to Connie, because Connie was worried about what Bella was doing. Could I listen to her? I took the phone and spoke to Connie and listened to her concern that what Bella was doing was not safe for the rest of them. Connie kept an eye on all the other parts and kept some form of stability among them.

I learned that one part could ask for help, and that often there is one part that has an overview of the internal system created by all the parts.

Gary (age 15) was able to talk to me about his parts, but found a younger one difficult to manage. For example, if Gary could play outdoor games the younger part was happy, but if he had to do schoolwork inside then this part could cause him bother.

One day he told me about an incident in a drama class at school when he had got into trouble for running around the hall blowing raspberries. I asked him what had happened before that and he said 'the teacher told us to find a space, shut our eyes and imagine that we were an animal'. I queried 'you were asked to shut your eyes? But you would find that very difficult!'. 'That's right. He said. I can't'. He suddenly connected his behaviour with the fear he had felt when he was asked to shut his eyes in a room full of other students. His younger protective part had taken him on a raspberry blowing trip to protect him from this fear. Sadly, the teacher did not appreciate the fact that three other pupils had copied him. We could then talk about what he could do next time this happened and what he could say to the teacher.

Therapeutic process

The therapy model used at Catchpoint with dissociative children and their parents is based on recognised three-stage trauma recovery models of stabilisation, integration and adaptation which have been documented by several authors (Hasler 2008, table 9.1, p. 172).

From these models, we devised a working four-stage therapy model for Catchpoint.

1 Disorder: the presenting stage – frustrating for parents and their community
2 Reorder: directive activities to establish security and stability – information to parents to increase understanding – developing a therapeutic network for support
3 Reframe: non-directive creative exploration of narrative and story – shared exploration, increasing skills of parents for managing difficulties at home – working with school staff
4 Reconnect: attunement and development of trust – expressing family joy

We discovered that these stages did not roll out in order, but that they cycle with the stage of 'Disorder' returning, causing parents considerable frustration and concern that the therapy was not working. At first we thought that this was a pothole on the path to healing, but we learned that this return to Disorder is a very necessary stage in recovery. In this stage, the child returns to beliefs and behaviours that had kept him safe and discovers that they don't work anymore. The people who love him and care about him are still present. This is frightening for the child who can go into panic mode leading to increased aggression. So when this happens in therapy, we return to 'reorder' stage to reset patterns of stability and increase support for parents before moving on again to the stage of reframing their experiences. We choose therapeutic activities according to where the child presents in the stages of the therapy model.

Key words in our therapy are 'Resonance' and 'Resilience'. How do we resonate with the child's fragmentation, anxiety, lack of trust and fear of being loved and cared for? How do we build up the child's resilience in a world that can be full of tripwires and potholes.

Resonance

It is the science of two frequencies and energies meeting in synchrony which increases their effectiveness. Resonance is about being attuned to the child's inner working model. Finding a way to resonate with a child's trauma without getting caught in a net of disturbance and destruction is an aim we try to help parents understand. We want parents to recognise how scary it is for a child who has suffered trauma and rejection to accept love. The more the child loves you, the greater the fear of being hurt through rejection. So the child fights hard to be in control trying to make happen what they most fear. Resonance is understanding this, using multi-sensory rhythmic patterns of relating playfully, creatively and with nurture. The effects of trauma are hard to resonate with, but worth working towards because when this is achieved the results can be amazing.

Resilience

It is the process of adapting positively in the face of adversity, trauma, tragedy, threats and stress. It is the ability to bounce back from stress and difficult times. Resilience can be developed through recovery from trauma. It is not the absence of stress, but the ability to manage and regulate stress and then recover. Dissociation forms part of resilience for some traumatised people. So we need to work with the dissociation to increase resilience in the areas that are problematic for the child.

Resilience factors include:

- Trusting that there are people who care for you, encourage you and listen to you.
- The ability to plan for the future and be able to put these plans into action.

- A positive view of yourself, and confidence in your strengths and abilities.
- Skills in identifying needs and solving problems.

Therapeutic activities

There are some common elements in therapeutic activities with the families of dissociative children that can be included whatever creative arts or play therapies are used. There are also other verbal based therapy approaches such as DDP that can be integrated with other creative therapy models. There are some that can be useful to parents at home such as Theraplay and NVR. As part of his Neurosequential Model of Therapeutics (NMT), Bruce Perry gives a list of factors, which he believes are required in healing trauma, and these factors can be included in activities at home. These are *relational, relevant, rhythmic, repetitive, rewarding and respectful* (Perry 2007–2018).

With Perry's recommendations in mind, I offer a list of key elements within the therapeutic process whether working on personal narrative, developing attachments or celebrating achievements.

A co-productive parent partnership

A visible partnership between parents and therapist demonstrates to children that the adults trust each other. This involves getting to know the parents before starting therapy, helping them understand their role in therapy and offering them time to talk about difficulties in the family or at home when the child is not present. We recommend that all family sessions have two therapists so that parents and children can be worked with both separately and together as necessary. Working in partnership with parents was explored in research by R. Bullivant who is an adoptive parent. Her PhD thesis was looking at 'the effectiveness of therapeutic interventions for attachment disturbances in children'.

> The use of integrated teams with a variety of specific skills that includes parents as part of the team reduces the risk of diagnosis based exclusively on one model e.g. Psychotherapy, attachment therapy, music therapy, family therapy etc. The needs of the child, parents and therapists can all be best served, and the inclination to become detached can be avoided by working together with mutual respect as an integrated team.
> (Bullivant 2005).

Bridging patterns

Many traumatised children and young people have difficulties with transitions from one space to another, from one activity to another and from one emotional experience to another. Developing bridging patterns at transition points in or at the end of the therapy session can help develop organisational skills, understanding of the sequential aspect of any situation, and increased confidence to manage transitions outside the therapy session. Bridging patterns can vary in length from moments of reflection on what has happened to a short activity with movement, rhythm and/or a chant. But the important thing is that there is a pattern to them. Some families enjoy making up an action for the beginning or end of therapy. These bridging patterns can help families attach and attune.

Reciprocity – turn taking

Turn taking is at the root of all communication – listening and responding. Whatever the mode of therapeutic communication, turn taking helps build up trust. A child with little trust may not believe she will get another turn again, so anxiety is raised. A rhythm of turn taking helps the child develop trust that she will be remembered and will get another turn.

Being heard – through a variety of creative experiences

'Being heard' can be a multi-sensory reflective experience. Sharing music together enables the child to hear that he is being listened to. If the therapist is playing in time with his beat, the child will have the active experience of 'being heard'. Sharing art work is also a form of 'being heard'. Sharing a dance or acting out stories creates space for revelations to be experienced, expressed and expanded on. Being heard is about being held in mind with resonance and respect. It develops self-esteem which is part of resilience.

A guide to asking for help

Dissociative children, when they start coming to therapy, are very anxious about asking for help because they don't trust that their needs will recognised never mind met. Different parts want to take control by telling the therapist what they want. 'Asking' is often seen as a sign of weakness which triggers controlling and dissociative behaviours. This connects to the previous key point of 'being heard'. If you don't believe anyone is listening then you won't believe that it is worth asking for something. Children need guidance about when and who they can ask for help, and also need guidance in understanding what they need. They can be guided to recognise what they need, ask for help and identify the person they need to ask. This can be done in a fun and playful way so that there is no negative element.

Being held in mind

Demonstrating that a child is held in mind is essential to the therapeutic process. This could mean reflecting on or continuing something that happened in the last session, or remembering what the child had been looking forward to and asking how it went – a birthday, a holiday or remembering something that had happened that the child had shared. The message to the child is that he/she exists in the therapist's mind between sessions. Being held in mind in the session is communicated through designing activities to suit the child and family by having an understanding of what they enjoy, what they need and what challenges them. Sessions are prepared for a family with respect for their specific needs. Being held in mind is about recognising the signals and trauma triggers that increase anxiety so that the therapist can respond by helping the child feel safe. This can also demonstrate to parents how to manage difficulties at home.

Multi-sensory experiences

Exploring and creatively using materials that have different textures, different actions, make different sounds and require different amounts of energy with key attachment figures can help develop integration and trust. These experiences can include bilateral coordination which are activities that use both sides of the brain alternately or together, but I also include in this field rocking, drumming and simply fiddling with many different objects and materials. The aim is to use as many different parts of the brain as possible and form links and paths that can help integration. I want a child to be presented with the question 'what can I do with this?' and then to share the result. If it is fun (rewarding) it will motivate the child to join in the activities again which helps build trust that shared positive experiences will be repeated.

MICRO moments

Progress towards healing and development of trust does not come in a smooth path. There are pits and troughs, but these dips can be interspersed with MICRO moments. These mini moments are like seeds which grow into sequences of positive interaction. A MICRO moment is a short time (sometimes only a few seconds) at any time of day which has the following ingredients:

M, Mindfulness; **I**, Insight; **C**, Connection; **R**, Resonance; **O**, Order.

So a MICRO moment is one where the child is held in the adult's mind, with insight into the child's trauma, making empathic connections, resonating with emotional energies and being part of a sequence that gives it order. A smile or sign of recognition can be a MICRO moment. If these moments become patterns then they can link to form the building blocks of trust, integration and resilience. These moments can be 'saved' by parents to draw on when times are difficult to keep a positive perspective on their parenting experience. Together parents and therapists can enjoy looking back on these MICRO moments rather than being overwhelmed by the destructive and dysregulated episodes.

Conclusion

My journey of discovery has taken me to many places and to meet many people. Working with dissociative children and their families requires a good understanding of the global effects of trauma and how these can impact on each child, their family and their education. There can be some common assumptions but generally the therapist needs to gain an understanding of how each child and family experience trauma and dissociation, and prepare the therapy programme accordingly. Each child will be at a different stage of progress which will determine whether activities are directive or non-directive. Each child will have their own triggers to trauma leading to raised anxiety, and then each child will respond differently to these triggers. So, combining key elements from the research of the pioneers in this field, with many different creative media, therapists can help a family develop positive attachment patterns, build family trust, become resilient in the face of future stress factors and increase the child's creative potential.

I will leave the end of this chapter to the voices of the young people and their parents.

Family: parents with three birth sons adopted Bella at age 18 months (now 24)

Bella's story

I wasn't pleased to be attending therapy as a child, but without the support I had I don't believe I would be here now, happily married with my own family and a good job.

I still occasionally switch off and am slightly forgetful at times but that might be to do with having just had a baby.

My past will always be there in some ways, but through therapy and support I have learned ways to cope with any issues which arise now, and my parents still provide support when I want it and ask for it.

My husband is very caring and understanding. I feel most safe when I am with my friends and my family with whom I can be myself.

Bella's parents' story

We looked for help because Bella's extreme behaviours were out of control and outside our experience with our birth children. Her escalating violence both in terms of frequency and extent towards things, herself and us was the catalyst to seeking professional help. At the time we had a strange mixture of shame, desperation, anticipation, apprehension and excitement. We were afraid it would not work and could not see an alternative. It felt empowering to be part of the team and the process. It was inciteful, but also gruelling and exhausting. The accompanying contra-intuitive parenting techniques were difficult. It was frightening and upsetting to be confronted by the depth and effects of the damage caused by her early trauma. Now we view it as a journey of discovery, grateful, proud and relieved that we could see the process through. It was successful and essential. We were guided to good reading material and the parenting techniques remained useful for many years.

Good and continuing feedback regarding specific behaviours and their roots in the trauma reinforced our understanding. There were different layers which needed different inputs at different times.

All our children were offered support on a continuous basis but only the youngest and closest in age to our daughter attended many of the early sessions. All were involved in the 'recovery' process after the 'intensive' process (a therapy week). The relationship with our daughter is now close, positive, mature, reciprocal and loving.

Family: parents adopted three children, Georgie, age nine (now 21) and Kim, age six (now 18) and their younger brother, age five (now 17)

Georgie's story

Initially I was not happy about my parents being in therapy with me. I thought they were 'snitching' on me for when I had behaved badly, making me feel angry. Why were my parents telling other people? With hindsight, having my parents there meant that, subconsciously, I felt safe enough to act the way I did. Once I got used to therapy, I began to enjoy having Dad in the sessions and would sometimes feel upset if he didn't join in, and I now know that this was so I could have space to rant.

Now when I am stressed, at work or feel under pressure, I do forget a lot but I cope with this by writing everything down. I often switch off when I am not interested which I now feel is a natural reaction and not because of my traumatic upbringing (which has been a huge realisation for me). At other times I have felt lost and stuck, but I am now able to recognise that feeling and take sometime out for myself.

I feel safe in several places – work, my flat and back at home. It was important for me to have a flat where I feel comfortable. I am able to separate work and home as I did with school and home. I am surrounded by good people who I can rely on and who will help me if I need it, no matter what.

More often than not, if I am feeling lost or need help, I go back home where I am surrounded by people who know me and understand me.

Georgie's parents' story

Georgie's behaviour was beyond our experience of anyone else and we couldn't understand it. Georgie was clearly distressed by her inner world.

Taking part in therapy was good. Dad particularly enjoyed the journey and taking part. We needed to see that there was a route out and Catchpoint provided this. They did not tell us which way to go, just that there was route. They allowed us to work within a framework which we could understand. Valerie also helped us understand Georgie's different parts with a framework to communicate, then carried on by Catchpoint.

We feel very privileged to be their parents, all three. Their early trauma has contributed to them becoming incredible people with insight into life and other people. They have an awareness of who they are and are proud.

Family: parents with a son and daughter adopted Greg, age seven (now 17) and his younger sister, age five (now 15)

Greg's story

When I started coming to therapy I was nervous about what it would be like. I didn't know if I would be accepted. Now it's fine. I know Joy and feel relaxed. I could mess about and be a six-year-old. She wasn't stern and I felt safe. She is someone who understands me that I can talk to.

I do switch off if I don't understand something, and I often lose things. When I get stressed, I run around and sometimes I can't understand things. Or I hide in screens, then I can switch off. Sometimes when I am on a screen for half an hour it seems like just two minutes.

I feel safe and comfortable when I am at home with our dog. I can ask my Mum and Dad for help, and at school I can ask Miss B. She understands. I've got some good friends now and I like messing about with my big brother.

Greg's mother's story

As a teacher and a parent I felt exhausted and did not understand Greg. I realised that it was beyond me so we needed help to make sure things didn't get worse. He was very different from other kids. He didn't respond to rewards or consequences.

At first going to therapy was a lot of travel but I was impressed with the expertise we found. Joy helped us understand why he was doing something and also what he was not doing – sharing thing and turn taking were hard for him. The journey home was always difficult. Now it's a relief that Greg and I can talk about things together.

We've learned about what happened to his brain, we've helped him understand that he is not stupid and we have strategies. It helped me to know that I was not the only one. My confidence increased and I stopped shouting. Now Greg will come and ask for help or a hug.

The other children in our family were quite traumatised. His older sister has been hurt but is getting on better with Greg now. His older brother has always been able to talk about difficulties so he has been OK.

We're still in progress. Nothing is simple and straightforward. There are still battles over simple things like self-care. We nearly didn't survive as a family, but now there is hope for Greg and he has lots more opportunities.

Family: single mother adopted Larna, age six (now age 23)

Larna's story

I felt confused as all my life, I was so sure that I wouldn't be wanted that I was afraid to attach and afraid to settle. It was also very hard because you feel a sense a loyalty to your biological parents and when I was younger I hadn't really accepted what they had done etc. so I found it very difficult. Now I wish I had settled and been like we are now.

Having therapy with my mum was hard because I started to learn to trust my mum and open up. I started to form an attachment and my personalities tried everything they could to stop it because every time I trusted and attached when I was young, we always ended up being moved or abandoned. It was like a war inside of me: on one side I was happy to finally be making progress but on the other hand I was furious because I was making myself vulnerable – something my personalities saw as weakness because that's what they'd been taught. Then you have the other side of therapy with my mum. It helped me and my personalities learn very valuable and important things about trust, and the therapy worked in such a way that my mum was understood and supported but I was also understood and support, to this day it's the only therapy I've ever had that made me feel cared about by not just my mum but by the person helping me and that was in my opinion the most important part.

I feel the most safe with my mum. I can be at my house or my mum's house, in the car or in a supermarket and if my mum is there I feel safe. However I'd have to say I feel most safe in my house because all of my belongings are here and if you make a house your own a place you feel comfortable and secure. I love travelling and staying at my mum's who lives about five minutes away so that makes it even better.

When me and my mum would drive around in the car or come for therapy, etc. we'd listen to music together, we loved to sing together and our favourite soundtrack was Mamma Mia and we'd always sing 'Slipping Through My Fingers'. I remember it as clear as day and I remember just lighting up completely and now even though we don't go for drives as much, I still listen to that song and I sing it when I am sad or scared or even if I just miss my mum and I smile and just remember all of those wonderful times that I now hold so close to my heart. We all do, all of my personalities.

Larna's mother's story

At first it was really hard. Larna was six when she came to live with me. She had different voices, and talked about different personalities inside her.

I tried to tell local therapists about this but they did not understand, and I was told that she 'hasn't got multi-personalities'. When we came to Catchpoint when Larna was ten, they confirmed what I thought, that she was dissociative. It was important that we were seen together so we made the journey once a month. In therapy she could not control me, and I learned an awful lot by seeing the things that she acted out. She joined in the activities, we had a lot of fun and she was able to talk about her other parts. Then the parts also talked to Joy.

Larna is now 23 and our relationship is good. She lives with a lot of difficulties – getting out is very difficult for her and she needs a lot of support. She lives in a flat but if she comes to the house, she takes over her room again and feels safe. She is my daughter.

References

Bullivant, R. (2005). Treatment Strategies and Outcomes for Attachment Disordered Children. Unpublished PhD dissertation.

Golding, K. and Hughes, D. (2012). *Creating Loving Attachments*, p. 46. London: JKP.

Hasler, J. (2008). A Piece of the Puzzle: Music Therapy with Looked-after Teenagers and Their Carers, pp. 159–176 in Oldfield, A. and Flower, C. (Eds), *Music Therapy with Children and Their Families*. London: JKP.

Hendry, A. and Hasler, J. (2017). *Creative Therapies for Complex Trauma*. London: JKP.

Perry, B. (2006). Applying Principles of Neurodevelopment to Clinical Work with Maltreated and Traumatized Children, p. 46. In Boyd Webb, N. (Ed), *Working with Traumatised Youth in Child Welfare*. New York: Guildford Press.

Perry, B. (2007–2018). Source: childtrauma.org/wp-content/uploads/2018/01/CTA_NMT_Core-Slides_2018r.pdf p. 7.

Perry, B. (2009). Examining Child Maltreatment through a Neurodevelopmental Lens: Clinical Applications of the Nuerosequential Model of Therapeutics, pp. 240–255. In *Journal of Loss and Trauma*, Volume 14. Taylor & Francis Group. doi.org/10.1080/15325020903004350

Perry, B. and Szalavitz, M. (2006). *The Boy Who Was Raised as a Dog*. New York: Basic Books.

Putnam, F.W., Helmers, K. and Trickett, P.K. (1993). Development, Reliability and Validity of a Child Dissociation Scale, pp. 731–741. In *Child Abuse and Neglect*, Volume 17, Issue 6.

Silberg, J.L. (1998). Preface, pp. xx-xx in Silberg, J. (Ed), *The Dissociative Child*, 2nd edition. Maryland: The Sidran Press.

Sinason, V. (2010) (Ed) Attachment, Trauma and Multiplicity: Working with Dissociative Identity Disorder. 2nd edition. Hove, UK: Routledge

Solomon, M.F. and Siegel, D.J. (2003). *Healing Trauma*. New York and London: W.W. Norton and Co.

Van der Kolk, B. (2015) The Body Keeps the Score: Mind, brain and body in the transformation of trauma. London, UK: Penguin.

Waters, F. and Silberg, J.L. (1998). Therapeutic Phases in the Treatment of Dissociative in Silberg, J. (Ed), *The Dissociative Child*, 2nd edition. Maryland: The Sidran Press.

Wieland, S. (2011). *Dissociation in Traumatised Children and Adolescents*. London: Routledge.

Chapter 14

The price that society and the individual victim pay

Zoe Hawton

It is widely recognized that children suffer trauma; however, the post-traumatic impact is often overlooked. This chapter does not intend to try and explain this anomaly, rather to explore it with a view to opening further discussion.

There is a cost to society of failing to recognize dissociation and post-traumatic stress symptoms in children and young people (referred to in this report as 'children' to highlight their fragility to the reader). Post-traumatic stress disorder with a dissociative subtype (PTSD+DS) was first recognized in diagnostic manuals in 2013 (American Psychiatric Association, 2013).

The stories of the children in the case studies illustrate the symptoms of this disorder. While the majority of us take it for granted that we have an autobiographical sense of self and clear sense of our life history, these studies show that the highlighted children's sense of an 'I' self after suffering trauma is not consistent. The catastrophic impact on their lives of the fragmented state that results from trauma prevents that. This is in line with Modrowski and Kerig's sample of justice-involved youth (detained in a short-term juvenile detention centre) which found a 50% prevalence of PTSD+DS, and found an association between PTSD+DS and both peritraumatic dissociation and emotion dysregulation (Modrowksi & Kerig, 2017 in Schiavone et al. 2018).

It is my hope that these illustrations will show that the eventual socio-economic cost of leaving such problems unresolved far exceeds the much lower financial cost of early intervention. It is more fiscally prudent to address the challenge of dissociation and post-traumatic stress symptoms in the early years than to pay for the consequences of leaving them unresolved.

To manage the impact of such adverse childhood experiences, children often dissociate. While this is adaptive at the time of trauma, the problems within children do not seem to recede naturally as the child matures; rather, the dissociated states get more separated off from the main personality states. The singular functional 'apparently normal personality' state that is left to be seen in common public presentations, such as to health

DOI: 10.4324/9781003246541-15

professionals, to educational settings and to some peers, masks an array of internal personality states, which one client aptly referred to as her "own hidden psychiatric unit".

These states carry the submerged trauma and often intensify behind closed doors, where their manifestations and actions can include unpredictable violence, self-harm and engagement in gang activities which negatively impact both the sufferer and a wider society.

Research by Vince Felitta and Robert Anda on a large sample of 17,000 clients found direct links between people who had experienced multiple adverse childhood experiences and their increased likelihood of early death, disease, disability and social problems, adoption of high-risk behaviours and social, emotional and cognitive impairment (Felitta, Anda et al 1998).

Many adult dissociative clients have endured a life marked by poor mental and physical health, a life punctuated by terms in prison or a mental health institution followed by short-term care. They are left vulnerable while also being generally excluded from the opportunity to be economically productive. This raises additional costs in terms of housing provision, welfare benefit, accident and emergency treatment, medical care with lifelong high pharmaceutical costs, use of voluntary agencies and any return to work; this would seem an area in which more research is needed to highlight why short-term lack of therapeutic interventions is so short sighted in the longer term.

Some statistics around costs include the following:

- Mental illness is the second largest source of burden of disease in England. Mental illnesses are more common, long-lasting and impactful than other health conditions (Public Health England, 2019).
- Mental ill health is responsible for a loss of 72 million working days and costs £34.9 billion each year (Centre for Mental Health, 2017).
  Note: Different studies will estimate the cost of mental ill health in different ways. Other reputable research estimates this cost to be as high as £74–£99 billion (Stevenson and Farmer, 2017).
- The total cost of mental ill health in England is estimated at £105 billion per year (Mental Health Taskforce, 2016).
- Half of mental ill health starts by age 15 and 75% develops by age 18 (Kessler, Berglund, Demler, Jin, Merikangas and Walters, 2005).
- 12.8% of young people aged 5–19 meet clinical criteria for a mental health disorder (Sadler, Vizard, Ford, Goodman, Goodman, and McManus, 2018).
- Only one in eight children who have been sexually abused comes to the attention of statutory agencies (Children's Commissioners, 2015).
- In an average classroom, ten children will have witnessed their parents separate; eight will have experienced severe physical violence, sexual

- abuse or neglect; one will have experienced the death of a parent and seven will have been bullied (Faulkner, 2011).
- There is an increase of 21% in hospital admissions of children and young people (aged 10–24 years old) as a result of self-harm. Numbers rose from 347 per 100,000 population in 2011/2012 to 421 per 100,000 population in 2017/2018 (Nuffield Trust, 2021).
- In 2018/19, ChildLine provided 13,406 counselling sessions about self-harm across the UK (NSPCC, 2021).
- People who self-harm are approximately 49 times more likely to die by suicide (Hawton, Bergen, Cooper, Turnbull, Waters, Ness, Kapur, 2015).
- 86% of boys and 79% of girls in custody aged between 15 and 18 years had at some time been excluded from school. The cost per place per year in a secure children's home is £215,000; in a secure training centre it is £160,000 and in a young offender institution it is £60,000 (Prison Reform Trust, 2010).
- At the end of March 2010 there were 9,823 young people aged 18–20 years in prisons in England and Wales. There were 2,148 children aged 15–18 years in custody, 470 fewer than a year ago. 71% of children in custody have been involved with, or in the care of, local authority social services before entering custody (Prison Reform Trust, 2010).

The cost of private counselling with a therapist can range from £10 up to £70, depending on where you live. The costs of treatment are infinitely smaller than the cost for psychiatric or prison provision

It is a paradox that this condition that breaks the mind into smaller and separate pieces that can become detached from the majority of the person's understanding or awareness is also paralleled in society and many medical staff being cut off or unaware of this diagnosis (Figure 14.1).

Schooldays

It is crucial that medical and mental health professionals and practitioners involved in social care of children, including teachers, have a better understanding of dissociation in children so that they can provide appropriate support and treatment. To this effect the case studies below aim to enhance awareness.

This selection represents the more extreme cases, but trauma is not rare. Recent research by Danese at Kings College London found that of all 18-year-olds in England and Wales, one in 13 has had post-traumatic stress disorder at some point (Lewis, Arseneault et al., 2019). If left untreated, adult client histories suggest dissociation intensifies and so the more 'damaged' end appears 'fine' on the surface to teaching staff, while harbouring fragmented personalities or structured dissociation just under the surface.

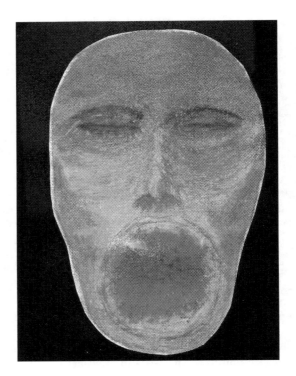

Figure 14.1 Screaming inside

DID has been determined to affect between 7.5% to 10% of those in an inpatient setting (Ross, Duffy, and Ellason, 2002). DID was found to affect 6% of psychiatric inpatients in a Canadian hospital (Horen, Leichner, and Lawson, 1995) and an American outpatient setting (Foote et al., 2006). Nevertheless as Renee Marks from Integrating Families asserts:

> Dissociative disorders are not generally recognised or diagnosed in children and adolescents by mainstream psychiatry. Of course, it is much easier to diagnose ADHD, autism or other more familiar psychiatric disorders, while dissociative disorders in children are still struggling to be accepted as formal diagnosis. The usual fantastical thinking of dissociative children is often normalised, voices that children might report, minimised. In this process the opportunity to access the rich information of the dissociative child's internal landscape is lost.
>
> (Marks, 2019)

Children displaying PTSD and dissociation can become a source of frustration and confusion for peers and teachers because they are unpredictable. Educative environments are increasingly focused on achieving academic targets. These children are often then categorized as 'difficult' pupils, while their real diagnosis is unrecognized. As a result, some of these children often end up excluded very early on. Being loose on the streets increases their likelihood of becoming involved in criminality and adds to their existing sense of exclusion and displacement. Having been hurt or having witnessed violence, they remain the victim, yet are not widely treated in a caring reparative manner by education or society.

Youth counselling services have a track record of successful interventions in children displaying trauma behaviours, but only within a wider context of Teams Around the Child (TAC) with cooperation from multiple professionals alongside, for the most at risk. At best, such care also offers long-term therapy and esteem-building activities outside of the school. Once again, the cost of such care can be substantially less than disruption to peer learning and future social care costs in later life.

Teacher referral notes to school counselling services note such common issues as:

- Inability to focus
- Difficulty absorbing or remembering information
- Blank/disorientated expression
- Inconsistent behaviour patterns characterized by rapid fluctuation between states
- Daydreaming (sometimes including vivid flashbacks)
- Aggression
- Tension and hyper-vigilance
- An increased startle response
- Moody outbursts
- Bullying of peers
- Sensitivity to loud noise
- Difficulty separating day-to-day rough and tumble play from actual physical attack

All of these common issues are also indicators of dissociation and dissociative states (American Psychiatric Association, 2013) and indicate that children are displaying hyper-vigilance linked to an overactive amygdala, which is the brain's fear-sensing centre. Like an over-responsive smoke alarm, an overactive amygdala may perceive mundane day-to-day events (such as a rough schoolyard game) as an attack. When the brain does this, it floods the child with cortisol and automatically invokes a defensive, fight or flight, response. This response can be occurring to a child with PTSD several times an hour, triggering in the present whatever horror they have experienced in the past. From this perspective, it is easy to understand why these children are 'jumpy'.

Listen to the children

It is important to notice, when children engage with counselling services, if they are displaying some of the symptoms below which would attest that they may have experienced extreme trauma with ongoing chronic symptoms. These symptoms might include at least two of the following:

- Nightmares, disturbed sleep and accompanying irritability
- Waking flashbacks
- Feeling over sensitized
- Somatic, body memories of past events intruding on them in the class
- Seemingly random fight, flight or freeze responses
- Feelings of fear and/or anxiety over any change in structure – this is particularly evident on entering a new school year, new classroom, or being assigned a new teacher
- Unusual thought patterns leading to maladaptive coping strategies. Children might internally rehearse their coping strategy, which appears as a trance-like (dissociated) external state
- Primary age children with bouts of regressed behaviour such as thumb-sucking, holding toys, chewing shirts, needing cuddles, etc.

Lack of diagnosis seems to contribute to rising levels of violence in their school years for some, as they lash out through fear and PTSD. This violent reactive behaviour can become normalized as a male attribute by society, and validated by gang identification, which increases young peoples' risk of institutionalization in later life.

The frequent misdiagnosis of PTSD and dissociation (DS) by local services as a form of personality disorder (often linked to its confusing presentation and funding issues – meaning assessment are time limited) can become a significant issue resulting in a failure of the service to provide appropriate care. In order to have a better understanding of such behaviours, it is beneficial for those working with or supporting children to be more informed and aware of the signs. The Mind website gives a full explanation of Complex PTSD (Mind, 2021).

Some of the symptoms of complex C-PTSD+DS are very similar to those of borderline personality disorder (BPD), but not all professionals are aware of complex PTSD which is the result of repeated trauma that the victim cannot escape from. This often results in a significant misdiagnosis. As a result, some people are given a diagnosis of BPD or another personality disorder when complex PTSD fits their experiences more closely after longer scrutiny.

If C-PTSD+DS is left undiagnosed and therefore untreated, this can launch children into a lifetime cycle of self-medication, anti-social behaviour and gang involvement, with a huge long-term social cost.

> Andrea Danese, co-author of the research from King's College London, citing that one in 13 teenagers has experienced PTSD (Lewis, Arseneault et al., 2019), is quoted in an article in the Guardian Newspaper as saying: *"Trauma is really a public health concern, it is very prevalent."* He added that it is not only associated with developing PTSD and other mental health conditions, but also linked to self-harm and suicide, and can have a profound effect on education and work. *"What was most distressing for us to see is that only a small proportion of these young people are in a position to receive treatment."* He stressed there is a huge gap in healthcare provision for young people who have experienced trauma.
>
> The team said that, as well as potentially leading to PTSD, trauma can have other profound ramifications: participants who had been exposed to traumatic events had higher rates of mental health-related problems in the previous year – ranging from anxiety to psychosis and drug dependence – than those unexposed to trauma. Such problems were even more prevalent among those who had had PTSD, with three in four experiencing another mental health problem.
>
> (Davis, 2019)

Young males are particularly vulnerable as their chronic internal landscape of lack of safety gives them a heightened need for security and they see involvement with gangs as a route to this. The typical hyper-vigilance that defines a PTSD diagnosis could easily be seen as contributing to random outbreaks of street violence in reaction to minor slights, such as being jostled in the street or a loud noise. The neuroscience of trauma suggests such damaged children begin their lives with the formation of damaged neural pathways. These lead to them develop 'trigger-happy' danger responses. Left unattended, these pathways become 'hardwired', creating a seeming permanence of internal meaning and fostering the development of patterns that reinforce the sensation of being constantly surrounded by danger (McCrory, De Brito and Viding, 2011).

> One common way of involvement in youth violence is engaging in gang membership, which can take on different meanings according to the environment and urban context in which gangs operate (CSJ, 2009; UK Government, 2011). Gang membership is increasingly evident in the UK's main cities such as London (UK Government, 2011) and has recently been found to be significantly associated with high levels of psychiatric morbidity (Coid, Ullrich, Keers, Bebbington, DeStavola, et al., 2013). Recent evidence has shown how being a gang member leads to trauma and fear of further violence, with clear implications for mental health (Coid et al., 2013)
>
> (Jovchelovitch and Concha, 2013)

The following two case studies are composite vignettes offering commonly presented real-life examples, in which extreme trauma has caused serious dissociative disorders. They illustrate the long-term consequences and social cost of failing to provide sufficient resources to address these problems.

A factor here, as well as funding problems and inadequate length of treatment, was also the existence of generational trauma in the history of the children's parents, including domestic violence, murder, imprisonment, sexual and physical abuse and organized paedophile ring abuse. The nature of the parents' own childhood trauma might suggest they had problems recognizing that the behaviour of their own children was not 'normal', which meant they did not seek help earlier for their children. It also suggests traumatic attachment issues in both the parents and their offspring, as a result of the parents' own poor mental health following trauma.

Children who experience repeated extreme trauma have literally split internally at the horror of these events, entering the world of clinical dissociation. The cases that follow are simplified and present dissociation of only one other personality 'state' of the client. However, there are often multiple selves inside even young clients. Many adult clients remember 'switching' into different parts consciously and unconsciously as children, to manage terrifying and life-threatening situations. For example, a child enduring the pain and physical torment of prostitution at night would easily switch to another 'self' in order to function during the day (Figure 14.2).

As part of their abuse, children are often threatened with death if they 'tell' whatever secrets they hold. Facing such a threat, the child's will to survive takes over. Such extreme fears make a personality split more likely, to ensure their survival, when their life depends on unsafe and terrifying caretakers. The child may not remember that they are in fact unsafe during the day, by inhabiting a different part of their personality. Their brain is creating a mechanism to keep them alive and sane by keeping terrifying memories dissociated and separate.

For example, one client recalls at age seven being able to play cards with himself as three different parts who he had named: *me, myself* and *I*. He clearly recalls instructing them not to cheat and how he was completely unaware of which cards his fragmented identity state selves were holding. This activity comprised part of the child's defence against the loneliness and fear of unexpected physical and sexual attack in his home.

Another adult DID client who presented at school as an 'eager to please, happy child' recalls her confusion and mounting terror as she walked home from school. She lost time and a sense of this functional self as she walked up the garden path. She was too scared to go home and so a dissociated fragmented version of her inside would endure her abusive home life. The 'happy child' (the 'apparently normal personality' or ANP, Van der Hart, Nijenhuis, and Steele, 2006) would resume only on the school route next day, having no memory of the abuse and then the entire cycle would repeat.

Figure 14.2 Matchstick men

Both of the case studies include suggestions of how to help support young people and their families by identifying helpful strategies in these to keep them safe and process their trauma and move forward in their lives.

All names and personal details in these case studies have been altered for confidentiality.

Case study 1: Tom, ten years old

Tom was a six-year-old boy (Figure 14.3). Tall for his age and slightly underweight, he carried an air of threat through his body language. He was observed in class and in the playground sitting watchfully with clenched fists, even when he seemed otherwise calm. His peers were wary of him after various incidents during which he had become exceptionally violent when he felt 'picked on'.

He was ambivalent about attending therapy. Part of him hated being removed from class for therapy, because of the stigma which resulted. Yet another part of him enjoyed the attention he got during therapy and knew he needed help. The boy was solemn when he revealed how he was plagued by night terrors and nightmares. He was not keen to feel like a victim and

Figure 14.3 Child and The Hulk

described sleeping with weapons as he had fears of being attacked in the night by people and animals.

The child was very fearful of adults, especially in one-to-one situations, and he would panic if an adult stood over him (which was impossible to avoid in a school setting). Tom became aggressive around raised voices, and noises like doors slamming or the sound of children playing in breaks. These would provoke a 'freeze' response in which he would sit, rocking and hunched on the floor, or a 'flight' response where he would run out of the room, causing his peers to mock him and exacerbating his feeling of difference from others.

Tom had problems interacting with peers. He would perceive playful teasing as attacks and would see any kind of play fighting as a challenge in which he had to force the other into submission. He had been a talented rugby player but had been excluded from the team, after a vicious attack on another player, who he believed had deliberately hurt him. His behaviour led staff and pupils to perceive him as a bully.

Tom had younger siblings and was deeply troubled because at home he valued having his belongings in a very set order he knew to be consistent. The young toddlers would often move or break these things, which Tom said made him feel, "Nowhere is safe".

Often tearful, Tom described, "setting my face and cutting off from these feelings". Initial work explored his feeling rejected by his mother who had a new boyfriend and new siblings to care for. She would urge him to "be a man" if he sought attention, and tell him he was "too old for cuddles". He was deeply ashamed when he became tearful at seeing flashbacks of past abuse which he described as "pictures in his head". He admitted he had learned to "put these away somewhere else inside".

Tom believed that if he maintained his macho exterior, he would be safe. He felt that he needed to remove any traces of the "scared baby" he felt inside. He felt under pressure from home, society and his peers to "man up and cope" and said he was "trying his hardest" to achieve this.

Tom's friends said that when Tom grew angry, he "switched" and his eyes became hard. They could tell the difference. He maintained this more guarded exterior when he first began attending therapy.

Tom was embarrassed to be seen in the playroom and would want to tape paper over the viewing panel in the door to ensure privacy if he showed any vulnerability. This suggested compartmentalization and reflected his ability to seal off parts of himself, or to display himself in specific ways.

During play therapy he would act out scenes in which two plastic figure characters would fight endlessly without resolution or narrative. He always looked tired, with dark circles under his eyes.

Life mapping techniques helped illuminate his distress. Later in therapy while using narrative-building exercises and illustrating a comic book about his life, the child revealed his harrowing memories of his violent father. He had witnessed horrific violence against his mother including stabbing, and her being sexually assaulted. The abuser then doused her with petrol in front of her child's gaze. At that time, Tom was often left harnessed in his pram, watching events unfold in a state of terror and helplessness.

His father's behaviour meant Tom learned not to cry or scream in front of daddy, as doing so would cause dad to become violent towards him. Fear of such assault caused him to sit in silence while these events took place. Tom told his therapist he had learned to "go elsewhere inside my head" when the cries of his mother became too overwhelming or he just could not stand to watch any more. When blood was drawn, he would often enter this dissociated state.

Then his world became that of Barney the Dinosaur, a character he had seen on television. Barney was seen as a safe and caring figure. Tom described learning to count by remembering TV episodes featuring Barney. In these he would repeat the numbers inside himself, following a story line in which Barney was teaching him to count or to speak the alphabet.

Tom's inner 'Barney World' was a safe place in which the child could express his feelings and ask to be held by the warm, furry, cuddly dinosaur. The child's vulnerable self could only exist inside this safe world. 'Tom' would refer to his self in this world by his full name, 'Thomas'. However, 'Tom' reviled 'Thomas' – who he already saw in the third person – calling him a 'silly baby'. During therapy, Thomas would sometimes enter the room and engage in sand- and preschool-type play.

Tom's father was imprisoned when the child was still a toddler. His mother 'decided' that Tom could not remember any of the events of the domestic violence. She was also attempting to process events herself. If the child mentioned this traumatic history, she would angrily deny that it took place. In doing this she fed a perception of a reality in which Thomas's needs were silenced or unmet.

Seven years on, Thomas could describe every detail of the domestic violence including the room and events. These events fuelled the creation of Tom, the other self who was angry with Thomas. Tom was angry with Thomas because it was Thomas' nightmares that haunted him; it was Thomas who had been helpless and restrained and failed to assist as a rescuer; it was Thomas who was unable to talk or defend himself.

Today, in the here and now, Tom was determined never ever to be like Thomas, 'the coward'. Yet at times, when Tom felt fearful, Thomas would surface internally – Thomas, the silent cry baby whose wet but soundless tears would run down his face. Tom hated Thomas, was cut off from him, yet relived these feelings inside himself when he experienced fear.

The boy's mother's denial of these events worsened this splitting and fostered a sense of unreality and Tom feared all men around him would attack him if they were in private. This fear left the boy in a terror state with fist clenched as he readied himself for imminent attack.

Tom had previously withdrawn from therapy originally offered by CAMHS because he felt therapy made "everything in my head worse, it brings it up." This had not been trauma-informed therapy, but he did however complete a short intervention in youth therapy. We worked with Tom's primary school teacher working out strategies she could use to calm him, such as:

- Avoiding looming over the child
- Avoiding accidental contact, such as brushing past him
- When approaching Tom she would try to do so head on and look him in the eye to assure he was present
- She would speak softly where she could or say his name gently if he looked 'unfocussed'
- Tom was given a pass out card which allowed him to leave the classroom for a few minutes without explanation in the event he felt overwhelmed by the noise

His school also created 'jobs' for him to do at lunchtime. These were sensitively chosen to enable release for the caring side of his nature and included such tasks as keeping school pets clean. This enabled him to avoid the stress he felt in the playground.

When Tom was in the playground, supervisors were watchful and intervened early if he got into arguments. When they did so they ensured he had the chance to exit the situation and calm down. They also kept their body language open and responsive (open palms and arms).

In summary, in primary school therapy, Tom had begun naming and accepting that he did remember the events which took place during the domestic violence episodes. Accepting these had enabled the separate parts of him to begin to merge and create a more realistic narrative concerning his safety levels. Unfortunately, his therapy ended when he completed primary education and even at ten years old, therapy had really begun too late to easily assist Tom.

The child also attended a local after school club where he enjoyed interaction with the youth workers. Unfortunately, this club lost its funding and he lost that avenue to social contact in a situation he felt comfortable in.

Then, when he went to a large secondary school in a socio-economic black spot, the going got difficult for Tom. He found himself surrounded by boys who looked like men. He was the youngest child making a long daily journey to attend a school in an area in which street violence and bullying were a problem.

He struggled to form new attachments with pastoral staff, there was no availability of continuity of care with his previous therapist and he was soon excluded for violence. He first entered the criminal justice system at 13 years old after assaulting another young man. There were concerns he had joined a gang, about which he had already said he believed membership offered him 'protection'. This need for protection could be seen as an overcompensatory attempt to achieve security he had never had. In his early life there was no early therapeutic intervention, no family work and no provision of one-to-one support for his mother.

His mum was not sufficiently confident or capable to find therapy for herself which could have helped her deal with her own trauma and difficulties.

Without trusted support in secondary school, Tom soon slipped into becoming hard eyed 'Tom' all the time, adopting the perpetrator role in which he believed he was 'safe'. By the time this child was in his mid-teens, he was being held in a specialist juvenile unit at a cost of around £3,000 a week, after a violent attack on another boy. He was by now also a father himself, evidencing early onset sexual activity and an urge to "have my own family". His baby was already the subject of possible care proceedings and he later had spells as an inpatient in psychiatric hospital.

To set this in context, the Government's figures for youth custody in 2016–17 show that the cost of an average place in a children's home is £210,000 a year. The cost of a secure training centre is £160,00 a year and of an under 18s young offender institution is £76,000 a year (Lee, 2018).

I often think sadly of Tom and the others who fall through the net due to funding restrictions, which often seem to have the biggest impact on those already societally disadvantaged and vulnerable. The mental health systems in place presume that parents are able to fill in forms, be articulate, trust authority figures and engage by bringing their children to sessions and having the travel fares to do so. It does not seem to account for people with severe financial restraints, poor education, no self-confidence, language barriers, severe social issues, underlying substance misuse, their own poor mental health and cultural restraints, and biases about mental health provision.

I know the outcomes in this case, as while Tom was an inpatient, he located me via the internet. He phoned and apologized for intruding but said he wanted to thank me and let me know that while incarcerated, he had time to think, he had recalled how understood and helped, he felt by his early counselling sessions. This had led him to engage with a therapist while institutionalized, when he had an opportunity, something which most of the other young men had rejected. It had not solved Tom's issues but he was continuing to attend. Tom gave permission for this to be used to highlight to others that 'kids need help'.

It also spotlights that Tom was a child victim and even as an adult, wanted to be back in society being productive and was attempting steps to do so as no early intervention had been in place, Tom's social costs were high and generational. It seems likely that longer term, specialist early intervention could have changed the difficult path his life later became. While his phone call may seem a heartening outcome, it is a great strain continuing to be part of a system, that due to funding restraints, has its hands so tied with offering provision, when many 'Toms' have told me similar later life experiences.

> The United Kingdom spent approximately 4.56 billion British pounds on its prison system in 2018/19, an increase when compared to the previous year.
>
> (Clark, 2021)

> In 2017 there were over 29 thousand assaults among prisoners, and a further 8.4 thousand assaults on prison staff in England and Wales. Just a few years earlier in 2014, there were 16.2 thousand assaults among prisoners and 3.6 thousand attacks on staff.
>
> (Clark, 2021)

Case Study 2: Salma, 15 years old

Salma did disclose the abuse at 15 years old. She was staring out of a top floor school window and considering suicide, a kindly teacher asked her gently what was wrong. For the first time, after a lifetime of abuse she told first the teacher and then the required social worker and a uniformed policeperson that she was being abused by her father and a wider group.

Most people who don't work in child protection have a romanticized view of how disclosure works. It is hard for the child, like in this case, as they have to tell a series of uniformed professionals a consistent version, knowing the first thing those people will do is go back to the same parents and disclose what the child has said. Knowing that after that's happened, the child may well have to go home to the same family, as the case is investigated. In many cases when that happens, clients describe that the family threaten the child with death or the shock of being placed alone in a kids home, means that the child later withdraw 'the allegations'.

Within mental health services if any are provided they are often labelled as 'fantasists' and if they ever disclose again, then these withdrawn allegations will work against them if they go back to the police. Coupled with their mental health problems, the Crown Prosecution Service (CPS) will not even try the case in a court.as the clients are dismissed as 'attention seeking' or 'unstable'.

Salma tells her own story:

She remembers the first social worker saying "you've been making allegations, I want to know your side of the story" and I hadn't a clue what she was talking about. There was no sort of, real introduction, no sensitivity, and it wasn't until my head mistress turned around and said, you know that thing you were telling me about your father, then suddenly the penny dropped.

The social worker spent more time with my mother than she did with me. Every time I said something, my social worker would go and ask my mum, if it was "true". The social worker used to go, repeat everything I said, and my mother would say, "no she was lying", and they would come back, and tell me that I was lying. So, in the end I stopped saying anything.

Looking back, I don't know how any social worker in their right mind, would consider that as being acceptable, because I am pretty sure my mother would never ever turn around and say, "yes of course my husband raped her most nights and sometimes tied her to a bale of hay outside and was paid by other men, so as they could go and do whatever they wanted with her while we both turned a blind eye."(See Figure 14.4.)

"I had a difficult life, I assumed everybody else had a difficult life. I assumed that if you were in a big family there was always one of you that was going to be a mixture of a slave and a toy for others. I didn't know any different. The lifestyle is very difficult to explain, but because I was so used to doing it, it stopped hurting. I just became someone else (through dissociative switching), whoever they wanted, a crying child or a nymphomaniac. That made it over quicker, made it stop."

Figure 14.4 Child Alone

She explained that at 15 after the disclosure she 'fell' into the care system and allowed herself to think things might change for the better. She was medically examined there and found to have gynaecological damage and sexually transmitted diseases. Doctors asked if this 'meant she liked the boys'. She had been a top student but now, with no routine to allow the dissociation to function easily, the splitting began to leak out, she had lapses in time and was accused of daydreaming and being uncooperative. She told care staff that she had also been taken and abused by a wider group of people and social workers began to question her credulity. They could believe her father and her uncle. They began to question if it was really possible that all her brothers could have been involved when she talked about what we would now understand as being child prostitution, exploitation and incest. After these comments she didn't talk about that anymore, adding to the confusion.

In care because of the dissociative mechanisms, she could often still appear 'normal'. This led to the barrister in the case telling her that:

I did not fit my circumstances, I do not appear to be a victim. I could be a bright, well mannered, nice person and there I was turning around and saying that, all these horrible things happened to me, and I don't know whether it was because nobody wanted to believe, or people looked at you and thought well, if that amount of horrible things happened to you, why aren't you behaving differently. I didn't know what to do. I didn't know how to act, I didn't know how to talk to people. Everything became louder, it became more confusing. I got a bed, I never really had a bed before. I could actually go to the bathroom and have a shower, but I couldn't, because I didn't know how. It was all those sorts of things, I didn't know how to do, I didn't know what to do. My stepfather always used to rape me after I had a bath, so I think that is one of the reasons I have this fear of water and the bathroom. But it was all those sorts of things where people were saying, "there's your toothbrush, there's your toothpaste, this is your room, there's the shower", and I am thinking, well what am I supposed to do, I don't know. I walked around in a daze most of the time. I was accused of something that I didn't do, the problem is…half the time you don't know whether it's the voices in your head or whether it's the voices externally, to you. So anyway, I carried on doing whatever I was doing, and I remember coming down the stairs and hearing the care team screaming and calling me all the names under the sun, I just remember standing there listening to them, and then when I turned the corner, they just looked at me and I looked at them, and all of a sudden you realise how badly they must of thought of me, but it just reinforced how badly I thought of myself. I got my school bag and went to school.

They left me in the same area, I went to a new set of foster parents and then to a child psychiatric unit. My main abusers were taken to court, pleaded guilty, which the judge saw as showing 'remorse' so they were jailed for under six months. The local paper reported this as 'the shame of the ultimate Mr Average' and everyone there around me read his version as if it were fact, it labelled me as 'quite obliging' and a psychologist read that to me, as if it was nothing.

In the care system Salma recalls

Nobody ever asked you anything, nobody asked you whether you were happy there, whether you had any problems with any staff, whether you needed anything. I couldn't eat. It's in my care file, that I didn't eat, but no external care staff asked me why. If somebody had come up to me and said, "well why aren't you eating", the chances are I would have turned around and said, "well I don't know how to use a knife and fork". The only thing I have ever done is eat with my hands. Then maybe I would have learnt a bit quicker. Nobody said, "well, hang on a minute, when was the last time you got in the bath" then maybe I would have been able to explain that I don't know how, every time I go in the bathroom, everything goes blank.

I had this charge nurse who was a bully. He actually sat in this group one day and he threatened violence towards one of the lads in the group, and I am sitting there thinking, well if he can hurt him, what sort of a danger is he to me. Yet in this group was a psychiatrist, school teachers, social workers, it's one of those team psychiatric group, and not one of them said anything.

I finished my exams and I then went back to my foster parents. The foster father raped me one night. Bearing in mind that now I was 17 and a half. My social worker at the time was in the process of moving jobs anyway, and I was not allocated another social worker, so all the time I was going through the Courts and speaking to the police, until the age of 18, I was never allocated another social worker. Basically, I was pretty much dropped by social services, because I had made an allegation against a foster parent. Which I might add was proved in Court, and he was sentenced.

I started self-harming then, I actually started self-harming in the first children's home after a gang rape by the boys there at night. I didn't stop after that. It became everything. People think self-harm is about wanting to kill yourself, it's not about wanting to kill yourself, for me it was never about wanting to die. When you have these voices, I assumed that I had something really bad, I had the demons inside me.

Part of it was trying to let them out, part of it was trying to follow what they were saying, them saying "see that fork, stick it in your leg" and part was that I was in pain, but I didn't know what the pain was for. I couldn't put anything together. And when you can't remember why, it's almost like you have to try and create it. It's like "I'm in pain" but there is nothing wrong with me, "oh there's a fork, let me stab myself", now I know why I am in pain.

I had to move back to my family, because there was nowhere else for me to go to. Social services seemed to just say goodbye. My father on my 18th birthday, he was standing outside the place I was staying, I don't know how he managed to get me in the car, but he just took me back home, and I have never left since. I wanted to die all my life, I have never viewed that there was a tomorrow, forget there was a yesterday, you live your life not knowing who people are, where they come from, life remained confusing.

I met Salma 20 years later after she was finally diagnosed as being dissociative. Initially she barely talked and was suspicious and hostile to authority figures, after her life being a 'merry go round' of hospitalizations (at around £4,000 a week in secure units) and return to the community. She had never been able to work, described having been abused for most of her adult life, having no sense of time and being in the world only by presenting a wide range of parts with different ages and different genders to cope with any external contact. She has almost no quality of life and had in effect become a victim of modern-day slavery in the sex worker field, still exploited by people linked to her father.

The social costs were high for a life on benefits – large costly amounts of medication, housing benefits, A and E attendance, GP visits and psychiatric attendance. It was a tragic loss of a life for someone who had good grades and had dreamed of being in the military. She has allowed this transcript to be used in the hope of educating others to be more alert to the signs of abuse and consider how children in the system are treated. It also serves only too well to highlight the tragedy of her lost life and the costs of not receiving the correct early interventions.

The fact that this case study is related by an adult should not cause the reader to presume that very similar scenarios do not continue, just as Salma's case shows, every year I meet a young person with a similar story.

Conclusion

Dissociation seems common across both sexes but boys are often only identified and labelled instead around their violent acting out (Figure 14.5). Dissociation and PTSD occur in all genders following repeated unavoidable trauma. Interestingly, research suggests that as adults females are more likely to be diagnosed with DID, but that there is no gender discrepancy in diagnoses visible in children or adolescents. This again supports the idea that later in life men are more likely to be incarcerated or deny their symptoms and trauma history, be that consciously or unconsciously linked to their dissociative presentations (Horen, Leichner, and Lawson, 1995).

The presentation of PTSD+DS symptoms, among primary school age boys, may remain unnamed as phrases such as 'be a man' enforce cultural stereotypes that imply a sense of shame and weakness in expressing vulnerability. This group even then seems to have a clear awareness that being a perpetrator rather than a victim makes parts of them feel safer.

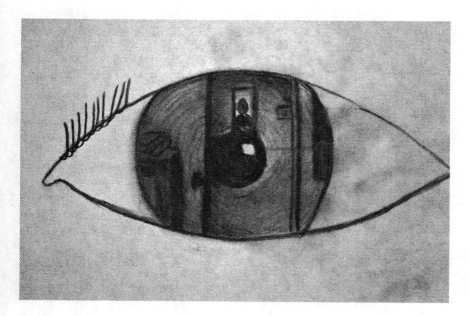

Figure 14.5 Blind eye

This aggressive abuser introject can develop into the main functional part of the child – a brutal and hypersensitive ANP often characterized by extreme triggering (PTSD+DS) and over-reaction to any small stimuli, which is seen as a threat. This is accompanied by a tendency to bully anybody showing vulnerabilities, which reminds them of their own profound experiences of helplessness at an early age.

This tallies with the experience of some of those identified as suffering DID late in life. Many of these adults have remained undiagnosed with a mental health condition despite their being repeatedly jailed or excluded for violent crime from an early age, as well as also repeatedly being traumatized and hurt themselves by criminal groups who recognize the dissociation as an exploitable weakness (Jovchelovitch and Concha, 2013).

People describe how their experience in the penal system reinforced the need to present a brutal front in order to survive; I suggest much of this demographic is largely overlooked. Ignoring the existence of the problem then creates a vast cost in terms of provision of prison and health system resources, quite apart from the physical and economic consequences of their crimes.

It is interesting that some of the teenage slang for violence is now often referred to as 'switching'. This describes people rapidly ascending into an out of control violent state, which they later struggle to remember or explain. This is remarkably close to the diagnosis of Dissociative Identity Disorder which is a presentation:

> ... characterized by the presence of two or more distinct identities or personality states, each with its own relatively enduring pattern of perceiving, relating to and thinking about the environment and self – that recurrently take control of the individuals behaviour, accompanied by an inability to recall important personal information that is too extensive to be explained by normal forgetfulness .... In children, symptoms cannot be attributable to fantasy play or imaginary playmates.
> (American Psychiatric Association, 2013)

I suspect many of these people hear internal voices they choose to ignore in order to avoid the stigma and shame of entering the mental health system. Their previous adverse experiences leave them feeling that they must avoid a vulnerable state at all costs.

Many adult clients describe negative experiences with all manner of authority figures: benefits officials, housing association, GPs, teachers. The "ANP" front personality state often presents a hostile front to such authority, and would not provide personal histories. This behaviour echoes dissociation; John Briere said that 'Dissociation can be defined as a disruption in the normally occurring linkages between subjective awareness, feelings, thought, behavior and memories consciously or unconsciously invoked to reduce psychological distress' (Briere, 1993) (Figure 14.6).

Figure 14.6 Fragmented

The dissociated client's condemnation of their own self as 'bad' fuels an internalized belief system in which they already feel they, and their failings as younger children, are the issue. This in turn can make them even more defensive and dissociated.

Professor Peter Fonagy and others have shown that *'the most common etiology for DID is a disorganized attachment followed by severe and long-term abuse at the hands of a care-giver'* (McQueen, Kennedy, Itzin, Sinason, and Maxted, 2008).

The best approach seems to be that outlined by the European Society for Trauma and Dissociation (ESTD, 2017) in its staged treatment interventions model, incorporating relational non-invasive, client-led treatments characterized by clear boundaries and therapist honesty and transparency. Often only in that environment and with the safety of long-term intervention will such clients present their varied selves, sharing and processing the tragedies that have befallen them through no fault of their own. These clients are, in a sense, society's most vulnerable members, often left locked inside generational cycles of unrecognized trauma. However we label these people,

I would urge you to consider that the only difference between them and you is the luck of being born into different circumstances.

Image credits

Zoe Hawton – play therapy photo used with client permission.

'Fragmented', 'Guarded' and 'Child Alone' by survivor artist K.S. used with kind permission.

'Eye' and 'Screaming Head' by survivor artist M.R. used with kind permission.

References

American Psychiatric Association. (2013). Dissociative disorders. *Diagnostic and statistical manual of mental disorders* (5th ed.). Washington, DC: American Psychiatric Publishing.

Briere, J. (1993). Self-reported amnesia for abuse in adults molested as children. *Journal of Traumatic Stress*, 6(1), pp. 21–31.

Centre for Mental Health. (2017). *Mental health at work: The business costs ten years on*. www.centreformentalhealth.org.uk/publications/mental-health-work-business-costs-ten-years.

Children's Commissioners. (2015). *Protecting children from harm: A critical assessment of child sexual abuse in the family network in England and priorities* for action. www.childrenscommissioner.gov.uk/wp-content/uploads/2017/06/Protecting-children-from-harm-full-report.pdf

Clark, D. (2021). *Public sector expenditure on prisons in the United Kingdom from 2009/10 to 2018/19*. https://www.statista.com/statistics/298654/united-kingdom-uk-public-sector-expenditure-prisons/

Coid, J. W., Ullrich, S., Keers, R.E., Bebbington, P., Destavola, B.L., Kallis, C., Yang, M., Reiss, D., Jenkins, R., Donnelly, P. (2013). Gang membership, violence and psychiatric morbidity. *American Journal of Psychiatry*, 170(9), pp. 985–93.

Davis, N. (2019). 'One in 13 teenagers has experienced PTSD, research finds'. *The Guardian Newspaper* 21Feb 2019. https://www.theguardian.com/society/2019/feb/21/one-in-13-teenagers-has-experienced-ptsd-research-finds

ESTD. (2017). *Guidelines for the assessment and treatment of children and adolescents with dissociative symptoms and dissociative disorders*. Child and Adolescent Committee of the European Society on Trauma and Dissociation (ESTD). https://www.estd.org/sites/default/files/files/estd_guidelines_child_and_adolescents_first_update_july_2.pdf

Faulkner, J. (2011). *Class of 2011 Yearbook: How happy are young people and why does it matter?* Relate www.relate.org.uk/sites/default/files/publication-class-2011-yearbook-2011.pdf.

Felitta, V. J., Anda, R. F., Nordenberg, D., Williamson, D.F., Spitz, A.M., Edwards, V., Koss, M.P., Marks, J.S. (1998). Relationship of childhood abuse and household dysfunction to many of the leading causes of death in adults. The Adverse

Childhood Experiences (ACE) Study. *American Journal of Preventative Medicine.* 14 (4) pp. 245–258.

Foote, B., Smolin, Y., Kaplan, M., Legatt, M.E., Lipschitz, D. (2006). Prevalence of dissociative disorders in psychiatric outpatients. *American Journal of Psychiatry,* 163(4) pp. 623–629.

Hawton, K., Bergen, H., Cooper, J., Turnbull, P., Waters, K., Ness, J., Kapur, N. (2015.) Suicide following self-harm: Findings from the Multicentre Study of Self-Harm in England, 2000-2012. *Journal of Affective Disorders* 175 pp.147–151.

Horen, S. A., Leichner, P., Lawson, J.S. (1995). Prevalence of dissociative symptoms and disorders in an adult psychiatric in-patient population in Canada. *The Canadian Journal of Psychiatry,* 40(4), pp. 185–91.

Jovchelovitch, S., Concha, N. (2013). *Kids Company: A Diagnosis of the Organisation and its Interventions.* The London School of Economics and Political Science, London. http://eprints.lse.ac.uk/id/eprint/52856

Kessler, R. C., Berglund, P., Demler, O., Jin, R., Merikangas, K. R., Walters, E. E. (2005). Lifetime prevalence and age-of-onset distributions of DSM-IV disorders in the National Comorbidity Survey Replication. In *Arch Gen Psychiatry.* 62(6) pp. 593–602.

Lee, P. (2018). Youth custody: Costs. Ministry of Justice. https://www.parliament.uk/business/publications/written-questions-answers-statements/written-question/Commons/2018-05-15/144303/

Lewis, S. J., Arseneault, L., Caspi, A., Fisher, H. L., Matthews, T., Moffitt, T. E., Odgers, C.L., Stahl, D., Teng, J.Y. & Danese, A. (2019). The epidemiology of trauma and post-traumatic stress disorder in a representative cohort of young people in England and Wales. *The Lancet Psychiatry* 6(3) pp.247–256.

Marks, R.P. (2019). *Assessment of dissociative disorders in children and adolescents.* Introduction to video presentation at the Second International Summit of Child abuse: Screening, Detection and Assessment. https://pracdemia.haifa.ac.il/index.php/he/video-conference-june-2019/449-renee-potgieter-marks-assessment-ofdissociative-disorders-in-children-and-adolescents

McCrory, E., De Brito, S. A. & Viding, E. (2011). The impact of childhood maltreatment: A review of neurobiological and genetic factors. *Frontiers in Psychiatry,* 2(48) doi: 10.3389/fpsyt.2011.00048

McQueen, D., Kennedy, R., Itzin, C., Sinason, V., Maxted, F. (2008). *Psychoanalytic psychotherapy after child abuse: The treatment of adults and children who have experienced sexual abuse, violence, and neglect in childhood.* London: Routledge.

Mental Health Taskforce (2016). *The five year forward view for mental health.* www.england.nhs.uk/wp-content/uploads/2016/02/Mental-Health-Taskforce-FYFV-final.pdf

MIND. (2021). *What is Complex PTSD?* https://www.mind.org.uk/information-support/types-of-mental-health-problems/post-traumatic-stress-disorder-ptsd-and-complex-ptsd/complex-ptsd/

Modrowski, C. A., Chaplo, S. D., Kerig, P. K., Mozley, M. M. (2019). Trauma exposure, posttraumatic overmodulation and undermodulation and nonsuicidal self-injury in traumatized justice-involved adolescents. *Psychological Trauma: Theory, Research, Practice and Policy,* 11(7), pp. 743–750. doi: org/10/1037/tra0000469

Modrowski, C. A., & Kerig, P. K. (2017). Investigating factors associated with PTSD dissociative subtype membership in a sample of traumatized justice-involved youth. *Journal of Child & Adolescent Trauma*, 10, pp. 343–351.

NSPCC. (2021). *Childline Annual Review 2018/19*. https://learning.nspcc.org.uk/media/1898/childline-annual-review-2018-19.pdf

Nuffield Trust. (2021). *What are the trends in hospital admissions as a result of self-harm in children and young people?* https://www.nuffieldtrust.org.uk/chart/what-are-the-trends-in-hospital-admissions-as-a-result-of-self-harm-in-children-and-young-people-3

Prison Reform Trust. (2010). Prison briefing – May 2010. http://www.prisonreformtrust.org.uk/uploads/documents/prisonbriefingsmall.pdf

Public Health England. (2019). Health profile for England: 2019. www.gov.uk/government/publications/health-profile-for-england-2019.

Ross, C.A., Duffy, C.M., Ellason, J.W. (2003). Prevalence, reliability and validity of dissociative disorders in an inpatient setting. *Journal of Trauma and Dissociation*, 3(1), pp. 7–17.

Sadler, K., Vizard, T., Ford T., Goodman A., Goodman R., McManus S. (2018). *Mental health of children and young people in England, 2017: Trends and characteristics.* Leeds, UK: NHS Digital https://openaccess.ciy.ac.uk/id/eprint/23650

Schiavone, F.L., Frewen, P., McKinnon, M & Lanius, R.A. (2018). The Dissociative Subtype of PTSD: An update of the literature. In *PTSD Research Quarterly* 29(13) pp. 1050–1835.

Stevenson, D. & Farmer, P. (2017). *Thriving at work: The independent review of mental health and employers.* www.gov.uk/government/publications/thriving-at-work-a-review-of-mental-health-and-employers.

Van der Hart, O., Nijenhuis, E. R. S., Steele, K. (2006). *The haunted self: Structural dissociation and the treatment of chronic traumatization.* Illustrated edition. New York, NY: W. W. Norton & Company

UK Government. (2011). Home office policy paper ending gang and youth violence. Cross Government Report ISBN 9780101821124.

Chapter 15

Covid-19 – the challenge, the solution and the unknown

Treating dissociative children online

Renée Potgieter Marks

Covid began to affect us all in 2020 and before the book went to press we considered it important to provide some insight on the impact on clinical work. This chapter shows how a clinic for children, adolescents and parents changed to manage this challenge. In the beginning, there was an attempt to keep face-to-face work with careful sanitising and ventilation but as the virus took hold that was not adequate. Technology was needed for safe work and the ethical issues around privacy to consider. As children could be seen in their own rooms and homes, help was needed for parents as to how they supported therapy in their own homes. Resilience in therapists and families was remarkable and children who did well face-to-face continued to do well virtually and those who found sessions harder continued to. Adolescents tended to prefer sessions in their own rooms. This chapter provides examples of the creative ways of working that helped as well as showing the powerful impact of Covid on all of us.

Introduction

Covid. It was far away, early 2020, somewhere in China, and for me, not having time to listen to the news, life went on as usual. Little people and young adolescents with complex trauma and dissociation were streaming into our well-equipped therapy offices. They brought themselves (whoever was present) as well as all their other parts. It was a beehive of business. The pulsing of buzzers around the building could at times be felt in my therapy room, while sitting on the floor where I was with a little four-year-old. The sound of bilateral stimulation alternatively beeped from four speakers across the room. Little Tom and I were trying to understand what was happening with the baby whose legs were hurt. And why Angry was causing chaos in the family by attacking the mother. One after the other little person, older children and adolescents walked through the doors, all unaware of what would shortly happen.

DOI: 10.4324/9781003246541-16

Somewhere early March 2020, I had to listen to the news. We ordered alcohol-based hand sanitiser. All that arrived were many bottles of pure alcohol! By Monday, 16 March 2020, sitting with my team of seven therapists, I knew we needed to prepare, but for what and how? We had a full day of 'checking in', advanced training and supervision. For some reason, the large men's tissue box was being passed around. Each one of us was deeply affected. I could no longer visit my very elderly parents and family in South Africa. The country shut its airports for all air traffic from Europe. Each person had some concerns about vulnerable parents, family and partners and there was a dread of the unknown. This time, in an eerie, unfamiliar and different way, was like a big cloud slowly moving towards us, threatening to envelop us. And we had absolutely no template for how to manage what was coming – no books, no literature, no Google, no experience, nothing!

Planning and preparation

We started to plan and by the end of the day we had a plan. All that we knew as a starting point was that we had no template or guidelines for what we needed to do and had to move to overdrive to invent new plans. As an agency we were treating children with complex trauma and dissociation and there was no way that we could just 'drop' the children and families. We had to prioritise the children we were working with as well as their parents, who often were suffering from secondary trauma, while also protecting ourselves and our families. The complexity and emotions of that day can never be described in words. How do you focus on two unfamiliar, complex things that you have to do, where life and death were at stake?

We ended the day with me asking my esteemed colleagues to make a choice. We could either from now on spend our time being anxious, panicking and worrying (and perhaps later deeply regret that we wasted so much time) or we could grab this moment as the biggest challenge in the history of our professional careers. We all opted for the conscious decision to embrace the challenge instead of the panic and anxiety. While we were having the meeting, our manager was mixing alcohol-based hand sanitiser, with precision, like a scientist. The operations team was restless, wondering what would happen next, while frantically working to finish the critically important tasks. The otherwise peaceful atmosphere in the building was replaced by something else, strange and unfamiliar.

After multiple plausible suggestions, we slowly realised that attempting to sanitise surfaces with approximately 25 people entering the building the next day (some of them quite unruly) would be a total impossibility. The next day we all eagerly started to use the alcohol sanitiser on our hands before and after sessions while suspiciously reading the unfamiliar notices across the building to wash hands and sanitise. We slowly but certainly realised that we could no longer just eradicate the virus in the building, if somebody brought it in. The dread was growing. Some of the sessions were cancelled – people were becoming sick.

Armed with a large amount of information from the World Health Organization, medical advisers and rumours that schools might shortly close, the management team took the very difficult decision on Wednesday, 18 March 2020 that we would have to close the building. The cloud was moving rapidly across Europe and the UK were obviously next.

From that moment it was chaos. Letters went out to inform parents and social workers of our decision.

The manager was doing research and sending information about confidentiality while working on line, trying to work out which online facility was the most secure. The operations team was trying to gather and move electronics, files and work to their homes, while wondering how confidential information would be shared without seeing each other.

Therapists were packing everything they could possibly get hold of in boxes to take home. We drew up new contracts for parents, got help to urgently design booklets for the children and adolescents. We started a WhatsApp group for the therapists and information was flying around. Not of panic or fear but of anticipation. We were about to embark on the biggest challenge ever, not alone, but as a team. But denial was never part of the messages shared. We shared the moments of fear, stress, concerns and family complications while also focussing and celebrating what was busy happening. We were most certainly going to continue with therapy with all our children and families without delay or missing sessions. We also felt contained in a cocoon of support from each other. It suddenly felt different, warm and comforting as if we were all together at war and kind of sure of a victory. The schools officially closed on Friday, 20 March 2020 and we were in a full lockdown where all our movements were restricted. We could no longer go to work and we could no longer visit family and friends. Life as we knew it changed overnight. But on WhatsApp we were huddling together like deer when they detect the lion around.

The first bits of information that were shared with parents of our very traumatised and dissociative children were how to keep the children busy at home. We also requested parents to keep them away from the screens, as much as possible, as it mostly enhanced their dissociation. Parents were asked to keep the children present and in relationship as much as possible. There was, in any case, now no longer the luxury of clubs, groups and extra lessons or sport. For the first time in many families there was time for relationship and being with.

But the task was too big for the parents alone as many of them already suffered from secondary trauma, so they received reinforcement in the form of practical fun, games, activities and relational strategies of what to do, how to be with and alongside their children. How to embrace the gift of time. The second big piece of information, which was shared with parents, was the new agreement and guidelines for online therapy.

Can online therapy work?

On Monday, 23 March 2020 our first official online therapy sessions started. A booklet for the children and another for adolescents were hastily prepared by a very creative family member. It explained the biggest transition the children had ever experienced in their therapy and that the environment of therapy would change. We waited with bated breath. The children we treat are highly traumatised and mostly unable to manage transitions. Now we were all forced into the most unusual transition ever with no preparation, but the booklet trying to prepare our children and families for online therapy.

Shortly after the first online therapy sessions took place, the therapists started to share information and we quickly found a couple of very important and encouraging pieces of information. The vast majority of children responded exactly the same way at home with online therapy as they did in the therapy room. They either worked or created chaos. Whatever they did, the therapists knew them sufficiently and managed complex behaviours in a similar way to how they usually would in the therapy room. Parents who usually attended therapy with their children continued supporting their children at home while the therapist worked from the screen in the room. Sometimes the therapist was sitting on the floor with the child; sometimes the therapist was on the table, chair, on some books, on the fridge; sometimes fell off and sometimes the therapist was on the ceiling! Each family made marvellous plans on how to accommodate the therapist on screen as well as keeping their expensive electronic devices safe from unpredictable children, who could one moment be kind and friendly and the next moment could create chaos. Our guidelines also provided clear information to parents about how they could manage complicated situations at their end during therapy.

Parents could relax in the room and were not responsible to 'chase' the child with the computer if the child moved out of the sight of the therapist. Many of our children move around during therapy and we continued with the therapy process, whether we could see the child or not. Parents were prepared to help us when we wondered where the child was or what the child was doing or what the body of the child was doing. Therapy as usual. Some adolescents did more work in their first sessions than what they had done in many months. It appeared easier for them to see their therapist on screen and they started to share much deeper insights. Perhaps we, as therapists, have finally entered their world.

For the very first time therapists started to meet the cats, dogs and hamsters which we just heard about before. For the first time we became real people and children found out we had dogs, cats, children, washing machines in our houses which beeped at the wrong times and deliveries of food at the door. But all of this took a moment of acknowledgement, sometimes fun, but strangely enough not intrusive to the therapy process. All these day-to-day realities became like the background sound of a truck passing in the street at the therapy rooms.

There was the child who worked well with the mother, but then at the end slammed the laptop closed and chaos ensued. But the phone and contact with the mother brought peace. And of course, in another family, we met Angry who disrupted the session for some time and provided ample information to discuss with parents as we had suddenly seen and heard the reality that parents were living with.

The WhatsApp which we shared as therapists produced more than 50 messages a day of sharing and supporting of each other. We specifically shared ideas and good sessions. But also asked help for difficult situations. Suddenly there was a closeness and a moment by moment sharing of a new challenges, experiences, successes and chaotic moments.

Something good started to grow and developed. All the children, apart from two, were continuing with therapy. In these cases, it was the decision of the parents and it appeared it had more to do with their personal preferences, rather than the child's inability to engage with online therapy. Parents were receiving their usual support. The time of some therapy sessions was reduced to accommodate the children's needs and/or providing time for parents to receive more support.

We realised at that stage that it was very early days, but somewhere, something good had to come out of this very horrible, shocking cloud that was hanging over earth.

The challenge

This overnight change, and the shocking, radical shift from being with colleagues, surrounded by toys, sand trays, big balls, tents, tunnels, and revelling in the therapeutic space, quickly took its toll on the therapists. The therapy rooms, richly stacked with every thinkable resource for doing therapy with children and adolescents, were deserted. We were suddenly dumped in a desert of sitting in front of a screen, day in and day out, sometimes elated by the good therapy, and sometimes staring at an upset child who wanted to be with us in the therapy room, sometimes utterly deprived of toys and metaphors.

I still don't know who had the biggest internal earthquake in this sudden desert experience, the therapists or the children? The challenge to the team was to find resources, to innovate. We worked hard to do just that. But we quickly also started to suffer. Being alone in front of a screen has never been our world. We were stripped from the most important things in our life, people, relationship, interaction, toys, tools, resources. We were stripped from the wonderful privilege of quickly sharing in the corridor, staff room, kitchen that we had a "fabulous" session or that we really struggled with a very uncooperative child. We missed the sharing with our colleagues and the quick encouragement.

After our first week of doing online therapy, we were exhausted. The WhatsApp group contained now up to 40 messages a day from desperate, tired, exhausted therapists who were stuck in a world we could never love to be in. Apart from being tired, therapists complained about feeling sick after long hours on the screen, headaches, nausea, burning eyes. The question "when will it end?" was on everyone's lips but we did not dare express it. As we all knew, this was only the beginning.

The reality is that the books we sent to the children to prepare them for the online therapy worked well and there was an element of exhilaration for some children to see us online, in our own homes. Other children continued with therapy but missed specific toys they needed to express themselves with. Generally, therapists reported that the transition went much better than expected and the vast majority of parents echoed this.

We decided to have a weekly support group for all the therapists of the agency, where we could just support each other in this desert of limited human contact. These weekly sessions became our lifeline, the place we could complain, share difficult sessions, cry, get help and above all experience the support from devoted therapists all feeling exactly the same. Our ethical responsibility, despite our own hardship, was a priority.

The solution

Five months later, the scenario looked very different. All the therapists have adapted, no, had to adapt. Some therapists now had a big screen on the wall, due to the irritation to their eyes being long hours in front of the screen.

Early on, we found that without the toys and concrete metaphors, we could not really function well in therapy. Multiple trips back to empty therapy room, arriving back home with bags full of toys and metaphors relieved the stress on therapists significantly. Suddenly there was no longer only the chair and the computer. There were toys all over, in some rooms, well organised in cupboards and shelves and others in boxes, containers and spread around the chair where the therapist sat in front of the computer. Puppets, soft toys, brain puzzles, sand tray figurines, physical metaphors and everything which could comfortably migrate from the therapy rooms to the home offices.

Responses of the children

We have learned so much about our own adaptability and the ingenuity of the children:

The biggest surprise was that children and adolescents who were usually doing well in therapy in the therapy room continued to do well with online therapy.
Children and adolescents who struggled with therapy, or who were inconsistent in their engagement in the therapy room, were doing exactly the same with the online therapy.

Most adolescents were doing much better with online therapy. It is possible that this is the space where adolescents nowadays share their most intimate details with people they have barely met. Perhaps the therapists finally adapted to the adolescents' world!

Some younger children initially struggled as they missed the toys and metaphors they used. We initially showed them the toys but interaction with the toys was very limited. Document cameras appeared on desks. This is a camera on the desk next to the computer and covers an area of two A4 papers. This area became the space where smaller toys could be used as it would be used in the therapy room while the image was projected on the screen for the child to see. Of course, at times it takes a bit longer to find the 'correct' baby or horse as the children did not just accept any toy.

Many children missed the sand tray. Creative parents bought a plastic tub, painted the bottom blue, put sand in and bought sand tray toys and this fully replaced the frustration of not being able to use the sand tray. In some cases the 'sand tray' became the desk with the use of the document camera. In other cases, small blown up sand trays used with the document camera, replaced the much bigger sand tray in the therapy rooms. Pictures in Powerpoint magically became life stories!

Some younger children started to bring their own toys into the therapy space and they always imported amazing metaphors of their own life which was used during the therapy.

Other children used cushions, blankets, rackets, bats, Lego and toys to externalise their internal world.

Children enjoy therapeutic reading and therapists started to use Kindle and screen share to make this possible. Others use the document camera to read the book.

Children are using movement, physical games and dancing in the therapy space in a similar way they used to do in the therapy room, although they can't always be seen. The conversation with the therapist continues 'holding' the child in the therapy space. Joining in with these activities also provided some exercise for the otherwise very passive therapists.

Children were enjoying writing and drawing on the whiteboard on the screen exactly the same way they used pens and paper in the therapy room. The save function ensured that the drawings were imported into the child's file. Children also continued to use art or drawings on paper and showed it to the therapist.

At times some adolescents and children didd not want to be seen. Instead of having to go and hide under a blanket or cushion, they moved their screen, feeling safer while continuing with the therapy session. Parents reflected what the child was doing if needed, but this never stopped the therapy process.

Using EMDR/BLS in the majority of therapy sessions, we also had to adapt this process. Some parents obtained a set of buzzers; some parents opted to buy Touchpoint, which we also use in the therapy rooms. Most parents have downloaded the app which enables them to get the bilateral sounds. Many parents have connected their device to stereo speakers in the room to enable bilateral sound stimulation. Some children were using eye movements while following the dot on the screen, choosing their own colour, size and sound (iEmdr). Other children used ear pods hanging over their ears, providing bilateral sounds. Some parents were tapping shoulders, feet or knees. Other children were marching up and down. The adaptions and improvisations continued endlessly.

We are continued to explore online sand tray work, social stories and other metaphors.

A couple of children left the therapy space in their house; most of them returned for the rest of the session. The few children and adolescents who refused to return clearly made a significant therapeutic statement which was then later discussed.

Unusual experiences

Of course, there had also been the very awkward moments. Seeing an adolescent in their own bedroom, without a parent present, initially felt very uncomfortable. If the bedroom of the child or adolescent was the only private space to conduct the therapy session, there were few options left in a lockdown household. No adolescent was seen on his/her own, without the parents knowing about the time of the therapy session while mostly using the parents' device. The parents were also invited to come into these sessions unannounced to check whether the adolescent was fine or needed anything to eat or drink. Adolescents just accepted this in their stride and continued with therapy.

There had also been some extra visitors in the therapy space, apart from pets. In some cases, siblings arrived and refused to leave the therapy space. Sometimes a bit of patience from everybody enabled the sibling to leave. In other cases, if the child who was seen accepted it, the session continued to discuss the siblings' relationship or sibling rivalry. In this process valuable information was gathered about boundaries in families and behaviours of children at home.

Then there was Jamie, who apparently arrived in a different dissociative state and had no idea who was on the screen. He was furious and demanded that the parents immediately switch off the screen as he did not know the person on the screen. No amount of explanation from parents helped. Jamie was adamant, shouting and screaming. With the first moment of silence the therapist said, "Hallo, I am so glad to meet you. I see you don't know me" and introduced herself to the child. Calm descended as another state arrived and consoled the new dissociative state that this is the friendly therapist who helps Jamie and the therapy session resumed.

Something similar happened to Joyce. As soon as the face of the therapist appeared on the screen she ran and hid behind the settee. The only responses were non-verbal sounds. Finally, parents figured out that Joyce was afraid of the therapist. The therapist said, "I see that Joyce is not here today? I wonder who is hiding behind the settee?". Finally, in a very infantile voice somebody said "Amy". The therapist responded with "Oh Amy, I am so glad that you are here today. I can see you are afraid of me, but I am the therapist of Joyce who comes every Thursday to see her. I will not hurt you or Joyce and I would love to get to know you."

Amy then peeped out and the therapy continued with Amy creeping closer and closer to the camera, inquisitive and engaging.

One adolescent crawled under the table which the computer was on. The therapist was unable to see him and reflected on the hiding. This state that could not be seen continued to attend therapy regularly and it became an enormous challenge to respond only on the infantile sounds and empathise with the little baby who could not be seen many years ago. For the first time this young person started to become more aware and accepting that another part was present, especially seeing that the 15-year-old could be very well functioning during other times.

Therapists also started to 'feel' the atmosphere in some houses. Overstressed parents were identified, and many parents also received increased support during lockdown. Therapists finally accept that anything can happen at any time. To get the perfect therapeutic setting in the house of a family who live with highly dissociative children or child, was not easy. The answer appeared to be that it is easier for the therapist to adapt the therapy than to fight the inevitable. Parents worked very hard to create a therapy space, but it was not always successful, yet therapy continued. It appeared that most of the children were resolute that they will continue to use their own therapy space, notwithstanding the changes and challenges.

Therapists' support

The initial despair of therapists also slowly made space for silent acceptance of 'this is life, right now'. The main benefit was that the vast majority of children's therapy continued with a smooth transition from face-to-face therapy to online therapy within one week. In the weekly therapists' support group, there were regularly 'celebrations' when therapy went well or a new 'gadget' or a new method or therapy tool was shared.

But the therapists generally remained very tired and extremely exhausted at the end of each week. We quickly found that it wasd better to have space between sessions in order to move, drink something and recover somewhat. Continuous back to back sessions caused significant stress, exhaustion and eye problems. One theme remained – we all wanted to return to the therapy rooms as soon as possible! The children were starting to miss us more, the novelty was gone, but therapy continued. Some sessions had to be shortened as the 1.5-hour sessions that we usually had became too long for some younger children.

Due to many children waiting for assessments, we could no longer allow them to wait and we also started to assess children online. We all thought it was impossible, yet found excellent results. All parent discussions, parent groups, parent training, reviews, meetings and also family observations were done online. It was business as usual, except that in the hearts and minds of the therapists, there remained an enormous need for the 'normal'.

The unknown

By autumn 2020, some lockdown restrictions were lifted and it appeared that we could move back to face to face therapy, but, with tight sanitising, masks and social distancing in place. It somehow felt like we have reached the eye of the storm, we survived the first part but had the unknown in front of us. This was not only because of the children, but because of the gnawing need to return to the therapy rooms to be physically with the children and to be together again. Perhaps, we are just a species where physical 'being with' is critically important. But the unknown was equally critically frustrating. However, only time would tell. There were children who were very impulsive, who would not be able to abide by the rules of social distancing. Then there were those who impulsively made physical contact with the therapist and the ones who love spitting, bumping into and hitting. Then there was the reality of not being able to use the waiting room, not being able to use the sand trays, the toys, the play dough. How do we navigate that, when that was our normal life? How does the therapy room look without using what is in it? Each child having their own individual 'therapy box' was a good start so far. What about our big objects we use in therapy; do we ban them? Do we sanitise after each child? What was the most effective way to sanitise these?

What was the safest? Sanitising, reducing people, opening windows between sessions? Then there was the problem with masks. How do you fully read the child's expressions with a face mask – that is if the child would wear a face mask which was highly unlikely in the vast majority of cases. Would transparent masks for therapists work? What would happen if the child would sneeze or cough? Should we also use a visor to protect our eyes, or a screen? None of the therapists could rely on the highly dissociative child to adhere to social expectations, and would a screen stop them from accessing the therapist or would it become a challenge to break the rules? We thought moving therapy online was the actual challenge, but perhaps moving back to the therapy rooms, was the actual challenge. We as therapists as well as small number of children, who were struggling to access therapy on line due to the fact that they could not express their distress sufficiently with the limited resources, were all desperate to return to face-to-face therapy.

We completed risk assessments on therapists and children to return to the therapy rooms as soon as possible. Some vulnerable therapists and parents would not be able to return prior to them receiving their vaccinations. A number of therapists were deemed safe enough to return to face to face therapy and some families opted to bring their children for face to face therapy, despite the obstacles of waiting in the car, wearing face masks, sanitising, temperature checks and adhering to the social distancing rules where the children were unable to access the 'no man's land' between the space allocated to parent and child and the space 1.5 meters apart which was allocated to the therapist'. Each child had their own box with pens, papers, selected toys, play dough etc. Rooms were ventilated between sessions and toys and chairs were sanitised after sessions. Nothing felt 'normal', but therapy continued.

At times I felt the silence, the eerie, similar to the evening before hurricane Matthew arrived over the New Providence island in the Bahamas, in October 2016. Then I remember my momentary anxiety, roof tiles flying from our roof early the next morning, the leaks, the running around when Hurricane Matthew bent the steel church tower in a U-shape, uprooted massive trees, stripped a whole forest of all the leaves on the trees, leaving it bare and the island devastated. But now five years later, with the signs still visible in New Providence, healing and new growth has also arrived. So, there is always hope, despite the pain of the immediate past and the present, but are we only now in the eye of the storm? What was still coming?

The Second Wave

The end of 2020 brought more unpredictability, as huge amounts of people in the southern parts of England started to die of the Alpha variant of Covid. There were signs of a possible new variant in South Africa as well, but devastation came when the Delta variant cruelly marched across the world and millions more people died. Lockdown in England came early in January 2021. All our well thought through plans to see the children face to face vanished like mist in the sun and everybody was back at home, solely relying on online therapy, once again. This time the pain of moving away from the therapy room was intense, mixed with frustration. But there was some hope, there was news of possible vaccines which would be released shortly.

For me life was upside down. I was finally in South Africa to manage a desperate crisis with my very elderly parents and due to the lockdowns across the world became stuck in South Africa for 7 months. The most negative aspect of the first experience of lockdown, now became my biggest gift. With airports closed, I used my time in South Africa to continue to see all the children and families online, as if I was at home. Of course I had to urgently buy in some toys, but therapy continued now across continents and I remained part of my team in England where we eventually managed to emotionally survive the second, much harsher and dangerous second wave of Covid.

Finally airports started to open and I returned home at the end of June and the lockdown restrictions were finally lifted in July 2021.

The Present

The vaccinations and the lifting of restrictions finally brought some relief. We once again conducted risk assessments and families started to return to face-to-face therapy. Elated therapist and operational staff was able to see each other once again after being 15 months apart.

Children and young people returned with big smiles and some of the little people were totally overjoyed to start seeing their therapists again and to be able to start to use the familiar toys again.

Although face-to-face therapy is now available, some families opted to remain online while other families now prefers a hybrid approach where they attend therapy both online and face-to-face.

The future is still unknown, further lockdowns might not totally be excluded, but somewhere there is a team that knows that we can survive as a team with continued support, sharing, improvising, crying and laughing together.

Summary

Despite all the complexities, therapy continued seven days a week as usual through all the lockdowns and a big cheer for all the brave therapists who moved with the times, survived the shocks and adapted to keep the therapy process for the children rolling. Trauma was still being processed, attachment was still happening, dissociative states were still revealed, worked with, and integrations were still taking place. Some children's therapies were even completed and ended.

We have experienced therapists, family members, clients and children becoming ill. We experienced loss with our colleagues, friends and clients. But somehow, we also know that once we win the Covid-19 war, we will collectively mourn, but we will also rejoice in the knowledge and experience which was forced upon us. New growth and new opportunities opened up.

We found more ways to help the children of the earth. We have more tools, techniques and improvised in the most unique ways, how to continue therapy with children suffering from attachment difficulties, complex trauma and dissociation.

There are those living close to us who we now have to see online, while we cannot see them face to face, and we also realise that we can similarly work with children living far away. And most of all use the new tools to enable the children and young people, to liberate themselves of the trauma and dissociation cloak they are carrying, especially in areas of the country and the world where there are no therapists trained in working with children and adolescents with complex trauma and dissociation!

Perhaps the past restrictions of place and distance to the very scarce resource of trained therapists, working with this population of children, will finally be overcome, not through an achievement highlighted on the news but through walking together through a very deep valley. And we will smile and remind each other once again that the sun shines on the other side and the trees have leaves again.

Acknowledgements

A very special thank you to my dear colleagues at Integrate, Les Ryan, Lynne Ryan, Wanda Dobson, Lynsey Everson, Claire Thackrah, Abbie Gregory, Sarah Brackenbury, Caroline Booth, Carol Wright, Gemma Taylor, Pam Dawson and Stephan Marks for your relentless bravery, resilience and tenacity to walk this road with me. I have no words to express my thanks and appreciation to you all – Renée.

Resources for treating complex trauma in children and adolescents

Literature

The list of books and chapters below is not exhaustive, but provides recent up-to-date literature for clinicians working with children and adolescents with complex trauma and dissociation.

1 Sandra Baita, a Latin American clinician, wrote the first book on childhood trauma and dissociation published in the Spanish language. It is a guide to the basic concepts of complex trauma, attachment and the development of dissociation during childhood, providing diagnostic criteria and including screening tests, differentiation between dissociation and developmental normative phenomena, clinical observation and inquiry, and also a guide to assess attachment in the parents' history (birth parents as well as adoptive parents) and the child's history, and the assessment of dissociative self-states. The last chapters of the book are devoted to psychoeducation for the child, but with a special emphasis on how to inform parents and schools about what dissociation is, how it manifests and how it is related to the child's behavioural manifestations.

   Baita, S. (2015b). *Rompecabezas: Unaguíaintroductoria al trauma y la disociación en la infancia.* Amazon: CreateSpace.

   The book was also translated into Italian:

   Baita, S. (2018). *Puzzles. Una guida introduttiva al trauma e alla dissociazione nell'infanzia.*

   (Translation, Viola Galleano / Carolina Ochsenius. Milan, Italy: Mimesis Edizioni. Collana Clinica del trauma e della dissociazione n.6.)

2 Niki Gomez Perales describes in a systematic way the treatment of children with complex trauma and dissociation. The book emphasises the importance of a phased approach, including attachment-focused therapy, and provides multiple examples of treating children. It also explains the transition to trauma processing and discusses comprehensively the most common assumptions about trauma therapy and her responses on

these, based on many years of experience. Gomez-Perales provides an excellent approach and illustrates flexibility and insight in the dynamics of treating the child with complex trauma and dissociation.

Gomez-Perales, N. (2015). *Attachment-Focused Trauma Treatment for Children and Adolescents: Phase Oriented Strategies for Addressing Complex Trauma Disorders.* New York & London: Routledge.

3 Renée Potgieter Marks describes a complicated problem with dissociative children where they have introjected the perpetrator and at times act with the similar power and intent of their original perpetrator. This causes significant behavioural difficulties, which often threaten to disrupt the children's placements at home and school. The victims are often parents, siblings and other children. Potgieter Marks describes different perpetrator introjects in children as well as treatment suggestions.

Potgieter Marks, R. (2012b). When the Sleeping Tiger Roars – Perpetrator Introjects in Children. In R. Vogt (Ed.), *Perpetrator Introjects – Psychotherapeutic Diagnostics and Treatment Models* (pp. 87–110). Kroning: AnsangerVerlag.

This chapter was also published in German:

Potgieter Marks, R. (2012a). Täterintrojekte in der Behandlung von dissoziativen Kindern. In R. Vogt (Ed.), *Täterintrojekte: Diagnostische und therapeutische Konzepte dissoziativer Strukturen* (pp. 139–160). Kroning: AnsangerVerlag.

4 Renée Potgieter Marks discusses the process of memory recall in dissociative children, at the hand of clinical cases. In these cases, both children were significantly 'stuck' in therapy due to their dissociative experiences. Through the process of externalising their internal experiences, the children were able to access significant memories and successfully integrate their dissociative states.

Potgieter Marks, R. (2019). The Frozen Child: The Process of Memory Recall in Children with Complex Trauma and Dissociation. In R. Vogt (Ed.), *The Traumatised Memory – Protection and Resistance: How Traumatic Stress Encrypts Itself in the Body, Behaviour and Soul and How to Detect It* (pp. 61–78). Hanover: Lehmanns Media.

A similar chapter was also published in German:

Potgieter Marks, R. (2018). Errinerungsagieren mit morderischen Taterintrojeckten bei dissoziativen Kindern. In R. Vogt (Ed.), *Das traumatisierte Gedächtnis – Schutz und Widerstand: Wie sich traumatische Belastungen in Körper, Seele und Verhalten verschlüsseln und wieder auffinden lassen.* (pp. 63–81). Berlin: Lehmanns Media GmbH.

5 Joyanna Silberg encountered her first dissociative child in the 1980s and she started a journey of connecting to experts in the field of dissociation. This journey took Silberg over many years of treating dissociative children in the Shepperd Pratt hospital in Baltimore. In 1996, Silberg

published her first book *The Dissociative Child*, which was the first book ever published on assessing and treating dissociative children. Many years later with much more experience treating dissociative children, Silberg developed the EDUCATE model which is the most extensively described model on how to treat dissociative children. This model was described in her book, *The Child Survivor*, in 2013. In this book, Silberg also described the concept of affect avoidance, which explains the problem with children who are unable to move to feeling as in essence they dissociated through affect avoidance. This book is filled with case examples and therapeutic techniques, and it is a must read for every therapist treating children and adolescents.

Silberg, J. (2013). *The Child Survivor: Healing Developmental Trauma and Dissociation.* New York: Routledge.

6 Joyanna Silberg also provides links to articles that she has written, on her webpage, on trauma and dissociation in children. See https://www.thechildsurvivor.com/publications.

7 Frances Waters encountered her first dissociative child in the 1980s when she realised the child had amnesia. A long journey followed where Waters connected to experts in the field of dissociation and over a period of many years she gathered information through her practical experience with dissociative children. Her wealth of information was finally compiled in 2016 in her book *Healing the Fractured Child*. This book is a comprehensive handbook which is a must for all therapists who are working in the field of child trauma and dissociation. It does not only contain a comprehensive chapter on assessment, but also contains multiple practical case studies and case examples and therapeutic techniques embedded in invaluable ideas on how to work with the child and adolescent who suffered complex trauma and dissociation.

Waters, F.S. (2016). *Healing the Fractured Child: Diagnoses and Treatment of Youth with Dissociation.* New York: Springer Publishing Company.

8 Fran Waters has developed a new checklist of indicators of trauma and dissociation in youth called 'CIT-DY'. It is a comprehensive checklist geared for parents/caregivers, clinicians and educators to fill out electronically or a hand filled version for children as young as three years old through adolescence. It is a guide to assist in assessing and diagnosing children with complex trauma.

You can download the checklist at her website: waterscounselingandtraining.com/cit-dy-checklist.

The Introductory Letter re: CIT-DY, CIT-DY's electronic version (enable macros and scores will be added automatically) and hand filled version of CIT-DY, and a Consent Form for research and publication of the results. She welcomes comments as well.

9   Sandra Wieland was a child and adolescent psychologist in British Columbia, Canada. In 2011, she edited the first book in 15 years on child trauma and dissociation. This book was updated and the second edition was published in 2015. The book consists of an introduction to the theoretical and neurobiological concepts regarding trauma and dissociation. This is followed by six very comprehensive case studies, written by international experts in the field, on how to treat children with complex trauma and dissociation. This book is a must read for all clinicians who have some experience of treating dissociative children and who want to access the reality of the practice.
    Wieland, S. (2012, 2015). *Dissociation in Children and Adolescents Theory and Clinical Interventions* (2nd ed.). London: Routledge.
    This book was also translated into German:
    Wieland, S. (2018). *Dissoziation bei traumatisierten Kindern und Jugendlichen: Grundlagen, klinische Fälle und Strategien*. Stuttgart: Klett-Cotta-Verlag.
10 Sandra Wieland focuses in this book on parenting the traumatised child from a systemic perspective. Children who suffered complex trauma need more than therapy once a week. They need parents, foster carers and adopted parents who are able to support and help them adapt to a safe environment. Parents and carers often struggle in this process due to transference and countertransference. Wieland describes how the parent, our other client, needs specific support and help, enabling them to find the patterns in their parenting that might block the therapeutic process in their children. The book contains excellent ideas on how we as therapists can help parents, but also be aware of our own countertransference which might interfere with the therapeutic process of the child and family.
    Wieland, S. (2017). *Parents Are Our Other Client – Ideas for Therapists, Social Workers Support Workers, and Teachers*. New York & London: Routledge.
11 Adrian Stierum describes the major problems with the effectiveness of medication for dissociative children and adolescents. This is an objective perspective, looking at the pharmacological, ethical and practical aspects of prescribing medication to this population of children. It also contains valuable content in a table to identify the different types of medication as well as their use and impact on children and adolescents.
    Stierum, A.J. (2016). Medication as an Intervention in the Treatment of Dissociative Disorders and Complex Trauma with Children and Adolescents. In F.S. Waters (Ed.), *Healing the Fractured Child: Diagnoses and Treatment of Youth with Dissociation* (pp. 249–282). New York: Springer Publishing Company.
12 Bradley Stolbach describes in this article the treatment of a child with severe burns at an earlier age. The value of this article is in the dissociative experiences of this child due to medical problems and it provides an

insight in how children with medical trauma make sense of overwhelming experiences through dissociative processes.

Stolbach, B. (2005). Psychotherapy of a Dissociative 8-Year-Old Boy Burned at Age 3. *Psychiatric Annals*, 35(8), pp. 685–694.

13 Arianne Struik focuses in this book on the importance not to ignore the trauma that children experienced in the past. Many therapists are of the opinion that it is better to leave the trauma but according to Struik trauma allows the sleeping dogs to lie as at some stage they will wake up. Struik makes a strong argument in this book to address the traumatic experiences of the child as soon as possible, and also provides practical steps to ensure the child's internal and external safety in the process.

Struik, A. (2019). *Treating Chronically Traumatized Children: The Sleeping Dogs Method*. London: Routledge.

14 Na'ama Yehuda is a speech and language pathologist who, in treating children in a school in New York, found significant signs of dissociation in many of the children she treats. This process started to make Yehuda increasingly aware of the impact of trauma and dissociation of children in school, their unusual ways of communicating as well as academic and social difficulties that they encounter. In 2016, Yehuda released her book *Communicating Trauma*. This book provides the most extensive information about the traumatised child's struggle to communicate. It also provides excellent suggestions of practical ways on how the needs of the traumatised and dissociative child in school can be met. There are also tools that can be used to enhance emotional regulation and grounding. The book provides valuable information on multi-professional collaboration regarding treating the child with trauma and dissociation as well as preventing vicarious trauma in the professionals.

Yehuda, N. (2016). *Communicating Trauma: Clinical Presentations and Interventions with Traumatized Children*. New York: Routledge.

15 Dr Arnon Bentovim, a psychiatrist, psychoanalyst and family therapist, who founded the first child abuse workshop in the UK at Great Ormond Street Hospital, provides a developmental understanding of the impact of trauma on children and adolescents. He shows how secrecy, denial and blame keep victim and perpetrator trapped, there is an absence of a protector and potential protectors are neutralised. Avoidance as well as dissociation maintains the ongoing secrecy.

Bentovim, A. (2002). Dissociative Identity Disorder, a Developmental Perspective. In V. Sinason (Ed.), *Attachment Trauma and Multiplicity* (pp. 21–36). Hove: Routledge.

16 Psychiatrist Dr Joan Coleman, the founder of RAINS (Ritual Abuse Information Network Support), provides, from an analysis of all disclosures she heard, a summary of treatment of children born into abusive cults.

Coleman, J. (1994). Satanic Cult Practices. In V. Sinason (Ed.), *Treating Survivors of Satanist Abuse* (pp. 242–253). London: Routledge.

17 The late Pamela Hudson, a Clinical Social Worker and Child Therapist in the USA, describes treating children whose dissociation came from ritual abuse. She also had the onerous experience of seeing 27 children from the same day nursery.

Hudson, P. (1994). The Clinician's Experience. In V. Sinason (Ed.), *Treating Survivors of Satanist Abuse* (pp. 71–81). London: Routledge.

18 American psychologist and psychotherapist Dr Mary Sue Moore, a past holder of the Fulbright scholarship, details the particular difference in drawings by ritually abused children.

Moore, M.S. (1994). Common Characteristics in the Drawings of Ritually Abused Children and Adults. In V. Sinason (Ed.), *Treating Survivors of Satanist Abuse* (pp. 221–242). London: Routledge.

19 American psychologist Dr Mary Sue Moore continues her analysis of drawings and the process of drawing in children with dissociative disorders, including the unconscious communication the drawings can represent.

Moore, M.S. (2012). Children's Art and the Dissociative Brain. In V. Sinason (Ed.), *Trauma, Dissociation and Multiplicity* (pp. 51–64). Hove: Routledge.

20 This is a major clinical chapter on the psychoanalytic psychotherapy of a young woman with Dissociative Identity Disorder who also had an intellectual disability. It highlights both the extra confusion this combination causes and areas of courage and hope.

Sinason, V. (2010). Dissociation and Disability, Cassie's Tale. In *Mental Handicap and the Human Condition, An Analytic Approach to Intellectual Disability* (pp. 263–276). Revised Edition. London: Free Association Books.

21 Whilst psychoanalysis often privileges the symbolic this chapter looks at the crucial importance of the literal in this work.

Sinason, V. (2012). The Verbal Language of Trauma and Dissociation. In *Trauma, Dissociation and Multiplicity* (pp. 37–50). Hove: Routledge.

22 Valerie Sinason looks at the lack of writing and understanding of children with dissociative disorders in the UK, including a case study where she herself was not able to deal with the dissociation because she had received no training in it.

Sinason, V. (2016). The Seeming Absence of Children with DID. In E.F. Howell & S. Itzkowitz (Eds.), *The Dissociative Mind in Psychoanalysis Understanding and Working with Trauma* (pp. 221–227). New York: Routledge.

23 An accessible guide to the key concepts involved in trauma and dissociation, this book covers all degrees of trauma: complex, childhood attachment ruptures, sexual abuse, torture, war and the coronavirus

pandemic. Its aim is to help professionals understand some of the worst possible experiences without a loss of feeling.

Sinason, V. (2020). *The Truth about Trauma and Dissociation: Everything You Didn't Want to Know and Were Afraid to Ask*. London: Confer Books.

Guidelines

These guidelines provide excellent help and guidance for therapist treating children with complex trauma and dissociation. It is essential to be aware and work in line with these guidelines when treating dissociative children.

(2017) ESTD Guidelines for the Assessment and Treatment of Children and Adolescents with Dissociative Symptoms and Dissociative Disorders. See https://www.estd.org/sites/default/files/files/estd_guidelines_child_and_adolescents_first_update_july_2.pdf

(2003) ISSTD Guidelines for the Evaluation and Treatment of Dissociative Symptoms in Children and Adolescents. See https://www.isst-d.org/wp-content/uploads/2019/02/childguidelines-ISSTD-2003.pdf

Training courses

The training courses available provide comprehensive training for therapists on the assessment and treatment of dissociative children.

Children and Adolescent Assessment and Treatment. Hybrid Course (online video training and face-to-face contact), including videos of therapy with actual cases plus monthly group supervision for duration of training. See https://bictd.org/dissociation.html.

Assessment and Treatment of Traumatized Children and Adolescents with Dissociative Symptoms and Disorders (online video training). See https://www.isst-d.org/training-and-conferences/professional-training-program/ptp-course-descriptions/.

Frequently asked questions and answers

These questions and answers provide helpful information to clinicians, teachers and parents if they have concerns about a child's presentation in terms of possible dissociation.

Child and Adolescents FAQs. See https://www.isst-d.org/resources/child-adolescent-faqs/.

Teacher FAQs. See https://www.isst-d.org/resources/faqs-for-teachers/.

Index

Note: **Bold** page numbers refer to tables, *Italic* page numbers refer to figures and page number followed by "n" refer to end notes.

abduction 16, 57–58, **58**, 71
abuse disclosures: child sexual abuse imagery **59**, 59–61; emotional abuse 60; religious abuse 60–61
adjustment disorder (AD) 98
adolescent dissociative experience scale (A-DES) 105
adolescent multidimensional inventory of dissociation (A-MID) 105
adoption support agencies 199
adrenergic reactions 27
adult attachment interview (AAI) 11, 13
adult attachment projective system (AAP) 11
adult-on-child sex 59
affect avoidance theory 76, 159–160
agency 111–112
aggression 72
Ainsworth, M. 29
alcohol-based hand sanitiser 238
Alvardo, C. S. 3
amnesia 55, 72
Anda, R. 214
anxiety 43–44
attachment-based psychotherapy 10
attachment-caregiving strategy 20
Attachment, Separation and Loss (1969–1980) 29
attachment system: abnormal tensions 16, 17, 20; in action 199; child's neuronal networks 7; cooperative system 15; Darwinian perspective 17, 20; defence behaviour 16; difficulties 72; disorganised attachment model 7; emotions and behaviours 18; exploratory system 15; individual attachment figures 8; internal working model 8; psychological testing 7; unsolvable tension 19
attachment theory 10, 21, 74; clinical applications 13; human behaviour 13; inner experience 13; star theoretical model 81; *see also* attachment system
attention deficit hyperactivity disorder (ADHD) 37
autonomic nervous system (ANS) 78–79
Avon Longitudinal Study of Parent and Children (ALSPAC) 37

Babenko, O. 37
bad memories 53
Baita, S. 4, 251
Baker, W. L. 79
Barker, E. D. 37
Barney World 224
Bartholomew, K. 13
behavioural control system 15
Bentovim, A. 255
Bergman, K. 45
betrayal trauma theory 76
Biven, L. 14
Blakely, T. 79
Blaustein, M. 67
borderline personality disorder (BPD) 218
Bowlby, J. 13, 14, 29, 75, 81, 82, 83, 84, 85, 86; *see also* psychological responses, Bowlby's stages
brain-activated mechanism 28
brain networks 77–78

Index

Briere, J. 232
British psychoanalytic theory 156n1
Bucci, W. 19
Buchanan, K. L. 36

caregiver mental state 11, **12**
caregiving interview 13
caregiving system 14
case series: data sheet 52; methodology 51–53
Cassidy, J. 29
Catchpoint company 198, 199, 203; Circle of Support 202; informal support network 200
Caucasian race 50
cellular memory 38
Chamberlain, D. B. 38, 45
Cheit, R. 62
Child and Adolescent Guidelines 4
childhood Bipolar Disorder (BD) 98
childhood dissociation: conceptual models 76; Jackson's theory 79; psychological escape hatch 76–77; vs. trauma 74–75
child-on-child sex 59
child-parent interactions 20
children's nervous systems 79
child's barriers 120–127; child's attachment relationships 124–125, 134; cognitive shift 126–137, 134; daily life 124, 133; emotion regulation 125–126, 134; safety planning 121–123, 133
child's exploratory system 15
child sexual abuse imagery (CSAI): abduction 57–58, **58**; abuse disclosures **59**, 59–61; criminal investigations 50; demographic 53, **53**; illegal industry 51; indirect play therapy approach 63; mass hysteria hypothesis 64; symptomatic presentations 53–57, **54**; toileting issues 56; trauma symptoms tracking 51; treatment approach 65–67
The Child Survivor (Silberg) 51
ChildTrauma Academy 199
CIT-DY 253
clear-cut dissociative symptoms 21
clinical experience 169–173
Clonidine 106
Coleman, J. 255–256
collapsed immobility 55, 72
Colman, I. 36
communication patterns: star theoretical model 73

competitive system 20
complex trauma and dissociation 158–159, 257
connection, inside-outside technique 165–166
controlling caregiving strategy 20
controlling-punitive strategy 20
conversion disorder, attention deficit hyperactivity disorder (ADHD) 98
Coons, P. M. 77
cooperative system 15
co-productive parent partnership 205
Covid-19: adaptability and ingenuity 242–244; advanced training and supervision 238; alcohol-based hand sanitiser 238; challenge 241–242; online therapy sessions 240–241; planning and preparation 238–239; present 248; second wave 247–248; solution 242; therapists' support 245–246; the unknown 246–247; unusual experiences 244–245
Creative Therapies for Complex Trauma 199
crown prosecution service (CPS) 227
Cyber Child Pornography Rings (CCPRs) 49
cybercrime 50

daily life 124, 133
Dallam, S. 3; contingent communication 157; draw herself 156–158
Danese, A. 219
Darknet 50
Darwinian adaptations 14
dazed states 55, 72
defence system 14, 17; abnormal tensions 16, 17; emotions and behaviours 18; post-traumatic stress 17; unsolvable tension 19
den Boer, J. A. 78
de-potentiation 109
Despine, A. 3
developmental theory: star theoretical model 87–88, **89**
DID diagnosis: career patients 169; in children 168–169; group therapy 173; identity changes 168; infanticidal attachment behaviour 176; self-harm in adolescents 173; self-harm in people 173
DiPietro, J. A. 36
discrete behavioural states 76

disorganised attachment model 7
dissociation faces 158–159
dissociative children: characterising severe 173–174; clinical experience 169–173; means 176–177; motive 174–176; opportunity 177; unusual self-harm 173–174
dissociative disorders 203; age-appropriate behaviours 2; detecting self-states 5; diagnose and treat adults 1; DID vignette 2; mental health services 2; pathological process 3
dissociative escalation 149–151
dissociative identity disorder 1; diagnosis 98; ego state therapy 106–107; integration 111–112; ISSTD guidelines 105; medication stage 105–106; modified havening method 109–110; post-separation 99; self agency 111–112; sensorimotor psychotherapy 107–109, 111; separation 99; therapeutic process 110–111; turning tides 110
Dissociative Identity Disorder (DID) 22
dissociative theory: conceptual models 76; dissociation 75; infant trauma 75; psychological escape hatch 76–77; trauma *vs.* dissociation 74–75
draw herself 156–158
DSM-III 168
Dutra, L. 17

early life stress (ELS) 36–37; developmental programming hypothesis 36; externalizing problems 37; long-term maladaptive stress responses 37; stress during pregnancy 37
ego state theory 76
ego state therapy 106, 113
emotional abuse 60, 71
emotional dysregulation 19
Erickson, M. 23
Erikson, E. 87, 88
Erikson's theory 91
ESTD's Child and Adolescent Guidelines 4
European Society for Trauma and Dissociation (ESTD) 199, 233
Evans, J. 36
exceptional emotional outbursts 41
exploratory system 15
eye movement desensitization and reprocessing (EMDR) 46n2

Facebook 151
face-to-face therapy 245, 247, 248
family: Bella's story 208–209; Georgie's story 209–210; Greg's story 210–211; Larna's story 211–212
Family Court 155
family systems theory: star theoretical model 91–93
'fantasy' 34
Felitta, V. 214
feminist ego state therapy 106
fight-flight system 14, 15
"fight" response 28
First Person Plural 199
Flared-Up-Anger 185, 186, *187,* 188
"flee" response 27
flow chart: sleeping dogs method 117, *117*
forensic interviews 64
Fraiberg, S. 27, 75
Frewen, P. 78

Gaensbauer, T. J. 75
Gamma Hydroxy Butyrate (GHB) 60
generalize anxiety disorder (GAD) 98
George, C. 14
Gilad, M. 49
Gomez-Perales, N. 251–252
Google 238
group therapy 173

hallucinations 72
HaMakor 65
'happy child' 220
Harper, L. 109
Healing the Fractured Child (Waters) 51
healthy attachments 181, 182
Heinicke, C. M. 86
Horowitz, L. M. 13
hostile emotion 27
hostility 84–85
Hudson, P. 256
human behaviour 10, 13
"Hurtcore" 50

Iacoboni, M. 80
implicit memory system 75
inborn motivational system 14
infant and adult attachment styles: caregiver mental state 11, **12**; caregiving system 14; careseeking-caregiving interactions 17; classification schemes 11, **12**, 13;

clinical applications of 13; and defence system 15–19; dissociative process 19–21; intergenerational transmission 13; motivational systems 13–15; multi-motivational theory 15; robust evidence 19–20; unsolvable tension 19
infant attachment patterns 11, **12**; *see also* infant and adult attachment styles
infant-parent attachment 30
infant's defence system 16
insecure-ambivalent 11
insecure-avoidant 11
inside-outside technique: acknowledging 165–166; connecting 165–166; the first meetings 160–162; limitations 166; self displayed 162–165
intergenerational transmission 13
internal working models (IWMs) 8, 17–21, 141
International Society for the Study of Trauma and Dissociation (ISSTD) 4, 105, 199
interpersonal motivational systems 20
IWMs *see* internal working models (IWMs)

Jackson's theory 79
Jones, N. 39
Jovasevic, V. 77, 78

Karr-Morse, R. 38, 43
Kayleigh's story, dissociation child: compounding trauma 146; dissociative escalation 149–151; dissociative internal landscape 140–143; expression of 140; final thoughts 151–152; imaginary friend 143–145; infant's inborn motivational systems 141; manifestation of 140; physio-psychological states 142; precipitating trauma 145; sexual encounters 147–149; thematic analysis 139
Kelly, J. 43
Kerig, P. K. 213
Kingsbury, M. 36
Kinniburg, K. 67
Kluft, R. P. 3
Kohler, R. M. 44
Kovalchuk, I. 37

Lamont, A. 39
Lanius, R. A. 78

LaPrairie, J. L. 39
life-threatening event 110
limitations: inside-outside technique 166
Liotti, G. 30, 31n1, 141
low-dose naltrexone (LDN) 105
LUSTFUL system 14

MacKinnon, N. 36, 37, 44, 45
Mahedy, L. 36
malignant aggression 15
Mariette, M. M. 36
Marks, R. P. 4, 252
Martin, E. 164
mass hysteria 62
maternal prenatal depression 37
Maughan, B. 37
McMartin Day Care 64
medical abuse 71
memory 38, 67, 77–78
mental mechanisms 18
Metz, G.A.S. 37
MICRO moments 207
Midgley, N. 2
mirror neurons 80
Modrowski, C. A. 213
Moore, M. S. 256
motivational systems 11, 13–15
multi-motivational theory 15
multi-sensory experiences 207

National Health Service Treatment and Training Centre 1
Nazi genocide 5
neurobiology: autonomic nervous system 78–79; brain networks 77–78; dissociation 78–79; mechanisms 28; memories 77–78; mirror neurons 80; nuerosequential model 79–80; Polyvagal theory 78–79
neurosequential model of therapeutics (NMT) 205
nightmares 71, 218
Nijenhuis, E. R. S. 78
non-maltreating parent 13
nuerosequential model 79–80
NURTURANCE system 14

obsessive compulsive disorders (OCD) 98
online sex rings 50
online therapy 240, 245; agreement and guidelines 239; changes and challenges

245; "fabulous" session 241; Powerpoint 243; WhatsApp group 241
opportunity 177
oppositional defiance disorder (ODD) 98
organized abuse 51, 63, 67

PANIC system 14, 72
Panksepp, J. 14
parasympathetic nervous system 79
parent-child attachment relationship 74
Pathological Defences in Infancy 27
pathological mourning 81
Perry, B. D. 67, 79, 201
personality development 19, 21
physical abuse 71
physical collapse 53; *see also* collapsed immobility
pictures 71
Piontelli, A. 38, 39, 42
play space: child's internal dissociative system 184–194, *185, 186, 187, 188, 189, 190*; continuity 194–196, *195*; dissociative continuum 182; healthy attachments 181; playing 180; problematic dissociation 182; self-states 182–183; treatment 183–194
Pollard, R. 79
Polyvagal theory 78–79, 109, 113
Porges, P. 78
positive attachment patterns: rhythms and musical improvisations 198
Positive Outcomes for Dissociative Survivors (PODS) 199
post-traumatic stress disorder 17; case study 221–231, *222, 228*; challenge of 213; chronic symptoms 218–221, *221*; school counselling services 217; schooldays 215–218, *216*; symptoms of 213; treatment costs 214–215
Powerpoint 243
pre-adolescent child: dissociative symptoms 13
pre-birth memories 34, 40
prenatal dissociation 42–43; sensory experiences 42
prenatal memories 38–39; cellular memory 38; conventional behaviour modification 38; evolutionary advantage 39; motor development 38
prenatal stress 35
prenatal trauma: anxiety 43–44; concept of 35; early life stress 36–37; epigenetic factors 43; evolutionary advantage 35; framing the conversation 35; hypotheses 35; impact of sound 39–40; impact of touch 40–41; memory capacities 35; prenatal influences 36; prenatal memories 38–39; recall details 35; stress 43–44; vignette A 41; vignette B 44–45
primary school therapy 225
psychoanalytic theory: adrenergic reactions 27; brain-activated mechanism 28; child's innate dissociative 30; fight adrenergic responses 27; neurobiological survival mechanism 27, 28; protective attachment figure 30
psycho-education 65, 118, 120, *119, 120*, 183
psychological responses, Bowlby's stages: appeals for help 85; despair 86–87; disorganisation 86–87; hostility 84–85; regression 86–87; reorganisation 87; thought and behaviour 84; withdrawal 86–87
psychological test 7
psychopathological symptoms 21
psychotherapy 10, 180
Putnam, F. W. 3, 4, 5, 76, 77, 157

Quadri-Theoretical Model 73

Radulovic, J. 78
reconnect 203
referential activity/referential process 19
reframe 203
regression or state changes 72
Reinders, A. A. T. S. 78
reliability 52
religious abuse 60, 71
religiously devout community 50–51
reorder 203
reorganisation 87
resilience 204–205
resonance 204
responsiveness 29
ritualized aggressive behaviour 15
Rivlin, H. 65
Robertson, J. 82, 83
Russian Matryoshka doll 120

safe deposit box 124
safely risk rejection 127

safe place 124
safety planning 121–123, 133
Salter, A. C. 51
sand tray toys 34, 243
Sandusky, J. 64
Satir, V. 92
Schore, A. 17
second wave: covid-19 247–248
secret keeping 72
secure base concept 11, 15
self-determination theory 118
self-exploration 159–160
self-harm 72, 173–174; attachment 175–176; means 176–177; motive 174–176; opportunity 177
self-medication: lifetime cycle of 219
self-reflection 158–160
self-regulation 142
self-report questionnaire 13
self-states: play space 182–183
sensorimotor psychotherapy 107–109, 110, 111
sensory self 42
separation anxiety 56, 68, 72
sexual abuse 59, 71, 145; within family 15
sexualized behavior 72
sexual system 14
Shanley, P. 64
Sherman, L. J. 29
Shirar, L. 4
Siegel, D. J. 157
signs of safety 121
Silberg, J. 4, 51, 159, 252–253
Silberg, J. L. 3, 4, 67, 116
Sinason, V. 4, 256–257
Slade, A. 13, 21, 180
sleeping dogs method 116, 120; barriers action plan 135–137; case conceptualization form 130–131; child's barriers 120–127; flow chart 117, *117*; integration action plan 137–138; integration interventions 128–129; motivation and nutshell checks 118, 120, *119, 120*, 127, *128*, 133–134; nutshell check 133–134; principles 118; psychoeducation 118, 120, *119, 120*; trauma-focused therapy 116; trauma-processing interventions 128, *128*
sleep issues 71
social behaviour 14

social engagement system 109
Solomon, J. 14, 29
SPADE Project 49
Spiegel, D. 98
star theoretical model: assessment and treatment 73, *74*; attachment theory 81; Bowlby's internal working models 83; Bowlby's stages 84–87; communication patterns 73; developmental theory 87–88, **89**; dissociative theory 74–77; *vs.* Erickson's model *90*, 90–91; family systems theory 91–93; neurobiology 78–80; psychological stages 83; traumatic psychologically 81–83
Steele, K. 159
Steinberg, M. 3
Stephen Porges' Polyvagal Theory 185
Stern, D. 42
Stierum, A. 254
Stolbach, B. 254–255
strange situation procedure (SSP) 11
strange verbalizations 72
stress: prenatal trauma and dissociation 43–44
Struik, A. 4, 67, 255
survival mechanism 27
Szalavitz, M. 67

teams around the child (TAC) 217
"The Club" 49
therapeutic process: asking for help 206; being heard 206; bridging patterns 205–206; co-productive parent partnership 205; held in mind 206–207; MICRO moments 207; multi-sensory experiences 207; resilience 204–205; resonance 204; therapeutic activities 205
therapeutic web 202
toileting problems 72
Tomasello, M. 15
Topsey-Tangle 185, 186, 191
Trauma and Abuse Group (TAG) 199
trauma-processing therapy 116, 129; motivation and nutshell checks 127, *128*; trauma-processing interventions 128, *128*
Trauma Symptom Inventory 51
Treating Chronically Traumatized Children: The Sleeping Dogs Method 116

treatment: play space 183–194
trigger-happy 219

UK NHS community 151
unusual self-harm 173–174

van der Hart, O. 83, 159
Van der Kolk, B. 39
Verny, T. 43
Vigilante, D. 79
violation of community
  norms 72
Vos, H. P. J. 78

Waters, F. S. 4, 67, 116, 253
WhatsApp group 241
Wieland, F. S. 4, 67, 116, 254
Wiley, M. S. 38, 43
Willemsen, A. T. M. 78
window of tolerance 118
withdrawal 86–87
World Health Organization (WHO) 239

Yehuda, N. 4, 39, 255
YouTube 106

Zoroglu, S. 3

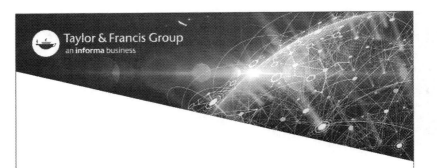

Taylor & Francis eBooks

www.taylorfrancis.com

A single destination for eBooks from Taylor & Francis with increased functionality and an improved user experience to meet the needs of our customers.

90,000+ eBooks of award-winning academic content in Humanities, Social Science, Science, Technology, Engineering, and Medical written by a global network of editors and authors.

TAYLOR & FRANCIS EBOOKS OFFERS:

- A streamlined experience for our library customers
- A single point of discovery for all of our eBook content
- Improved search and discovery of content at both book and chapter level

REQUEST A FREE TRIAL
support@taylorfrancis.com

Printed in the United States
by Baker & Taylor Publisher Services